LITERARY WASHINGTON, D.C.

LITERARY
WASHINGTON, D.C.

edited by

PATRICK ALLEN

foreword by

ALAN CHEUSE

TRINITY UNIVERSITY PRESS

SAN ANTONIO

Published by Trinity University Press
San Antonio, Texas 78212
Copyright © 2012 by Trinity University Press

Design by Anne Richmond Boston

Trinity University Press strives to produce its books using methods and materials in an environmentally sensitive manner. We favor working with manufacturers that practice sustainable management of all natural resources, produce paper using recycled stock, and manage forests with the best possible practices for people, biodiversity, and sustainability. The press is a member of the Green Press Initiative, a nonprofit program dedicated to supporting publishers in their efforts to reduce their impacts on endangered forests, climate change, and forest dependent communities.

The paper used in this publication meets the minimum requirements of the American National Standard for Information Sciences—Permanence of Paper for Printed Library Materials, ansi z39.48-1992.

Library of Congress Cataloging-in-Publication Data
Literary Washington, D.C. / edited by Patrick Allen ; foreword by Alan Cheuse.
     p. cm.
     Includes bibliographical references.
     Summary: "Memoir, fiction, essays, poetry, and songs blend to create a balanced and nuanced literary portrait of Washington, D.C. The voices of some 36 writers comprise the volume. Foreword by Alan Cheuse"—Provided by publisher.
     ISBN 978-1-59534-078-8 (pbk. : alk. paper)
     1. American literature—Washington (D.C.) 2. Washington (D.C.)—Literary collections. I. Allen, Patrick, 1965–
     PS548.D6L63 2012
     810.8'09753—DC23   2011051284

16   15   14   13   12   5   4   3   2   1

Cover illustration: The City of Washington, birds-eye view from the Potomac—looking north, drawn by C.R. Parsons. Library of Congress, Geography and Map Division.

Contents

CONTENTS

Foreword

A writer, the lore would have it, has to have a sense of place, some location that you were born in and grew up in and whose life you are steeped in until the work is stewed and ready for the table. That's the Eudora Welty gold standard for the making of good fiction, and it's a fine rule, if you can make it your own. If you apply it to most of the poets and novelists who have written about life in the District of Columbia, they will fail the test. Washington, D.C., has made a place for itself in the literary imagination of the nation, but it is, with few exceptions, mostly transients rather than permanent residents who have written well about it.

Part of this peculiar city's sense of place is that it serves as a capital for people who have no permanent sense of place. All of us came to this country from somewhere else, the American Indians by way of the land bridge from Siberia, Greenlanders and Irish monks (if you believe the myths) by storm-tossed oceangoing ships and rafts, explorers from the Mediterranean, settlers from just about every nation in Europe, railroad builders from China, black slaves untimely ripped from their native Africa, refugees from various historical holocausts around the world, people seeking good jobs or just good wage labor, people arriving on foot and by airplane, by train and truck and by ship. That is how we made our country, which remains a nation of transients still, where most people uproot themselves and move away from wherever they started at least several times in their lives.

It's fitting that every four years the nation has an opportunity to express its will on whether the incumbent president and his minions should vacate the White House or stay. In the worst of historical times, it seems as though the people base that will on certain social needs—jobs, food, housing, an end to oppression—but in the best of times, and we have been lucky enough recently to see some of those, the electorate just sometimes seems to desire to get things moving again. We're American, they say in one huge voice, so let's get on the road again and see if we can do better with the next place or, in the case of elections, with some new people.

Given that Washington is the capital of the country of movement and change, it's appropriate that most of us who have written about it have come from somewhere else and, who knows, may go somewhere else after a while here. Presidents come and go, senators come and go, and congresspeople come and go (although not as quickly as the velocity-driven sense of American transience would like them to move). Why not writers and poets?

Myself, I arrived here in 1987 and have lived here longer than I have lived anywhere else in my adult life (and if I think back on it, in my childhood either, since my mother, true first-generation American that she was, was constantly changing apartments and then houses and then towns within the northeast New Jersey county where I was born). Contemporary writers Susan Richards Shreve and Patricia Browning Griffith, whose work appears in this book, have lived here a number of decades. But they came here from elsewhere, Shreve from Ohio, when her father took a job in the Roosevelt administration, and Griffith from Texas more recently than that. Ward Just, who has taken on the admirable and terribly difficult role of becoming the chronicler of human sorrow within the governments that come and go, lived here a long time but came from elsewhere, and he now seems to spend most of his time in Europe and on Cape Cod.

The majority of the writers gathered in these pages are more obviously from elsewhere—Henry James and Walt Whitman, to name two of the most prominent transients who have used Washington as a subject in one way or another.

Gore Vidal, who wears lightly the cape of the chronicler of the pageantry and psychic foibles of historical Washington administrations from Jefferson to Lincoln and beyond, lived here as a boy, and in his memoir *Palimpsest* he describes how he led his grandfather, blind Senator Gore, among the newly constructed marble buildings on Constitution Avenue. Archibald MacLeish worked in the government for a time, then departed. Larry

McMurtry still keeps a residence, and a bookstore, in Georgetown, but has long since made his main residence in Texas. Rita Dove lives in Charlottesville, 100 miles down the road; she spent two good years here as poet laureate. (Robert Penn Warren, Richard Wilbur, Robert Pinsky—also a fellow New Jerseyan and the only three-term laureate—and Robert Hass, among others, have also served in that office, though not all spent the same number of days, weeks, and hours here.)

Passing through! The poets and fiction writers seem to move through with nearly the same velocity as presidents!

It's the rare writer, as I mentioned earlier, who opened his eyes on this turf at birth. That's why in the fiction of Edward Jones and Marita Golden, for example, we get a special perspective on the capital city, not as a place that many people refer to as the capital of the world, but as a true homeplace as Welty understands it, where people are born, live, love, make families or destroy them, suffer, laugh, and end only a little further along than where they began. This is not the Washington of the Smithsonian and the Jefferson Memorial and Foggy Bottom and the Mall. You get a different view of life when you're standing on the corner of Georgia Avenue and Harvard Street, looking south (especially if you have lived through the 1968 riots so terrifically described by Trinidadian writer V. S. Naipaul in his 1971 novella *One Out of Many*.)

And then there are the tourists, of one sort or another. When thinking about Washington, you can never leave out the tourists. And pretty high-class tourists are included here, Emily Dickinson and Charles Dickens among them.

War has brought us here, peace has brought us here, love has kept us here, and love or loss of love will give some of us reason again to leave. Which makes Washington, D.C., exactly like most other places in the rest of the country and the rest of the world—only more so.

ALAN CHEUSE

Preface

This book attempts to portray Washington through the eyes of its writers and poets. It does not have the easy bombast of a newspaper headline nor the orderly delineation of Pierre Charles L'Enfant's master plan for the Federal City. From its beginning, the city's essence has been polyglot and contradictory, and this book, composed of many writers from many eras working in a variety of forms, seeks, as much as a single volume can, to be likewise multifarious.

Ernest Knoll called Washington an "invented city, neither Rome nor home." A city reclaimed from swampland and based on imperial models, Washington is undoubtedly artificial, a construct. But that historical fact is only part of the story of the city's culture and way of life. In this stage set of a city, people make their homes, work, have families, go to school, worship, and are buried. While there is a dichotomy between "official Washington" and "domestic Washington," the two come together, both in the city itself and in this collection.

The attempt to present Washington's many truths mandated that the city's varied voices be heard through many forms—poetry, essays, fiction, memoirs, diaries, letters, and journalism—with preference given to the literary and to a balance between the familiar and the arcane. Some authors are represented in genres they are not often associated with, and a conscious effort has been made to represent the work of women, people of color, and others whose voices are often unheard.

The making of anthologies is an activity fated to inspire displeasure in some about what has been left out. Simple space considerations prohibit all the great work about the city in all genres from being included in a single volume. Presidential inauguration poems whose fame outlives their occasion—Robert Frost's and Maya Angelou's spring to mind—are not included, nor have I attempted to systematically include the works of the poets laureate and consultants in poetry to the Library of Congress unless their work related directly to the city. A long and diverse list of writers—Frederick Douglass, Georgia Douglas Johnson, Margaret Leech, Peter Taylor, Edmund Wilson, Ann Beattie, and Paul Lawrence Dunbar, to name a few—do not appear here, some because, though they may have been born and died in D.C., they did not commit their impressions of the city to paper, and others because their work does not lend itself to easy excerption. There are other belletristic traces of the city and its culture that I would have liked to include, such as George Watterson's *The L ... Family at Washington* (1822), perhaps the first novel set in Washington City, or some of the remarkable letters written by Washington painter Marcella Comès Wilson to her roster of literary friends and acquaintances, including her cousin Robert Lowell, as well as Allen Tate and Caroline Gordon, Katherine Anne Porter, Robert Penn Warren, Eudora Welty, Karl Shapiro, Ezra Pound, and Robert Frost. To avoid the risk of turning a roster of esteemed Washington writers, poets, and journalists into a grocery list, I attempt no definitive list of those writers whose work demands attention and ask that readers use this book as a guide to further reading as well as a reference.

Washington is a city that often looks back at its own history, perhaps because it is in part—in the form of the Library of Congress, the National Cathedral, the Smithsonian Institution, and its numerous monuments and public structures—the repository of all the things Americans hold dear. But the long and varied list of writers who make Washington and environs their home—Vassily Aksyonov, Dolores Kendrick, Beverly Lowry, and E. Ethelbert Miller, to name only a few—assures us that Washington is and will continue to be a progenitive part of the living culture of the land for which it acts as political capital.

from *The Domestic Manners of the Americans*

FRANCES TROLLOPE (1780–1863)

Born Frances Milton near Bristol, England, the clergyman's daughter married Thomas Anthony Trollope in 1809. Her husband had little success at the many careers he tried his hand at—lawyer, farmer, and merchant, among them—and in 1827 the feminist and reformer Frances Wright suggested the family emigrate to the United States. The Trollopes spent three financially and emotionally difficult years in Cincinnati before returning to England, and Frances began writing in order to support herself and her family. Her first book, written in 1831 and excerpted below, caused a furor in America, long under the sway of the manners and culture of its former colonists. Trollope's book was one of the most notorious of several books critical of American mores written by British travelers in the early nineteenth century. Inevitably, Americans retorted in book form to the various British charges. Perhaps the best of the American answers is *Notions of the Americans: Picked Up by a Travelling Bachelor* (1828), a two-volume collection of fictional letters written anonymously by James Fenimore Cooper in the guise of a British traveler; the second volume is datelined "Washington." Among Trollope's many other travel books and novels are *The Lottery of Marriage* (1846) and *The Life and Adventure of a Clever Woman* (1854). A daughter and two of her sons became writers, the best known being Anthony, author of *Barchester Towers* (1857) and *The American Senator* (1877).

I was delighted with the whole aspect of Washington; light, cheerful, and airy, it reminded me of our fashionable watering-places. It has been laughed at by foreigners, and even by natives, because the original plan of the city was upon an enormous scale, and but a very small part of it has been as yet executed. But I confess I see nothing in the least degree ridiculous about it; the original design, which was as beautiful as it was extensive, has been in no way departed from, and all that has been done has been done well. From the base of the hill on which the capitol stands extends a street of magnificent width, planted on each side with trees, and ornamented by many splendid shops. This street, which is called Pennsylvania Avenue, is above a mile in length, and at the end of it is the handsome mansion of the President; conveniently near to his residence are the various public offices, all handsome, simple, and commodious; ample areas are left round each, where grass and shrubs refresh the eye. In another of the principal streets is the general post-office and not far from it a very noble town-hall. Towards the quarter of the President's house are several handsome dwellings, which are chiefly occupied by the foreign ministers. The houses in the other parts of the city are scattered, but without ever losing sight of the regularity of the original plan; and to a person who has been travelling much through the country, and marked the immense quantity of new manufactories, new canals, new rail-roads, new towns, and new cities, which are springing, as it were, from the earth in every part of it, the appearance of the metropolis rising gradually into life and splendour, is a spectacle of high historic interest.

Commerce had already produced large and handsome cities in America before she had attained to an individual political existence, and Washington may be scorned as a metropolis, where such cities as Philadelphia and New York exist; but I considered it as the growing metropolis of the growing population of the Union, and it already possesses features noble enough to sustain its dignity as such.

The residence of the foreign legations and their families gives a tone to the society of this city which distinguishes it greatly from all others. It is also, for a great part of the year, the residence of the senators and representatives, who must be presumed to be the *élite* of the entire body of citizens, both in respect to talent and education. This cannot fail to make Washington a more agreeable abode than any other city in the Union.

The total absence of all sights, sounds, or smells of commerce, adds greatly to the charm. Instead of drays you see handsome carriages; and instead of the busy bustling hustle of men, shuffling on to a sale of "dry goods" or "prime bread stuffs," you see very well-dressed personages lounging leisurely up and down Pennsylvania Avenue.

Mr. Pishey Thompson, the English bookseller, with his pretty collection of all sorts of pretty literature fresh from London, and Mr. Somebody, the jeweller, with his brilliant shop full of trinkets, are the principal points of attraction and business. What a contrast to all other American cities! The members, who pass several months every year in this lounging easy way, with no labour but a little talking, and with the *douceur* of eight dollars a day to pay them for it, must feel the change sadly when their term of public service is over.

There is another circumstance which renders the evening parties at Washington extremely unlike those of other places in the Union; this is the great majority of gentlemen. The expense, the trouble, or the necessity of a ruling eye at home, one or all of these reasons, prevents the members' ladies from accompanying them to Washington; at least I heard of very few who had their wives with them. The female society is chiefly to be found among the families of the foreign ministers, those of the officers of state and of the few members, the wealthiest and most aristocratic of the land, who bring their families with them. Some few independent persons reside in or near the city, but this is a class so thinly scattered that they can hardly be accounted a part of the population.

But, strange to say, even here a theatre cannot be supported for more than a few weeks at a time. I was told that gambling is the favourite recreation of the gentlemen, and that it is carried to a very considerable extent; but here, as elsewhere within the country, it is kept extremely well out of sight. I do not think I was present with a pack of cards a dozen times during more than three years that I remained in the country. Billiards are much played, though in most places the amusement is illegal. It often appeared to me that the old women of a State made the laws, and the young men broke them.

Notwithstanding the diminutive size of the city, we found much to see and to amuse us.

The patent office is a curious record of the fertility of the mind of man when left to its own resources; but it gives ample proof also that it is not under such circumstances it is most usefully employed. This patent office contains models of all the mechanical inventions that have been produced in the Union, and the number is enormous. I asked the man who showed these, what proportion of them had been brought into use; he said about one in a thousand; he told me also, that they chiefly proceeded from mechanics and agriculturists settled in remote parts of the country, who had begun by endeavouring to hit upon some contrivance to enable them to *get along* without sending some thousand and odd miles for the thing they wanted. If the contrivance succeeded, they generally became so fond of this offspring of their ingenuity, that they brought it to Washington for a patent.

At the secretary of state's office we were shown autographs of all the potentates with whom the Union were in alliance; which, I believe, pretty well includes all. To the parchments bearing these royal signs manual were appended, of course, the official seals of each, enclosed in gold or silver boxes of handsome workmanship. I was amused by the manner in which one of their own, just prepared for the court of Russia, was displayed to us, and the superiority of their decorations pointed out. They were superior, and in much better taste than the rest; and I only wish that the feeling that induced this display would spread to every corner of the Union, and mix itself with every act and with every sentiment. Let America give a fair portion of her attention to the arts and the graces that embellish life, and I will make her another visit, and write another book as unlike this as possible.

from *American Notes*

CHARLES DICKENS (1812–1870)

British novelist Charles Dickens enjoyed a meteoric rise to literary fame with the series publication of *The Posthumous Papers of the Pickwick Club* (March 1836–November 1837). Subsequent years of popular and critical acclaim, success as a magazine editor, and acceptance into the most prestigious literary clubs and social salons in England marked a time of great fame and personal prosperity. Exhausted by the whirlwind of professional and social obligations, Dickens took a six-month visit to the United States in 1842. He longed to see the country he imagined free from class snobbery and official corruption—the perfect anecdote, he believed, both to the pain of his childhood spent partly in debtor's prison and to the graft of the England of his adulthood. Dickens and his wife, Catherine, were met at the Boston port by admiring throngs, a reception repeated over and over in the couple's stops in various cities from New England to New York, Philadelphia, Washington, and as far west as St. Louis. When the sketches Dickens composed along the way were published as *American Notes* (November 1842), his former hosts felt betrayed and belittled by the book's mix of gentle criticism and qualified praise of the American way of life and goverment. Of the American public reaction Thomas Carlyle wrote, "All Yankee-Doodle-dum blazed up like one universal soda bottle." The book's reception in England was likewise dismal. Dickens wrote *A Christmas Carol* (1843) partly to make up for the poor sales of *American Notes*. Despite the popular and critical success of Scrooge's story, sales were flat and the downturn in Dicken's career continued until the triumphant publication of *David Copperfield* (May 1849–1850).

We left Philadelphia by steamboat, at six o'clock one very cold morning, and turned our faces towards Washington.

In the course of this day's journey, as on subsequent occa-

sions, we encountered some Englishmen (small farmers, perhaps, or country publicans at home) who were settled in
America, and were travelling on their own affairs. Of all grades
and kinds of men that jostle one in the public conveyances of the
States, these are often the most intolerable and the most insuffer-
able companions. United to every disagreeable characteristic
that the worst kind of American travellers possess, these countrymen of ours display an amount of insolent conceit and cool
assumption of superiority, quite monstrous to behold. In the
coarse familiarity of their approach, and the effrontery of their
inquisitiveness (which they are in great haste to assert, as if they
panted to revenge themselves upon the decent old restraints of
home), they surpass any native specimens that came within my
range of observation: and I often grew so patriotic when I saw
and heard them, that I would cheerfully have submitted to a
reasonable fine, if I could have given any other country in the
whole world, the honour of claiming them for its children.

As Washington may be called the head-quarters of tobacco-
tinctured saliva, the time is come when I must confess, without
any disguise, that the prevalence of those two odious practices of
chewing and expectorating began about this time to be anything
but agreeable, and soon became most offensive and sickening. In
all the public places of America, this filthy custom is recognised.
In the courts of law, the judge has his spittoon, the crier his, the
witness his, and the prisoner his; while the jurymen and specta-
tors are provided for, as so many men who in the course of
nature must desire to spit incessantly. In the hospitals, the students of medicine are requested, by notices upon the wall, to eject
their tobacco juice into the boxes provided for that purpose, and
not to discolour the stairs. In public buildings, visitors are
implored, through the same agency, to squirt the essence of their
quids, or "plugs," as I have heard them called by gentlemen
learned in this kind of sweetmeat, into the national spittoons, and
not about the bases of the marble columns. But in some parts, this
custom is inseparably mixed up with every meal and morning call,
and with all the transactions of social life. The stranger, who fol-

lows in the track I took myself, will find it in its full bloom and glory, luxuriant in all its alarming recklessness, at Washington. And let him not persuade himself (as I once did, to my shame) that previous tourists have exaggerated its extent. The thing itself is an exaggeration of nastiness, which cannot be outdone.

On board this steamboat, there were two young gentlemen, with shirt-collars reversed as usual, and armed with very big walking-sticks; who planted two seats in the middle of the deck, at a distance of some four paces apart; took out their tobacco-boxes; and sat down opposite each other, to chew. In less than a quarter of an hour's time, these hopeful youths had shed about them on the clean boards, a copious shower of yellow rain; clearing, by that means, a kind of magic circle, within whose limits no intruders dared to come, and which they never failed to refresh and re-refresh before a spot was dry. This being before breakfast, rather disposed me, I confess, to nausea; but looking attentively at one of the expectorators, I plainly saw that he was young in chewing, and felt inwardly uneasy, himself. A glow of delight came over me at this discovery; and as I marked his face turn paler and paler, and saw the ball of tobacco in his left cheek, quiver with his suppressed agony, while yet he spat, and chewed, and spat again, in emulation of his older friend, I could have fallen on his neck and implored him to go on for hours.

We all sat down to a comfortable breakfast in the cabin below, where there was no more hurry or confusion than at such a meal in England, and where there was certainly greater politeness exhibited than at most of our stage-coach banquets. At about nine o'clock we arrived at the railroad station, and went on by the cars. At noon we turned out again, to cross a wide river in another steamboat; landed at a continuation of the railroad on the opposite shore; and went on by other cars; in which, in the course of the next hour or so, we crossed by wooden bridges, each a mile in length, two creeks, called respectively Great and Little Gunpowder. The water in both was blackened with flights of canvas-backed ducks, which are most delicious eating, and abound hereabouts at that season of the year.

These bridges are of wood, have no parapet, and are only just wide enough for the passage of the trains; which, in the event of the smallest accident, would inevitably be plunged into the river. They are startling contrivances, and are most agreeable when passed.

We stopped to dine at Baltimore, and being now in Maryland, were waited on, for the first time, by slaves. The sensation of exacting any service from human creatures who are bought and sold, and being, for the time, a party as it were to their condition, is not an enviable one. The institution exists, perhaps, in its least repulsive and most mitigated form in such a town as this; but it *is* slavery; and though I was, with respect to it, an innocent man, its presence filled me with a sense of shame and self-reproach.

After dinner, we went down to the railroad again, and took our seats in the cars for Washington. Being rather early, those men and boys who happened to have nothing particular to do, and were curious in foreigners, came (according to custom) round the carriage in which I sat; let down all the windows; thrust in their heads and shoulders; hooked themselves on conveniently, by their elbows; and fell to comparing notes on the subject of my personal appearance, with as much indifference as if I were a stuffed figure. I never gained so much uncompromising information with reference to my own nose and eyes, and various impressions wrought by my mouth and chin on different minds, and how my head looks when it is viewed from behind, as on these occasions. Some gentlemen were only satisfied by exercising their sense of touch; and the boys (who are surprisingly precocious in America) were seldom satisfied, even by that, but would return to the charge over and over again. Many a budding president has walked into my room with his cap on his head and his hands in his pockets, and stared at me for two whole hours: occasionally refreshing himself with a tweak of his nose, or a draught from the water-jug; or by walking to the windows and inviting other boys in the street below, to come up and do likewise: crying, "Here he is!" "Come on!" "Bring all your brothers!" with other hospitable entreaties of that nature.

We reached Washington at about half-past six that evening, and had upon the way a beautiful view of the Capitol, which is a fine building of the Corinthian order, placed upon a noble and commanding eminence. Arrived at the hotel; I saw no more of the place that night; being very tired, and glad to get to bed.

Breakfast over next morning, I walk about the streets for an hour or two, and, coming home, throw up the window in the front and back, and look out. Here is Washington, fresh in my mind and under my eye.

Take the worst parts of the City Road and Pentonville, or the straggling outskirts of Paris, where the houses are smallest, preserving all their oddities, but especially the small shops and dwellings, occupied in Pentonville (but not in Washington) by furniture-brokers, keepers of poor eating-houses, and fanciers of birds. Burn the whole down; build it up again in wood and plaster; widen it a little; throw in part of St. John's Wood; put green blinds outside all the private houses, with a red curtain and a white one in every window; plough up all the roads; plant a great deal of coarse turf in every place where it ought *not* to be; erect three handsome buildings in stone and marble, anywhere, but the more entirely out of everybody's way the better; call one the Post Office, one the Patent Office, and one the Treasury; make it scorching hot in the morning, and freezing cold in the afternoon, with an occasional tornado of wind and dust; leave a brick-field without the bricks, in all central places where a street may naturally be expected; and that's Washington.

The hotel in which we live, is a long row of small houses fronting on the street, and opening at the back upon a common yard, in which hangs a great triangle. Whenever a servant is wanted, somebody beats on this triangle from one stroke up to seven, according to the number of the house in which his presence is required; and as all the servants are always being wanted, and none of them ever come, this enlivening engine is in full performance the whole day through. Clothes are drying in the same yard; female slaves, with cotton handkerchiefs twisted round their heads, are running to and fro on the hotel business;

black waiters cross and recross with dishes in their hands; two great dogs are playing upon a mound of loose bricks in the centre of the little square; a pig is turning up his stomach to the sun, and grunting "that's comfortable!" and neither the men, nor the women, nor the dogs, nor the pig, nor any created creature, takes the smallest notice of the triangle, which is tingling madly all the time.

I walk to the front window, and look across the road upon a long, straggling row of houses, one story high, terminating, nearly opposite, but a little to the left, in a melancholy piece of waste ground with frowzy grass, which looks like a small piece of country that has taken to drinking, and has quite lost itself. Standing anyhow and all wrong, upon this open space, like something meteoric that has fallen down from the moon, is an odd, lop-sided, one-eyed kind of wooden building, that looks like a church, with a flag-staff as long as itself sticking out of a steeple something larger than a tea-chest. Under the window, is a small stand of coaches, whose slave-drivers are sunning themselves on the steps of our door, and talking idly together. The three most obtrusive houses near at hand, are the three meanest. On one—a shop, which never has anything in the window, and never has the door open—is painted in large characters, "THE CITY LUNCH." At another, which looks like a backway to somewhere else, but is an independent building in itself, oysters are procurable in every style. At the third, which is a very, very little tailor's shop, pants are fixed to order; or in other words, pantaloons are made to measure. And that is our street in Washington.

It is sometimes called the City of Magnificent Distances, but it might with greater propriety be termed the City of Magnificent Intentions; for it is only on taking a bird's-eye view of it from the top of the Capitol, that one can at all comprehend the vast designs of its projector, an aspiring Frenchman. Spacious avenues, that begin in nothing, and lead nowhere; streets, mile-long, that only want houses, roads and inhabitants; public buildings that need but a public to be complete; and ornaments of great thoroughfares, which only lack great thoroughfares to ornament—are its leading features. One might fancy the season over, and most of the houses gone out of town forever with their masters. To the admirers of cities it is a Barmecide Feast: a pleasant field for the imagination to rove in; a monument raised to a deceased project, with not even a legible inscription to record its departed greatness.

Such as it is, it is likely to remain. It was originally chosen for the seat of Government, as a means of averting the conflicting jealousies and interests of the different States; and very probably, too, as being remote from mobs; a consideration not to be slighted, even in America. It has no trade or commerce of its own: having little or no population beyond the President and his establishment; the members of the legislature who reside there during the session; the Government clerks and officers employed in the various departments; the keepers of the hotels and boarding-houses; and the tradesmen who supply their tables. It is very unhealthy. Few people would live in Washington, I take it, who were not obliged to reside there; and the tides of emigration and speculation, those rapid and regardless currents, are little likely to flow at any time towards such dull and sluggish water.

The principal features of the Capitol, are, of course, the two houses of Assembly. But there is, besides, in the centre of the building, a fine rotunda, ninety-six feet in diameter, and ninety-six high, whose circular wall is divided into compartments, ornamented by historical pictures. Four of these have for their subjects prominent events in the revolutionary struggle. They were painted by Colonel Trumbull, himself a member of Washington's staff at the time of their occurrence; from which circumstance they derive a peculiar interest of their own. In this same hall Mr. Greenough's large statue of Washington has been lately placed. It has great merits of course, but it struck me as being rather strained and violent for its subject. I could wish, however, to have seen it in a better light than it can ever be viewed in, where it stands.

There is a very pleasant and commodious library in the Capitol; and from a balcony in front, the bird's-eye view, of which I have just spoken, may be had, together with a beautiful prospect of the adjacent country. In one of the ornamented portions of the building, there is a figure of Justice; whereunto the Guide Book says, "the artist at first contemplated giving more of nudity, but he was warned that the public sentiment of this country would not admit of it, and in his caution he has gone, perhaps, into the opposite extreme." Poor Justice! she has been made to wear much stranger garments in America than those she pines in, in the Capitol. Let us hope that she has changed her dressmaker since they were fashioned, and that the public sentiment of the country did not cut out the clothes she hides her lovely figure in, just now.

The House of Representatives is a beautiful and spacious hall, of semicircular shape, supported by handsome pillars. One part of the gallery is appropriated to the ladies, and there they sit in front rows, and come in, and go out, as at a play or concert. The chair is canopied, and raised considerably above the floor of the House; and every member has an easy chair and a writing-desk to himself: which is denounced by some people out of doors as a most unfortunate and injudicious arrangement, tending to long sittings and prosaic speeches. It is an elegant chamber to look at, but a singularly bad one for all purposes of hearing. The Senate, which is smaller, is free from this objection, and is exceedingly well adapted to the uses for which it is designed. The sittings, I need hardly add, take place in the day; and the parliamentary forms are modelled on those of the old country.

I was sometimes asked, in my progress through other places, whether I had not been very much impressed by the *heads* of the law-makers at Washington; meaning not their chiefs and leaders, but literally their individual and personal heads, whereon their hair grew, and whereby the phrenological character of each legislator was expressed: and I almost as often struck my questioner dumb with indignant consternation by answering "No, that I didn't remember being at all overcome." As I must, at whatever hazard, repeat the avowal here, I will follow it up by relating my impressions on this subject in as few words as possible.

In the first place—it may be from some imperfect development of my organ of veneration—I do not remember having ever fainted away, or having even been moved to tears of joyful pride, at sight of any legislative body. I have borne the House of Commons like a man, and have yielded to no weakness, but slumber, in the House of Lords. I have seen elections for borough and county, and have never been impelled (no matter which party won) to damage my hat by throwing it up into the air in triumph, or to crack my voice by shouting forth any reference to our Glorious Constitution, to the noble purity of our independent voters, or, the unimpeachable integrity of our independent members. Having withstood such strong attacks upon my fortitude, it is possible that I may be of a cold and insensible temperament, amounting to iciness, in such matters; and therefore my impressions of the live pillars of the Capitol at Washington must be received with such grains of allowance as this free confession may seem to demand.

Did I see in this public body an assemblage of men, bound together in the sacred names of Liberty and Freedom, and so asserting the chaste dignity of those twin goddesses, in all their discussions, as to exalt at once the Eternal Principles to which their names are given, and their own character and the character of their countrymen, in the admiring eyes of the whole world?

It was but a week, since an aged, grey-haired man, a lasting honour to the land that gave him birth, who has done good service to his country, as his forefathers did, and who will be remembered scores upon scores of years after the worms bred in its corruption, are but so many grains of dust—it was but a week, since this old man had stood for days upon his trial before this very body, charged with having dared to assert the infamy of that traffic, which has for its accursed merchandise men and women, and their unborn children. Yes. And publicly exhibited in the same city all the while; gilded, framed and glazed; hung up for general admiration; shown to strangers not with shame, but pride; its face not turned towards the wall, itself not taken down and burned; is the Unanimous Declaration of the Thirteen

United States of America, which solemnly declares that All Men are created Equal; and are endowed by their Creator with the Inalienable Rights of Life, Liberty, and the Pursuit of Happiness!

It was not a month, since this same body had sat calmly by, and heard a man, one of themselves, with oaths which beggars in their drink reject, threaten to cut another's throat from ear to ear. There he sat, among them; not crushed by the general feeling of the assembly, but as good a man as any.

There was but a week to come, and another of that body, for doing his duty to those who sent him there; for claiming in a Republic the Liberty and Freedom of expressing their sentiments, and making known their prayer; would be tried, found guilty, and have strong censure passed upon him by the rest. His was a grave offence indeed; for years before, he had risen up and said, "A gang of male and female slaves for sale, warranted to breed like cattle, linked to each other by iron fetters, are passing now along the open street beneath the windows of your Temple of Equality! Look!" But there are many kinds of hunters engaged in the Pursuit of Happiness, and they go variously armed. It is the Inalienable Right of some among them, to take the field after *their* Happiness equipped with cat and cartwhip, stocks, and iron collar, and to shout their view halloa! (always in praise of Liberty) to the music of clanking chains and bloody stripes.

Where sat the many legislators of coarse threats; of words and blows such as coalheavers deal upon each other, when they forget their breeding? On every side. Every session had its anecdotes of that kind, and the actors were all there.

Did I recognise in this assembly, a body of men, who, applying themselves in a new world to correct some of the falsehoods and vices of the old, purified the avenues to Public Life, paved the dirty ways to Place and Power, debated and made laws for the Common Good, and had no party but their Country?

I saw in them, the wheels that move the meanest perversion of virtuous Political Machinery that the worst tools ever wrought. Despicable trickery at elections; under-handed tamperings with public officers; cowardly attacks upon opponents, with scurrilous newspapers for shields, and hired pens for daggers; shameful trucklings to mercenary knaves, whose claim to be considered, is, that every day and week they sow new crops of ruin with their venal types, which are the dragon's teeth of yore, in everything but sharpness; aidings and abettings of every bad inclination in the popular mind, and artful suppressions of all its good influences: such things as these, and in a word, Dishonest Faction in its most depraved and most unblushing form, stared out from every corner of the crowded hall.

Did I see among them, the intelligence and refinement: the true, honest, patriotic heart of America? Here and there, were drops of its blood and life, but they scarcely coloured the stream of desperate adventurers which sets that way for profit and for pay. It is the game of these men, and of their profligate organs, to make the strife of politics so fierce and brutal, and so destructive of all self-respect in worthy men, that sensitive and delicate-minded persons shall be kept aloof, and they, and such as they, be left to battle out their selfish views unchecked. And thus this lowest of all scrambling fights goes on, and they who in other countries would, from their intelligence and station, most aspire to make the laws, do here recoil the farthest from that degradation.

That there are, among the representatives of the people in both Houses, and among all parties, some men of high character and great abilities, I need not say. The foremost among those politicians who are known in Europe, have been already described, and I see no reason to depart from the rule I have laid down for my guidance, of abstaining from all mention of individuals. It will be sufficient to add, that to the most favourable accounts that have been written of them, I more than fully and most heartily subscribe; and that personal intercourse and free communication have bred within me, not the result predicted in the very doubtful proverb, but increased admiration and respect. They are striking men to look at, hard to deceive, prompt to act, lions in energy, Crichtons in varied accomplishments, Indians in fire of eye and gesture, Americans in strong and generous impulse; and they as well represent the honour and wisdom of their country at home, as the distinguished gentleman who is now its Minister at the British Court sustains its highest character abroad.

I visited both houses nearly every day, during my stay in Washington. On my initiatory visit to the House of Representatives, they divided against a decision of the chair; but the chair won. The second time I went, the member who was speaking, being interrupted by a laugh, mimicked it, as one child would in quarrelling with another, and added, "that he would make honourable gentlemen opposite, sing out a little more on the other side of their mouths presently." But interruptions are rare; the speaker being usually heard in silence. There are more quarrels than with us, and more threatenings than gentlemen are accustomed to exchange in any civilised society of which we have record: but farm-yard imitations have not as yet been imported from the Parliament of the United Kingdom. The feature in oratory which appears to be the most practised, and most relished, is the constant repetition of the same idea or shadow of an idea in fresh words; and the inquiry out of doors is not, "What did he say?" but, "How long did he speak?" These, however, are but enlargements of a principle which prevails elsewhere.

The Senate is a dignified and decorous body, and its proceedings are conducted with much gravity and order. Both houses are handsomely carpeted; but the state to which these carpets are reduced by the universal disregard of the spittoon with which every honourable member is accommodated, and the extraordinary improvements on the pattern which are squirted and dabbled upon it in every direction, do not admit of being described. I will merely observe, that I strongly recommend all strangers not to look at the floor; and if they happen to drop anything, though it be their purse, not to pick it up with an ungloved hand on any account.

It is somewhat remarkable too, at first, to say the least, to see so many honourable members with swelled faces; and it is scarcely less remarkable to discover that this appearance is caused by the quantity of tobacco they contrive to stow within the hollow of the cheek. It is strange enough too, to see an honourable gentleman leaning back in his tilted chair with his legs on the desk before him, shaping a convenient "plug" with his penknife, and when it is quite ready for use, shooting the old one from his mouth, as from a pop-gun, and clapping the new one in its place.

I was surprised to observe that even steady old chewers of great experience, are not always good marksmen, which has rather inclined me to doubt that general proficiency with the rifle, of which we have heard so much in England. Several gentlemen called upon me who, in the course of conversation, frequently missed the spittoon at five paces; and one (but he was certainly short-sighted) mistook the closed sash for the open window, at three. On another occasion, when I dined out, and was sitting with two ladies and some gentlemen round a fire before dinner, one of the company fell short of the fireplace, six distinct times. I am disposed to think, however, that this was occasioned by his not aiming at that object; as there was a white marble hearth before the fender, which was more convenient, and may have suited his purpose better.

The Patent Office at Washington, furnishes an extraordinary example of American enterprise and ingenuity; for the immense number of models it contains, are the accumulated inventions of only five years; the whole of the previous collection having been destroyed by fire. The elegant structure in which they are arranged, is one of design rather than execution, for there is but one side erected out of four, though the works are stopped. The Post Office is a very compact and very beautiful building. In one of the departments, among a collection of rare and curious articles, are deposited the presents which have been made from time to time to the American ambassadors at foreign courts by the various potentates to whom they were the accredited agents of the Republic; gifts which by the law they are not permitted to retain. I confess that I·looked upon this as a very painful exhibition, and one by no means flattering to the national standard of honesty and honour. That can scarcely be a high state of moral feeling which imagines a gentleman of repute and station, likely to be corrupted, in the discharge of his duty, by the present of a snuff-box, or a richly-mounted sword, or an Eastern shawl; and surely the Nation who reposes confidence in her appointed servants, is likely to be better served, than she who makes them the subject of such very mean and paltry suspicions.

At George Town, in the suburbs, there is a Jesuit College; delightfully situated, and, so far as I had an opportunity of seeing, well managed. Many persons who are not members of the Romish Church, avail themselves, I believe, of these institutions, and of the advantageous opportunities they afford for the education of their children. The heights of this neighbourhood, above the Potomac River, are very picturesque: and are free, I should conceive, from some of the insalubrities of Washington. The air, at that elevation, was quite cool and refreshing, when in the city it was burning hot.

The President's mansion is more like an English clubhouse, both within and without, than any other kind of establishment with which I can compare it. The ornamental ground about it has been laid out in garden walks; they are pretty, and agreeable to the eye; though they have that uncomfortable air of having been made yesterday, which is far from favourable to the display of such beauties.

My first visit to this house was on the morning after my arrival, when I was carried thither by an official gentleman, who was so kind as to charge himself with my presentation to the President.

We entered a large hall, and having twice or thrice rung a bell which nobody answered, walked without further ceremony through the rooms on the ground floor, as divers other gentlemen (mostly with their hats on, and their hands in their pockets) were doing very leisurely. Some of these had ladies with them, to whom they were showing the premises; others were lounging on the chairs and sofas; others, in a perfect state of exhaustion from listlessness, were yawning drearily.

The greater portion of this assemblage were rather asserting their supremacy than doing anything else, as they had no par-

ticular business there, that anybody knew of. A few were closely
eyeing the movables, as if to make quite sure that the President
(who was far from popular) had not made away with any of the
furniture, or sold the fixtures for his private benefit.

After glancing at these loungers; who were scattered over a
pretty drawing-room, opening upon a terrace which commanded
a beautiful prospect of the river and the adjacent country; and
who were sauntering, too, about a larger state-room called the
Eastern Drawing-room; we went upstairs into another chamber,
where were certain visitors, waiting for audiences. At sight of
my conductor, a black in plain clothes and yellow slippers who
was gliding noiselessly about, and whispering messages in the
ears of the more impatient, made a sign of recognition, and
glided off to announce him.

We had previously looked into another chamber fitted all
round with a great bare wooden desk or counter, whereon lay
files of newspapers, to which sundry gentlemen were referring.
But there were no such means of beguiling the time in this apartment, which was as unpromising and tiresome as any waiting-
room in one of our public establishments, or any physician's
dining-room during his hours of consultation at home.

There were some fifteen or twenty persons in the room. One,
a tall, wiry, muscular old man, from the west; sunburnt and
swarthy; with a brown white hat on his knees, and a giant
umbrella resting between his legs; who sat bolt upright in his
chair, frowning steadily at the carpet, and twitching the hard
lines about his mouth, as if he had made up his mind "to fix" the
President on what he had to say, and wouldn't bate him a grain.
Another, a Kentucky farmer, six-feet-six in height, with his hat
on, and his hands under his coat-tails, who leaned against the
wall and kicked the floor with his heel, as though he had Time's
head under his shoe, and were literally "killing" him. A third, an
oval-faced, bilious-looking man, with sleek black hair cropped
close, and whiskers and beard shaved down to blue dots, who
sucked the head of a thick stick, and from time to time took it
out of his mouth, to see how it was getting on. A fourth did

nothing but whistle. A fifth did nothing but spit. And indeed all these gentlemen were so very persevering and energetic in this latter particular, and bestowed their favours so abundantly upon the carpet, that I take it for granted the Presidential housemaids have high wages, or, to speak more genteelly, an ample amount of "compensation:" which is the American word for salary, in the case of all public servants.

We had not waited in this room many minutes, before the black messenger returned, and conducted us into another of smaller dimensions, where, at a business-like table covered with papers, sat the President himself. He looked somewhat worn and anxious, and well he might; being at war with everybody— but the expression of his face was mild and pleasant, and his manner was remarkably unaffected, gentlemanly, and agreeable. I thought that in his whole carriage and demeanour, he became his station singularly well.

Being advised that the sensible etiquette of the republican court, admitted of a traveller, like myself, declining, without any impropriety, an invitation to dinner, which did not reach me until I had concluded my arrangements for leaving Washington some days before that to which it referred, I only returned to this house once. It was on the occasion of one of those general assemblies which are held on certain nights, between the hours of nine and twelve o'clock, and are called, rather oddly, Levees.

I went, with my wife, at about ten. There was a pretty dense crowd of carriages and people in the court-yard, and so far as I could make out, there were no very clear regulations for the taking up or setting down of company. There were certainly no policemen to soothe startled horses, either by sawing at their bridles or flourishing truncheons in their eyes; and I am ready to make oath that no inoffensive persons were knocked violently on the head, or poked acutely in their backs or stomachs; or brought to a standstill by any such gentle means, and then taken into custody for not moving on. But there was no confusion or disorder. Our carriage reached the porch in its turn, without any blustering, swearing, shouting, backing, or other disturbance: and we dismounted with as much ease and comfort as though we had been escorted by the whole Metropolitan Force from A to Z inclusive.

The suite of rooms on the ground-floor, were lighted up; and a military band was playing in the hall. In the smaller drawing-room, the centre of a circle of company, were the President and his daughter-in-law, who acted as the lady of the mansion; and a very interesting, graceful, and accomplished lady too. One gentleman who stood among this group, appeared to take upon himself the functions of a master of the ceremonies. I saw no other officers or attendants, and none were needed.

The great drawing-room, which I have already mentioned, and the other chambers on the ground-floor, were crowded to excess. The company was not, in our sense of the term, select, for it comprehended persons of very many grades and classes; nor was there any great display of costly attire: indeed, some of the costumes may have been, for aught I know, grotesque enough. But the decorum and propriety of behaviour which prevailed, were unbroken by any rude or disagreeable incident; and every man, even among the miscellaneous crowd in the hall who were admitted without any orders or tickets to look on, appeared to feel that he was a part of the Institution, and was responsible for its preserving a becoming character, and appearing to the best advantage.

That these visitors, too, whatever their station, were not without some refinement of taste and appreciation of intellectual gifts, and gratitude to those men who, by the peaceful exercise of great abilities, shed new charms and associations upon the homes of their countrymen, and elevate their character in other lands, was most earnestly testified by their reception of Washington Irving, my dear friend, who had recently been appointed Minister at the court of Spain, and who was among them that night, in his new character, for the first and last time before going abroad. I sincerely believe that in all the madness of American politics, few public men would have been so earnestly, devotedly, and affectionately caressed, as this most charming writer: and I have seldom respected a public assembly more, than I did this eager throng, when I saw them turning with one mind from noisy orators and officers of state, and flocking with a generous and honest impulse round the man of quiet pursuits: proud in his promotion as reflecting back upon their country: and grateful to him with their whole hearts for the store of graceful fancies he had poured out among them. Long may he dispense such treasures with unsparing hand; and long may they remember him as worthily!

Letter to Mrs. J. G. Holland

EMILY DICKINSON (1830–1886)

Emily Dickinson spent the entirety of her quiet life in Amherst, Massachusetts. The poet made only a few trips away from the Dickinson homestead on Main Street, to neighboring towns, to Boston, and in 1855, as far away as Washington and Philadelphia. On this latter trip, Dickinson and her younger sister Lavinia lodged at Washington's Willard Hotel while visiting their father, then serving a term in Congress. With her father's service in mind, she wrote the gently mocking lines in one of her earliest poems (Number Three):

Unto the Legislature
My country bids me go;
I'll take my *india rubbers,*
In case the *wind* should blow!

Philadelphia, 18 March 1855

Dear Mrs. Holland and Minnie, and Dr. Holland too—I have stolen away from company to write a note to you; and to say that I love you still.

I am not at home—I have been away just five weeks today, and shall not go quite yet back to Massachusetts. Vinnie is with me here, and we have wandered together into many new ways.

We were three weeks in Washington, while father was there, and have been two in Philadelphia. We have had many pleasant times, and seen much that is fair, and heard much that is wonderful—many sweet ladies and noble gentlemen have taken us by the hand and smiled upon us pleasantly—and the sun shines brighter for our way thus far.

I will not tell you what I saw—the elegance, the grandeur; you will not care to know the value of the diamonds my Lord and Lady wore, but if you haven't been to the sweet Mount Vernon,

then I *will* tell you how on one soft spring day we glided down
the Potomac in a painted boat, and jumped upon the shore—
how hand in hand we stole along up a tangled pathway till we
reached the tomb of General George Washington, how we
paused beside it, and no one spoke a word, then hand in hand,
walked on again, not less wise or sad for that marble story; how
we went within the door raised the latch he lifted when he last
went home—thank the Ones in Light that he's since passed in
through a brighter wicket! Oh, I could spend a long day, if it did
not weary you, telling of Mount Vernon and I will sometime if
we live and meet again, and God grant we shall!

I wonder if you have all forgotten us, we have stayed away so
long. I hope you haven't—I tried to write so hard before I went
from home, but the moments were so busy, and then they *flew*
so. I was sure when days *did* come in which I was less busy, I
should seek your forgiveness, and it did not occur to me that you
might not forgive me. Am I too late today? Even if you are angry,
I shall keep praying you, till from very weariness, you will take
me in. It seems to me many a day since we were in Springfield,
and Minnie and the *dumb-bells* seem as vague—as vague; and
sometimes I wonder if I ever dreamed—then if I'm dreaming
now, then if I *always* dreamed, and there is not a world, and not
these darling friends, for whom I would not count my life too
great a sacrifice. Thank God there is a world, and that the friends
we love dwell forever and ever in a house above. I fear I grow
incongruous, but to meet my friends does delight me so that I
quite forget time and sense and so forth.

Now, my precious friends, if you won't forget me until I get
home, and become more sensible, I will write again, and more
properly. Why didn't I ask before, if you were well and happy?
Forgetful
Emilie.

from *Hospital Sketches*

LOUISA MAY ALCOTT (1832–1888)

Louisa May Alcott was born in Germantown, Pennsylvania, and grew up in Boston and Concord, Massachusetts. She received her only schooling informally from her father, Amos Bronson Alcott. Amos was a well-respected Transcendentalist, and Louisa May grew up in the world of Ralph Waldo Emerson and Henry David Thoreau. Much of Alcott's childhood was spent working to help support a family that could not live off the meager money her father made giving speeches on issues of the day. Alcott began writing at a young age, but her career showed little return until her letters written as a nurse in the Civil War were serially published in the *Commonwealth*, a Boston anti-slavery newspaper. Each issue of the newspaper containing an Alcott letter was an immediate sellout on the newsstand, and the writings were subsequently collected as *Hospital Sketches* (1863). After *Sketches*, other writings emerged, including her first novel for adults, *Moods* (1864), and her best-known book, *Little Women* (first published in 1868). After the success of these novels, Alcott had the financial security to work for the women's suffrage and temperance movements, as well as to continue her literary career. The following selection from *Hospital Sketches* recounts Alcott's experiences as a nurse serving at the Union Hotel Hospital, a former tavern commandeered for military purposes in 1861 and soon abandoned as unsafe and unsanitary.

Washington.—It was dark when we arrived; and, but for the presence of another friendly gentleman, I should have yielded myself a helpless prey to the first overpowering hack man, who insisted that I wanted to go just where I didn't. Putting me into the conveyance I belonged in, my escort added to the obligation by pointing out the objects of interest which we passed in our long drive. Though I'd often been told that Washington was a spacious place, its visible magnitude quite took my breath away, and of course I quoted Randolph's expression, "a city of magnificent distances," as I suppose every one does when they see it. The Capitol was so like the pictures that hang opposite the staring Father of his Country, in boarding-houses and hotels, that it did not impress me, except to recall the time when I was sure that Cinderella went to housekeeping in just such a place, after she had married the inflammable Prince; though, even at that early period, I had my doubts as to the wisdom of a match whose foundation was of glass.

The White House was lighted up, and carriages were rolling in and out of the great gate. I stared hard at the famous East Room, and would have like a peep through the crack of the door. My old gentleman was indefatigable in his attentions, and I said "Splendid!" to everything he pointed out, though I suspect I often admired the wrong place, and missed the right. Pennsylvania Avenue, with its bustle, lights, music, and military, made me feel as if I'd crossed the water and landed somewhere in Carnival time. Coming to less noticeable parts of the city, my companion fell silent, and I meditated upon the perfection which Art had attained in America—having just passed a bronze statue of some hero, who looked like a black Methodist minister, in a cocked hat, above the waist, and a tipsy squire below; while his horse stood like an opera dancer, on one leg, in a high, but somewhat remarkable wind, which blew his mane one way and his massive tail the other.

"Hurly-burly House, ma'am!" called a voice, startling me from my reverie, as we stopped before a great pile of buildings, with a flag flying before it, sentinels at the door, and a very trying quantity of men lounging about. My heart beat rather faster than usual, and it suddenly struck me that I was very far from home; but I descended with dignity, wondering whether I should be stopped for want of a countersign, and forced to pass the night in the street. Marching boldly up the steps, I found that no form was necessary, for the men fell back, the guard touched their caps, a boy opened the door, and as it closed behind me, I felt that I was fairly started and Nurse Periwinkle's Mission was begun.

. . .

The boy came in with the rest, and the man who was taken dead from the ambulance was the Kit he mourned. Well he might; for, when the wounded were brought from Fredericksburg, the child lay on one of the camps thereabout, and this good friend, though sorely hurt himself, would not leave him to the exposure and neglect of such a time and place; but, wrapping him in his own blanket, carried him in his arms to the transport, tended him during the passage, and only yielded up his charge when Death met him at the door of the hospital which promised care and comfort for the boy. For ten days, Teddy had shivered or burned with fever and ague, pining the while for Kit, and refusing to be comforted, because he had not been able to thank him for the generous protection, which, perhaps, had cost the giver's life. The vivid dream had wrung the childish heart with a fresh pang, and when I tried the solace fitted for his years, the remorseful fear that haunted him found vent in a fresh burst of tears, as he looked at the wasted hands I was endeavoring to warm:

"Oh! if I'd only been as thin when Kit carried me as I am now, maybe he wouldn't have died; but I was heavy, he was hurt worser than we knew, and so it killed him; and I didn't see him, to say good bye."

This thought had troubled him in secret; and my assurances that his friend would probably have died at all events, hardly assuaged the bitterness of his regretful grief.

At this juncture, the delirious man began to shout; the one-legged rose up in his bed, as if preparing for another dart; Teddy bewailed himself more piteously than before: and if ever a woman was at her wit's end, that distracted female was Nurse Periwinkle, during the space of two or three minutes, as she vibrated between the three beds, like an agitated pendulum. Like a most opportune reinforcement, Dan, the bandy, appeared, and devoted himself to the lively party, leaving me free to return to my post; for the Prussian, with a nod and a smile, took the lad away to his own bed, and lulled him to sleep with a soothing murmur, like a mammoth humble-bee. I liked that in Fritz, and if he ever wondered afterward at the dainties which sometimes found their way into his rations, or the extra comforts of his bed, he might have found a solution of the mystery in sundry persons' knowledge of the fatherly action of that night.

Hardly was I settled again, when the inevitable bowl appeared, and its bearer delivered a message I had expected, yet dreaded to receive:

"John is going, ma'am, and wants to see you, if you can come."

"The moment this boy is asleep; tell him so, and let me know if I am in danger of being too late."

My Ganymede departed, and while I quieted poor Shaw, I thought of John. He came in a day or two after the others; and, one evening, when I entered my "pathetic room," I found a lately emptied bed occupied by a large, fair man, with a fine face, and the serenest eyes I ever met. One of the earlier comers had often spoken of a friend, who had remained behind, that those apparently worse wounded than himself might reach a shelter first. It seemed a David and Jonathan sort of friendship. The man fretted for his mate, and was never tired of praising John— his courage, sobriety, self-denial, and unfailing kindliness of heart; always winding up with: "He's an out an' out fine feller, ma'am; you see if he ain't."

I had some curiosity to behold this piece of excellence, and when he came, watched him for a night or two, before I made friends with him; for, to tell the truth, I was a little afraid of the stately looking man, whose bed had to be lengthened to accommodate his commanding stature; who seldom spoke, uttered no complaint, asked no sympathy but tranquilly observed what went on about him; and, as he lay high upon his pillows, no picture of dying statesman or warrior was ever fuller of real dignity than this Virginia blacksmith. A most attractive face he had, framed in brown hair and beard, comely featured and full of vigor, as yet unsubdued by pain; thoughtful and often beautifully mild while watching the afflictions of others, as if entirely forgetful of his own. His mouth was grave and firm, with plenty of will and courage in its lines, but a smile could make it as sweet as any woman's; and his eyes were child's eyes, looking one fairly in the face, with a clear, straightforward glance, which promised well for such as placed their faith in him. He seemed to cling to life, as if it were rich in duties and delights, and he had learned the secret of content. The only time I saw his composure disturbed, was when my surgeon brought another to examine John, who scrutinized their faces with an anxious look, asking of the elder: "Do you think I shall pull through, sir?" "I hope so, my man." And, as the two passed on, John's eye still followed them, with an intentness which would have won a clearer answer from them, had they seen it. A momentary shadow flitted over his face; then came the usual serenity, as if, in that brief eclipse, he had acknowledged the existence of some hard possibility, and, asking nothing yet hoping all things, left the issue in God's hands, with that submission which is true piety.

The next night, as I went my rounds with Dr. P., I happened to ask which man in the room probably suffered most; and, to my great surprise, he glanced at John:

"Every breath he draws is like a stab; for the ball pierced the left lung, broke a rib, and did no end of damage here and there; so the poor lad can find neither forgetfulness nor ease, because he must lie on his wounded back or suffocate. It will be a hard struggle, and a long one, for he possesses great vitality; but even his temperate life can't save him; I wish it could."

"You don't mean he must die, Doctor?"

"Bless you, there's not the slightest hope for him; and you'd better tell him so before long; women have a way of doing such things comfortably, so I leave it to you. He won't last more than a day or two, at furthest."

I could have sat down on the spot and cried heartily, if I had not learned the wisdom of bottling up one's tears for leisure moments. Such an end seemed very hard for such a man, when half a dozen worn out, worthless bodies round him, were gathering up the remnants of wasted lives, to linger on for years perhaps, burdens to others, daily reproaches to themselves. The army needed men like John, earnest, brave, and faithful; fighting for liberty and justice with both heart and hand, true soldiers of the Lord. I could not give him up so soon, or think with any patience of so excellent a nature robbed of its fulfilment and blundered into eternity by the rashness or stupidity of those at whose hands so many lives may be required. It was an easy thing for Dr. P. to say: "Tell him he must die," but a cruelly hard thing to do, and by no means as "comfortable" as he politely suggested. I had not the heart to do it then and privately indulged the hope that some change for the better might take place, in spite of gloomy prophesies; so, rendering my task unnecessary. A few minutes later, as I came in again, with fresh rollers, I saw John sitting erect, with no one to support him, while the surgeon dressed his back. I had never hitherto seen it done; for, having simpler wounds to attend to, and knowing the fidelity of the attendant, I had left John to him, thinking it might be more agreeable and safe; for both strength and experience were needed in his case. I had forgotten that the strong man might long for the gentler tendance of a woman's hands, the sympathetic magnetism of a woman's presence, as well as the feebler souls about him. The Doctor's words caused me to reproach myself with neglect, not of any real duty perhaps, but of those little cares and kindnesses that solace homesick spirits, and make the heavy hours pass easier. John looked lonely and forsaken just then, as he sat with bent head, hands folded on his knee, and no outward sign of suffering, till, looking nearer, I saw great tears roll down and drop upon the floor. It was a new sight there; for, though I had seen many suffer, some swore, some groaned, most endured silently, but none wept. Yet it did not seem weak, only very touching, and straightway my fear vanished, my heart opened wide and took him in, as, gathering the bent head in my arms, as freely as if he had been a little child, I said, "Let me help you bear it, John."

Never, on any human countenance, have I seen so swift and beautiful a look of gratitude, surprise and comfort, as that which answered me more eloquently than the whispered—

"Thank you, ma'am, this is right good! This is what I wanted!"

"Then why not ask for it before?"

"I didn't like to be a trouble; you seemed so busy, and I could manage to get on alone."

"You shall not want it any more, John."

Nor did he; for now I understood the wistful look that some-times followed me, as I went out, after a brief pause beside his bed, or merely a passing nod, while busied with those who seemed to need me more than he, because more urgent in their demands; now I knew that to him, as to so many, I was the poor substitute for mother, wife, or sister and in his eyes no stranger, but a friend who hitherto had seemed neglectful; for, in his mod-esty, he had never guessed the truth. This was changed now; and, through the tedious operation of probing, bathing, and dressing his wounds, he leaned against me, holding my hand fast, and, if pain wrung further tears from him, no one saw them fall but me. When he was laid down again, I hovered about him, in a remorseful state of mind that would not let me rest, till I had bathed his face, brushed his "bonny brown hair," set all things smooth about him, and laid a knot of heath and heliotrope on his clean pillow. While doing this, he watched me with the satis-fied expression I so liked to see; and when I offered the little nosegay, held it carefully in his great hand, smoothed a ruffled leaf or two, surveyed and smelt it with an air of genuine delight, and lay contentedly regarding the glimmer of the sunshine on the green. Although the manliest man among my forty, he said, "Yes, ma'am," like a little boy; received suggestions for his com-fort with the quick smile that brightened his whole face; and now and then, as I stood tidying the table by his bed, I felt him softly touch my gown, as if to assure himself that I was there.

Anything more natural and frank I never saw, and found this brave John as bashful as brave, yet full of excellencies and fine aspirations, which, having no power to express themselves in words, seemed to have bloomed into his character and made him what he was.

After that night, an hour of each evening that remained to him was devoted to his ease or pleasure. He could not talk much, for breath was precious, and he spoke in whispers; but from occasional conversations, I gleaned scraps of private history which only added to the affection and respect I felt for him. Once he asked me to write a letter, and as I settled pen and paper, I said, with an irrepressible glimmer of feminine curiosity, "Shall it be addressed to wife, or mother, John?"

"Neither, ma'am. I've got no wife, and will write to mother myself when I get better. Did you think I was married because of this?" he asked, touching a plain ring he wore, and often turned thoughtfully on his finger when he lay alone.

"Partly that, but more from a settled sort of look you have, a look which young men seldom get until they marry."

"I don't know that; but I'm not so very young, ma'am, thirty in May and have been what you might call settled this ten years; for mother's a widow, I'm the oldest child she has, and it wouldn't do for me to marry until Lizzy has a home of her own, and Laurie's learned his trade; for we're not rich, and I must be father to the children and husband to the dear old woman, if I can."

"No doubt but you are both, John; yet how came you to go to war, if you felt so? Wasn't enlisting as bad as marrying?"

"No ma'am, not as I see it, for one is helping my neighbor, the other pleasing myself. I went because I couldn't help it. I didn't want the glory or the pay; I wanted the right thing done, and people kept saying the men who were in earnest ought to fight. I was in earnest, the Lord knows! but I held off as long as I could, not knowing which was my duty; mother saw the case, gave me her ring to keep me steady, and said, 'Go:' so I went."

A short story and a simple one, but the man and the mother

were portrayed better than pages of fine writing could have done it.

"Do you ever regret that you came, when you lie here suffering so much?"

"Never ma'am; I haven't helped a great deal, but I've shown I was willing to give my life, and perhaps I've got to; but I don't blame anybody, and if it was to do over again, I'd do it. I'm a little sorry I wasn't wounded in front; it looks cowardly to be hit in the back, but I obeyed orders, and it don't matter in the end, I know."

Poor John! it did not matter now, except that a shot in front might have spared the long agony in store for him, he seemed to read the thought that troubled me, as he spoke so hopefully when there was no hope, for he suddenly added:

"This is my first battle; do they think it's going to be my last?"

"I'm afraid they do, John."

It was the hardest question I had ever been called upon to answer; doubly hard with those clear eyes fixed on mine, forcing a truthful answer by their own truth. He seemed a little startled at first, pondered over the fateful fact a moment then shook his head, with a glance at the broad chest and muscular limbs stretched out before him:

"I'm not afraid, but it's difficult to believe all at once. I'm so strong it don't seem possible for such a little wound to kill me."

Merry Mercutio's dying words glanced through my memory as he spoke: "'Tis not so deep as a well, nor so wide as a church door, but 'tis enough." And John would have said the same could he have seen the ominous black holes between his shoulders, he never had; and, seeing the ghastly sights about him, could not believe his own wound more fatal than these, for all the suffering it caused him.

"Shall I write to your mother, now?" I asked, thinking that these sudden tidings might change all plans and purposes; but they did not; for the man received the order of the Divine Commander to march with the same unquestioning obedience with which the soldier had received that of the human one, doubtless remembering that the first led him to life, and the last to death.

"No, ma'am; to Laurie just the same; he'll break it to her best, and I'll add a line to her myself when you get done."

So I wrote the letter which he dictated, finding it better than any I had sent; for, though here and there a little ungrammatical or inelegant, each sentence came to me briefly worded, but most expressive; full of excellent counsel to the boy, tenderly bequeathing "mother and Lizzie" to his care, and bidding him good bye in words the sadder for their simplicity. He added a few lines, with steady hand, and, as I sealed it, said, with a patient sort of sigh, "I hope the answer will come in time for me to see it"; then, turning away his face, laid the flowers against his lips, as if to hide some quiver of emotion at the thought of such a sudden sundering of all the dear home ties.

These things had happened two days before; now John was dying, and the letter had not come. I had been summoned to many death beds in my life, but to none that made my heart ache as it did then, since my mother called me to watch the departure of a spirit akin to this in its gentleness and patient strength. As I went in, John stretched out both hands:

"I knew you'd come! I guess I'm moving on, ma'am."

He was; and so rapidly that, even while he spoke, over his face I saw the grey veil falling that no human hand can lift, I sat down by him, wiped the drops from his forehead, stirred the air about him with the slow wave of a fan, and waited to help him die. He stood in sore need of help and I could do so little; for, as the doctor had foretold, the strong body rebelled against death, and fought every inch of the way, forcing him to draw each breath with a spasm, and clench his hands with an imploring look, as if he asked, "How long must I endure this, and be still!" For hours he suffered dumbly, without a moment's respite, or a moment's murmuring; his limbs grew cold, his face damp, his lips white, and, again and again, he tore the covering off his breast, as if the lightest weight added to his agony; yet through it all, his eyes never lost their perfect serenity, and the man's soul seemed to sit therein, undaunted by the ills that vexed his flesh.

One by one, the men woke, and round the room appeared a circle of pale faces and watchful eyes, full of awe and pity; for, though a stranger, John was beloved by all. Each man there had wondered at his patience, respected his piety, admired his fortitude, and now lamented his hard death; for the influence of an upright nature had made itself deeply felt, even in one little week. Presently, the Jonathan who so loved this comely David, came creeping from his bed for a last look and word. The kind soul was full of trouble, as the choke in his voice, the grasp of his hand, betrayed; but there were no tears, and the farewell of the friends was the more touching for its brevity.

"Old boy, how are you?" faltered the one.

"Most through, thank heaven!" whispered the other.

"Can I say or do anything for you anywheres?"

"Take my things home, and tell them that I did my best."

"I will! I will!"

"Good bye, Ned."

"Good bye, John, good bye!"

They kissed each other, tenderly as women, and so parted, for poor Ned could not stay to see his comrade die. For a little while, there was no sound in the room but the drip of water, from a stump or two, and John's distressful gasps, as he slowly breathed his life away. I thought him nearly gone, and had just laid down the fan, believing its help to be no longer needed, when suddenly he rose up in his bed, and cried out with a bitter cry that broke the silence, sharply startling every one with its agonized appeal:

"For God's sake, give me air!"

It was the only cry pain or death had wrung from him, the only boon he had asked; and none of us could grant it, for all the airs that blew were useless now. Dan flung up the window. The first, red streak of dawn was warming the grey east, a herald of the coming sun; John saw it, and with the love of light which lingers in us to the end, seemed to read in it a sign of hope of help, for, over his whole face there broke that mysterious expression, brighter than any smile, which often comes to eyes that look their last. He laid himself gently down; and, stretching out his strong right arm, as if to grasp and bring the blessed air to his lips in a fuller flow, lapsed into a merciful unconsciousness, which assured us that for him suffering was forever past. He died then; for, though the heavy breaths still tore their way up for a little longer, they were but the waves of an ebbing tide that beat unfelt against the wreck, which an immortal voyager had deserted with a smile. He never spoke again but to the end held my hand close, so close that when he was asleep at last, I could not draw it away. Dan helped me, warning me as he did so that it was unsafe for dead and living flesh to lie so long together; but though my hand was strangely cold and stiff, and four white marks remained across its back, even when warmth and color had returned elsewhere, I could not but be glad that, through its touch, the presence of human sympathy, perhaps, had lightened that hard labor.

When they had made him ready for the grave, John lay in state for half an hour, a thing which seldom happened in that busy place; but a universal sentiment of reverence and affection seemed to fill the hearts of all who had known or heard of him; and when the rumor of his death went through the house, always astir, many came to see him, and I felt a tender sort of pride in my lost patient; for he looked a most heroic figure, lying there stately and still as the statue of some young knight asleep upon his tomb. The lovely expression which so often beautifies dead faces, soon replaced the marks of pain, and I longed for those who loved him best to see him when half an hour's acquaintance with Death had made them friends. As we stood looking at him, the ward master handed me a letter, saying it had been forgotten the night before. It was John's letter, come just an hour too late to gladden the eyes that had longed and looked for it so eagerly: yet he had it; for, after I had cut some brown locks for his mother, and taken off the ring to send her, telling how well the talisman had done its work, I kissed this good son for her sake, and laid the letter in his hand, still folded as when I drew my own away, feeling that its place was there, and making myself happy with the thought, that, even in his solitary place in the "Government Lot," he would not be without some token of the love which makes life beautiful and outlives death. Then I left him, glad to have known so genuine a man, and carrying with me an enduring memory of the brave Virginia blacksmith, as he lay serenely waiting for the dawn of that long day which knows no night.

from *Behind the Scenes, or Thirty Years a Slave and Four Years in the White House*

ELIZABETH KECKLEY (1818–1907)

Born into slavery in Hillsborough, North Carolina, at age eighteen Elizabeth Keckley was given to a white man, Alexander Kirkland, with whom she later had a son, George. After Kirkland died, she moved with her former slavemaster to St. Louis, Missouri, where she began learning the seamstress's trade. She then married James Keckley under the impression that he was a freeman, only to find out later that he was still bound to slavery. In 1855 she took her savings, borrowed $1,200 from a patron, and left her unpleasant marriage for freedom and independence with her young son. Her first home in freedom was in Baltimore, where she began a school teaching sewing and etiquette to young girls. She soon moved to Washington and established her own dressmaking business, a shop that became so successful that she employed up to twenty women at a time. She worked for Varina Davis, wife of Jefferson Davis, and formed a close relationship with Mary Todd Lincoln, to whom she became a personal maid and seamstress. Keckley's son was killed in service to the Union Army, which deepened her emotional bond with Mrs. Lincoln, who had also lost a son. Mrs. Lincoln became more supportive of black rights through her relationship with Keckley and helped contribute to the First Black Contraband Relief Association, which Keckley founded. Mrs. Lincoln refused to patronize Keckley after the 1886 publication of Keckley's memoir, and other Washington women of fashion followed. Keckley's business failed, and she died in the Washington Home for Destitute Women and Children. Besides the interest of her own biography, *Behind the Scenes* provides an interesting complement to the many literary portraits of Lincoln—among them George Washington Harris's, Emerson's, Hawthorne's, and Melville's.

WASHINGTON IN 1862-3

In the summer of 1862, freedmen began to flock into Washington from Maryland and Virginia. They came with a great hope in their hearts, and with all their worldly goods on their backs. Fresh from the bonds of slavery, fresh from the benighted regions of the plantation, they came to the Capital looking for liberty, and many of them not knowing it when they found it. Many good friends reached forth kind hands, but the North is not warm and impulsive. For one kind word spoken, two harsh ones were uttered; there was something repelling in the atmosphere, and the bright joyous dreams of freedom to the slave faded—were sadly altered, in the presence of that stern, practical mother, reality. Instead of flowery paths, days of perpetual sunshine, and bowers hanging with golden fruit, the road was rugged and full of thorns, the sunshine was eclipsed by shadows, and the mute appeals for help too often were answered by cold neglect. Poor dusky children of slavery, men and women of my own race—the transition from slavery to freedom was too sudden for you! The bright dreams were too rudely dispelled; you were not prepared for the new life that opened before you, and the great masses of the North learned to look upon your helplessness with indifference—learned to speak of you as an idle, dependent race. Reason should have prompted kinder thoughts. Charity is ever kind.

One fair summer evening I was walking the streets of Washington, accompanied by a friend, when a band of music was heard in the distance. We wondered what it could mean, and curiosity prompted us to find out its meaning. We quickened our steps, and discovered that it came from the house of Mrs. Farnham. The yard was brilliantly lighted, ladies and gentlemen were moving about, and the band was playing some of its sweetest airs. We approached the sentinel on duty at the gate, and asked what was going on. He told us that it was a festival given for the benefit of the sick and wounded soldiers in the city. This suggested an idea to me. If the white people can give festivals to raise funds for the relief of suffering soldiers, why should not the well-to-do colored people go to work to do something for the benefit of the suffering blacks? I could not rest. The thought was ever present with me, and the next Sunday I made a suggestion in the colored church, that a society of colored people be formed to labor for the benefit of the unfortunate freedmen. The idea proved popular, and in two weeks "The Contraband Relief Association" was organized, with forty working members.

In September of 1862, Mrs. Lincoln left Washington for New York, and requested me to follow her in a few days, and join her at the Metropolitan Hotel. I was glad of the opportunity to do so, for I thought that in New York I would be able to do something in the interests of our society. Armed with credentials, I took the train for New York and went to the Metropolitan, where Mrs. Lincoln had secured accommodations for me. The next morning I told Mrs. Lincoln of my project and she immediately headed my list with a subscription of $200. I circulated among the colored people, and got them thoroughly interested in the subject, when I was called to Boston by Mrs. Lincoln, who wished to visit her son Robert, attending college in that city. I met Mr. Wendell Phillips, and other Boston philanthropists, who gave me all the assistance in their power. We held a mass meeting at the Colored Baptist Church. Rev. Mr. Grimes, in Boston, raised a sum of money, and organized there a branch society. The society was organized by Mrs. Grimes, wife of the pastor, assisted by Mrs. Martin, wife of Rev. Stella Martin. This branch of the main society, during the war, was able to send us over eighty large boxes of goods, contributed exclusively by the colored people of Boston. Returning to New York, we held a successful meeting at the Shiloh Church, Rev. Henry Highland Garnet, pastor. The Metropolitan Hotel, at that time as now, employed colored help. I suggested the object of my mission to Robert Thompson, Steward of the Hotel, who immediately raised quite a sum of money among the dining-room waiters. Mr. Frederick Douglass contributed $200, besides lecturing for us. Other prominent colored men sent in liberal contributions. From England a large quantity of stores was received. Mrs.

Lincoln made frequent contributions, as also did the President. In 1863 I was re-elected President of the Association, which office I continue to hold.

For two years after [the Lincolns's son] Willie's death the White House was the scene of no fashionable display. The memory of the dead boy was duly respected. In some things Mrs. Lincoln was an altered woman. Sometimes, when in her room, with no one present but myself, the mere mention of Willie's name would excite her emotion, and any trifling memento that recalled him would move her to tears. She could not bear to look upon his picture and after his death she never crossed the threshold of the Guest's Room in which he died, or the Green Room in which he was embalmed. There was something supernatural in her dread of these things, and something that she could not explain. Tad's nature was the opposite of Willie's, and he was always regarded as his father's favorite child. His black eyes fairly sparkled with mischief.

The war progressed, fair fields had been stained with blood, thousands of brave men had fallen, and thousands of eyes were weeping for the fallen at home. There were desolate hearthstones in the South as well as in the North, and as the people of my race watched the sanguinary struggle, the ebb and flow of the tide of battle, they lifted their faces Zionward, as if they hoped to catch a glimpse of the Promised Land beyond the sulphurous clouds of smoke which shifted now and then but to reveal ghastly rows of new-made graves. Sometimes the very life of the nation seemed to tremble with the fierce shock of arms. In 1863 the Confederates were flushed with victory, and sometimes it looked as if the proud flag of the Union, the glorious old Stars and Stripes, must yield half its nationality to the tri-barred flag that floated grandly over long columns of gray. These were sad, anxious days to Mr. Lincoln, and those who saw the man in privacy only could tell how much he suffered. One day he came into the room where I was fitting a dress on Mrs. Lincoln. His step was slow and heavy, and his face sad. Like a tired child he threw himself upon a sofa, and shaded his eyes with his hands.

He was a complete picture of dejection. Mrs. Lincoln, observing his troubled look, asked:

"Where have you been, father?"

"To the War Department," was the brief, almost sullen answer.

"Any news?"

"Yes, plenty of news, but no good news. It is dark, dark everywhere."

He reached forth one of his long arms, and took a small Bible from a stand near the head of the sofa, opened the pages of the holy book, and soon was absorbed in reading them. A quarter of an hour passed, and on glancing at the sofa the face of the President seemed more cheerful. The dejected look was gone, and the countenance was lighted up with new resolution and hope. The change was so marked that I could not but wonder at it, and wonder led to the desire to know what book of the Bible afforded so much comfort to the reader. Making the search for a missing article an excuse, I walked gently around the sofa, and looking into the open book, I discovered that Mr. Lincoln was reading that divine comforter, Job. He read with Christian eagerness, and the courage and hope that he derived from the inspired pages made him a new man. I almost imagined that I could hear the Lord speaking to him from out the whirlwind of battle: "Gird up thy loins now like a man: I will demand of thee, and declare thou unto me." What a sublime picture was this! A ruler of a mighty nation going to the pages of the Bible with simple Christian earnestness for comfort and courage, and finding both in the darkest hours of a nation's calamity. Ponder it, O ye scoffers at God's Holy Word, and then hang your heads for very shame!

Frequent letters were received warning Mr. Lincoln of assassination, but he never gave a second thought to the mysterious warnings. The letters, however, sorely troubled his wife. She seemed to read impending danger in every rustling leaf, in every whisper of the wind.

"Where are you going now, father?" she would say to him, as she observed him putting on his overshoes and shawl.

"I am going over to the War Department, mother; to try and learn some news."

"But, father, you should not go out alone. You know you are surrounded with danger."

"All imagination. What does any one want to harm me for? Don't worry about me, mother, as if I were a little child, for no one is going to molest me"; and with a confident unsuspecting air he would close the door behind him, descend the stairs, and pass out to his lonely walk.

For weeks, when trouble was anticipated, friends of the President would sleep in the White House to guard him from danger.

Robert would come home every few months, bringing new joy to the family circle. He was very anxious to quit school and enter the army, but the move was sternly opposed by his mother.

"We have lost one son, and his loss is as much as I can bear, without being called upon to make another sacrifice," she would say, when the subject was under discussion.

"But many a poor mother has given up all her sons," mildly suggested Mr. Lincoln, "and Orson is not more dear to us than the sons of other people are to their mothers."

"That may be but I cannot bear to have Robert exposed to danger. His services are not required in the field, and the sacrifice would be a needless one."

"The services of every man who loves his country are required in this war. You should take a liberal instead of a selfish view of the question, mother."

Argument at last prevailed, and permission was granted Robert to enter the army. With the rank of Captain and A.D.C. he went to the field, and remained in the army till the close of the war.

I well recollect a little incident that gave me a clearer insight into Robert's character. He was at home at the time the Tom Thumb combination was at Washington. The marriage of little Hop-o'-my-thumb—Charles Stratton—to Miss Warren created no little excitement in the world, and the people of Washington participated in the general curiosity. Some of Mrs. Lincoln's friends made her believe that it was the duty of Mrs. Lincoln to show some attention to the remarkable dwarfs. Tom Thumb had been caressed by royalty in the Old World, and why should not the wife of the President of his native country smile upon him also? Verily, duty is one of the greatest bugbears in life. A hasty reception was arranged, and cards of invitation issued. I had dressed Mrs. Lincoln, and she was ready to go below and receive her guests, when Robert entered his mother's room.

"You are at leisure this afternoon, are you not, Robert?"

"Yes, mother."

"Of course, then, you will dress and come down-stairs."

"No, mother, I do not propose to assist in entertaining Tom Thumb. My notions of duty, perhaps, are somewhat different from yours."

Robert had a lofty soul, and he could not stoop to all of the follies and absurdities of the ephemeral current of fashionable life.

Mrs. Lincoln's love for her husband sometimes prompted her to act very strangely. She was extremely jealous of him, and if a lady desired to court her displeasure, she could select no surer way to do it than to pay marked attention to the President. These little jealous freaks often were a source of perplexity to Mr. Lincoln. If it was a reception for which they were dressing, he would come into her room to conduct her downstairs, and while pulling on his gloves, ask, with a merry twinkle in his eyes:

"Well, mother, who must I talk with to-night—shall it be Mrs. D.?"

"That deceitful woman! No, you shall not listen to her flattery."

"Well, then, what do you say to Miss C.? She is too young and handsome to practice deceit."

"Young and handsome, you call her! You should not judge beauty for me. No, she is in league with Mrs. D., and you shall not talk with her."

"Well, mother, I must talk with someone. Is there anyone that you do not object to?" trying to button his glove, with a mock expression of gravity.

"I don't know as it is necessary that you should talk to anybody in particular. You know well enough, Mr. Lincoln, that I do not approve of your flirtations with silly women, just as if you were a beardless boy, fresh from school."

"But, mother, I insist that I must talk with somebody. I can't stand around like a simpleton, and say nothing. If you will not tell me who I may talk with, please tell me who I may *not* talk with."

"There is Mrs. D. and Miss C. in particular. I detest them both. Mrs. B. also will come around you, but you need not listen to her flattery. These are the ones in particular."

"Very well, mother; now that we have settled the question to your satisfaction, we will go down-stairs"; and always with stately dignity, he proffered his arm and led the way.

from *The Gilded Age*

MARK TWAIN (1835–1910)

> Born in Florida, Missouri, Samuel Langhorne Clemens eventually took the pseudonym Mark Twain from the river pilot's term for water that is two fathoms deep and therefore safe for a riverboat. Clemens earned his pilot's license in 1888 after working for several years as a journeyman printer. After a year and a half on the river and an unsuccessful attempt at prospecting, he worked as a reporter for a Nevada newspaper. Twain became a household name after his tall tales and sketches began appearing in newspapers and his lectures on his travels were a hit. After the success of *Innocents Abroad* (1869) and with the help of his new father-in-law, Twain bought an interest in the Buffalo (New York) *Express* and intended to make journalism a career. When the venture failed in 1871, Twain and his wife moved to Hartford, Connecticut, the home of the subscription firm that had handled the publication of *Innocents*. There he made the acquaintance of the residents of the Nook Farm literary colony, which included Harriet Beecher Stowe, Charles Dudley Warner, and Theodore Hooker. *The Gilded Age* (1874) was Twain's first attempt at fiction. In it, he and coauthor Warner (1829–1900) satirized the speculative mania and graft of the Grant administration. Their characterization of the world of greedy Col. Beriah Sellers fixed the era with a sobriquet.

The capital of the Great Republic was a new world to country-bred Washington Hawkins. St. Louis was a greater city, but its floating population did not hail from great distances, and so it had the general family aspect of the permanent population; but Washington gathered its people from the four winds of heaven, and so the manners, the faces and the fashions there, presented a variety that was infinite. Washington had never been in "society" in St. Louis, and he knew nothing of the ways of its wealthier citizens and had never inspected one of their dwellings. Consequently, everything in the nature of modern fashion and grandeur was a new and wonderful revelation to him.

Washington is an interesting city to any of us. It seems to become more and more interesting the oftener we visit it. Perhaps the reader has never been there? Very well. You arrive either at night, rather too late to do anything or see anything until morning, or you arrive so early in the morning that you consider it best to go to your hotel and sleep an hour or two while the sun bothers along over the Atlantic. You cannot well arrive at a pleasant intermediate hour, because the railway corporation that keeps the keys of the only door that leads into the town or out of it takes care of that. You arrive in tolerably good spirits, because it is only thirty-eight miles from Baltimore to the capital, and so you have only been insulted three times (provided you are not in a sleeping car—the average is higher, there): once when you renewed your ticket after stopping over in Baltimore, once when you were about to enter the "ladies' car" without knowing it *was* a lady's car, and once when you asked the conductor at what hour you would reach Washington.

You are assailed by a long rank of hackmen who shake their whips in your face as you step out upon the sidewalk; you enter what they regard as a "carriage," in the capital, and you wonder why they do not take it out of service and put it in the museum: we have few enough antiquities, and it is little to our credit that we make scarcely any effort to preserve the few we have. You reach your hotel, presently—and here let us draw the curtain of charity—because of course you have gone to the wrong one. You being a stranger, how could you do otherwise? There are a hundred and eighteen bad hotels, and only one good one. The most renowned and popular hotel of them all is perhaps the worst one known to history.

It is winter, and night. When you arrive, it was snowing, when you reach the hotel, it was sleeting. When you went to bed, it was raining. During the night it froze hard, and the wind blew some chimneys down. When you got up in the morning, it was foggy. When you finished your breakfast at ten o'clock and went out, the sunshine was brilliant, the weather balmy and delicious, and the mud and slush deep and all-pervading. You will like the climate—when you get used to it.

You naturally wish to view the city; so you take an umbrella, an overcoat, and a fan, and go forth. The prominent features you soon locate and get familiar with; first you glimpse the ornamental upper works of a long, snowy palace projecting above a grove of trees, and a tall, graceful white dome with a statue on it surmounting the palace and pleasantly contrasting with the back-ground of blue sky. That building is the capitol; gossips will tell you that by the original estimates it was to cost $12,000,000, and that the government did come within $27,200,000 of building it for that sum.

You stand at the back of the capitol to treat yourself to a view, and it is a very noble one. You understand, the capitol stands upon the verge of a high piece of table land, a fine commanding position, and its front looks out over this noble situation for a city—but it don't see it, for the reason that when the capitol extension was decided upon, the property owners at once advanced their prices to such inhuman figures that the people went down and built the city in the muddy low marsh *behind* the temple of liberty; so now the lordly front of the building, with its imposing colonnades, its projecting, graceful wings, its picturesque groups of statuary, and its long terraced ranges of steps, flowing down in white marble waves to the ground, merely looks out upon a sorrowful little desert of cheap boarding houses.

So you observe, that you take your view from the back of the capitol. And yet not from the airy outlooks of the dome, by the way, because to get there you must pass through the great rotunda: and to do that, you would have to see the marvelous Historical Paintings that hang there, and the bas-reliefs—and what have you done that you should suffer thus? And besides, you might have to pass through the old part of the building, and you could not help seeing Mr. Lincoln, as petrified by a young lady artist for $10,000—and you might take his marble emancipation proclamation, which he holds out in his hand and contemplates, for a folded napkin; and you might conceive from his expression and his attitude, that he is finding fault with the washing. Which is not the case. Nobody knows what *is* the matter with him; but everybody feels for him. Well, you ought not to go into the dome anyhow, because it would be utterly impossible to go up there without seeing the frescoes in it—and why should you interested in the delirium tremens of art?

The capitol is a very noble and a very beautiful building, both within and without, but you need not examine it now. Still, if you greatly prefer going into the dome, go. Now your general glance gives you picturesque stretches of gleaming water, on your left, with a sail here and there and a lunatic asylum on shore; over beyond the water, on a distant elevation, you see a squat yellow temple which your eye dwells upon lovingly through a blur of unmanly moisture, for its recalls your lost boyhood and the Parthenons done in molasses candy which made it blest and beautiful. Still in the distance, but on this side of the water and close to its edge, the Monument to the Father of his Country towers out of the mud—sacred soil is the customary term. It has the aspect of a factory chimney with the top broken off. The skeleton of a decaying scaffolding lingers about its summit, and tradition says that the spirit of Washington often comes down and sits on those rafters to enjoy this tribute of respect which the nation has reared as the symbol of its unappeasable gratitude. The Monument is to be finished, some day, and at that time our Washington will have risen still higher in the nation's veneration, and will be known as the Great-Great-Grandfather of his Country. The memorial Chimney stands in a quiet pastoral locality that is full of reposeful expression. With a glass you can see the cow-sheds about its base, and the contented sheep nibbling pebbles in the desert solitudes that surround it, and the tired pigs dozing in the holy calm of its protecting shadow.

Now you wrench your gaze loose and you look down in front of you and see the broad Pennsylvania Avenue stretching straight ahead for a mile or more till it brings up against the iron fence in front of a pillared granite pile, the Treasury building—an edifice that would command respect in any capital. The stores and hotels that wall in this broad avenue are mean, and cheap, and dingy, and are better left without comment. Beyond the Treasury is a fine large white barn, with wide unhandsome grounds about it. The President lives there. It is ugly enough outside, but that is nothing to what it is inside. Dreariness, flimsiness, bad taste reduced to mathematical completeness is what the inside offers to the eye, if it remains yet what it always has been.

The front and right hand views give you the city at large. It is a wide stretch of cheap little brick houses, with here and there a noble architectural pile lifting itself out of the midst—government buildings, these. If the thaw is still going on when you come down and go about town, you will wonder at the short-sightedness of the city fathers, when you come to inspect the streets, in that they do not dilute the mud a little more and use them for canals.

If you inquire around a little, you will find that there are more boarding houses to the square acre in Washington than there are in any other city in the land, perhaps. If you apply for a home in one of them, it will seem odd to you to have the landlady inspect you with a severe eye and then ask you if you are a member of Congress. Perhaps, just as a pleasantry, you will say yes. And then she will tell you that she is "full." Then you show her her advertisement in the morning paper, and there she stands, convicted and ashamed. She will try to blush, and it will be only polite in you to take the effort for the deed. She shows you her rooms, now, and lets you take one—but she makes you pay in advance for it. That is what you will get for pretending to be a member of Congress. If you had been content to be merely a private citizen, your trunk would have been sufficient security for your board. If you are curious and inquire into this thing, the chances are that your landlady will be ill-natured enough to say that the person and property of a Congressman are exempt from arrest or detention, and that with the tears in her eyes she has seen several of the people's representatives walk off to their several States and Territories carrying her unreceipted board bills in their pockets for keepsakes. And before you have been in Washington many weeks you will be mean enough to believe her, too.

Of course you contrive to see everything and find out everything. And one of the first and most startling things you find out is, that every individual you encounter in the City of Washington almost—and certainly even separate and distinct individual in the public employment, from the highest bureau chief, clear down to the maid who scrubs Department halls, the night watchmen of the public buildings and the darkey boy who purifies the Department spittoons—represents Political Influence. Unless you can get the ear of a Senator, or a Congressman, or a Chief of a Bureau or Department, and persuade him to use his "influence" in your behalf, you cannot get an employment of the most trivial nature in Washington. Mere merit, fitness and capability, are useless baggage to you without "influence." The population of Washington consists pretty much entirely of government employees and the people who board them. There are thousands of these employees, and they have gathered there from every corner of the Union and got their berths through the intercession (command is nearer the word) of the Senators and Representatives of their respective States. It would be an odd circumstance to see a girl get employment at three or four dollars a week in one of the great public cribs without any political grandee to back her, but merely because she was worthy, and competent, and a good citizen of a free country that "treats all persons alike." Washington would be mildly thunderstruck at such a thing as that. If you are a member of Congress (no offence), and one of your constituents who doesn't know anything, and does not want to go into the bother of learning something, and has no money, and no employment, and can't earn a living, comes besieging you for help, do you say, "Come, my friend, if your services were valuable you could get employment elsewhere—don't want you here?" Oh, no. You take him to a department and say, "Here, give this person something to pass away the time at—and a salary"—and the thing is done. You throw him on his country. He is his country's child, let his country support him. There is something good and motherly about Washington, the grand old benevolent National Asylum for the Helpless.

The wages received by this great hive of employees are placed at the liberal figure meet and just for skilled and competent labor. Such of them as are immediately employed about the two Houses of Congress, are not only liberally paid also, but are remembered in the customary Extra Compensation bill which slides neatly through, annually, with the general grab that signalizes the last night of a session, and thus twenty per cent is added to their wages, for fun—no doubt.

Washington Hawkins' new life was an unceasing delight to him. Senator Dilworthy lived sumptuously, and Washington's quarters were charming—gas; running water, hot and cold; bathroom, coal fires, rich carpets, beautiful pictures on the walls; books on religion, temperance, public charities, and financial schemes; trim colored servants, dainty food—everything a body could wish for. And as for stationery, there was no end to it; the government furnished it; postage stamps were not needed—the Senator's frank could convey a horse through the mails, if necessary.

And then he saw such dazzling company. Renowned generals and admirals who had seemed but colossal myths when he was in the far west, went in and out before him or sat at the Senator's table, solidified into palpable flesh and blood; famous statesmen crossed his path daily; that once rare and awe-inspiring being, a Congressman, was become a common spectacle—a spectacle so common, indeed, that he could contemplate it without excitement, even without embarrassment; foreign ministers were visible to the naked eye at happy intervals; he had looked upon the President himself, and lived. And more, this world of enchantment teemed with speculation—the whole atmosphere was thick with it—and that indeed was Washington Hawkins' native air; none other refreshed his lungs so gratefully. He had found paradise at last.

The more he saw of his chief, the Senator, the more he honored him, and the more conspicuously the moral grandeur of his character appeared to stand out. To possess the friendship and the kindly interest of such a man, Washington said in a letter to Louise, was a happy fortune for a young man whose career had been so impeded and so clouded as his.

The weeks drifted by; Harry Brierly flirted, danced, added lustre to the brilliant Senatorial receptions, and diligently "buzzed" and "button-holed" Congressmen in the interest of the Columbus River scheme; meantime Senator Dilworthy labored hard in the same interest—and in others of equal national importance. Harry wrote frequently to Sellers, and always encouragingly; and from these letters it was easy to see that Harry was a pet with all Washington, and was likely to carry the thing through; that the assistance rendered him by "old Dilworthy" was pretty fair— pretty fair; "and every little helps, you know," said Harry.

Washington wrote Sellers officially, now and then. In one of his letters it appeared that whereas no member of the House committee favored the scheme at first, there was now needed but one more vote to compass a majority report. Closing sentence: "Providence seems to further our efforts."

(Signed,) "ABNER DILWORTHY, U.S.S.,
per Washington Hawkins, P. S."

At the end of a week, Washington was able to send the happy news—officially, as usual,—that the needed vote had been added and the bill favorably reported from the Committee. Other letters recorded its perils in Committee of the whole, and by and by its victory, by just the skin of its teeth, on third reading and final passage. Then came letters telling of Mr. Dilworthy's struggles with a stubborn majority in his own committee in the Senate; of how these gentlemen succumbed, one by one, till a majority was secured.

Then there was a hiatus. Washington watched every move on the board, and he was in a good position to do this, for he was clerk of this committee, and also one other. He received no salary as private secretary, but these two clerkships, procured by his benefactor, paid him an aggregate of twelve dollars a day, without counting the twenty per cent extra compensation which would of course be voted to him on the last night of the session.

He saw the bill go into Committee of the whole and struggle for its life again, and finally worry through. In the fullness of time he noted its second reading, and by and by the day arrived when the grand ordeal came, and it was put upon its final passage. Washington listened with bated breath to the "Aye!" "No!" "No!" "Aye!" of the voters for a few dread minutes, and then could bear the suspense no longer. He ran down from the gallery and hurried home to wait.

At the end of two or three hours the Senator arrived in the bosom of his family, and dinner was waiting. Washington sprang forward, with the eager question on his lips, and the Senator said:

"We may rejoice freely, now, my son—Providence has crowned our efforts with success."

from *Specimen Days*

WALT WHITMAN (1819–1892)

New York–born Walt Whitman had little formal education and spent most of his early life working as a printer, a schoolteacher, and later as an editor and writer for numerous newspapers. He is best known for his groundbreaking and controversial collection of poetry, *Leaves of Grass* (1855). In 1863, Whitman left his Brooklyn home to search for his wounded brother at the Virginia battlefront. George Whitman had suffered only minor wounds at the Battle of Fredericksburg, but Walt remained in the Federal City, drawn to the nation's capital by "a profound conviction of necessity, affinity." From 1863 until 1874, Whitman maintained a residence in Washington, D.C. While there, he produced the essay *Democratic Vistas* (1871); a number of poems about the Civil War, eventually published as *Drum-Taps* (1865); and his elegies for Lincoln, "When Lilacs Last in the Dooryard Bloom'd" and "O Captain! My Captain." In Washington, Whitman worked as a copyist and also, for a short time, as a clerk in the Indian Bureau of the Department of the Interior. However, he felt what he called "a divine attraction" to the hospitals and battlefields, volunteering his time to sit with and care for the injured and dying. Whitman also ventured onto the battlefield to aid nurses and tend to the injured, and once, near Culpepper, Virginia, he was just a mile from the front lines of the war. Whitman spent many hours in the Armory Square Hospital engaging patients in conversation, writing letters for them, and quoting Shakespeare and sometimes his own writings. He believed that, by the close of the Civil War, he had made over 600 hospital visits and tours and, in some way, had made contact with almost 100,000 injured soldiers from both the North and South. During his visits, the poet could also be found writing his personal memoranda of the war on homemade notebooks of paper pinned together. *Memoranda during the War* was published in 1875. Like his extended poem "The Wound Dresser," it describes his work in the Union hospitals. The following selection is taken from the 1883 edition of

Specimen Days and Collect. In it Whitman describes scenes in what was then the Patent Office and is now the National Portrait Gallery.

BACK TO WASHINGTON.

January, '63.—Left camp at Falmouth with some wounded, a few days since, and came here by Aquia creek railroad, and so on government steamer up the Potomac. Many wounded were with us on the cars and boat. The cars were just common platform ones. The railroad journey of ten or twelve miles was made mostly before sunrise. The soldiers guarding the road came out from their tents or shebangs of bushes with rumpled hair and half-awake look. Those on duty were walking their posts, some on banks over us, others down far below the level of the track. I saw large cavalry camps off the road. At Aquia creek landing were numbers of wounded going north. While I waited some three hours, I went around among them. Several wanted word sent home to parents, brothers, wives, &c., which I did for them, (by mail the next day from Washington.) On the boat I had my hands full. One poor fellow died going up.

I am now remaining in and around Washington, daily visiting the hospitals. Am much in Patent-office, Eighth street, H street, Armory-square, and others. Am now able to do a little good, having money, (as almoner of others home,) and getting experience. To-day, Sunday afternoon and till nine in the evening, visited Campbell hospital; attended specially to one case in ward I, very sick with pleurisy and typhoid fever, young man, farmer's son, D.F. Russell, company E, 60th New York, downhearted and feeble; a long time before he would take any interest; wrote a letter home to his mother, in Malone, Franklin county, N. Y., at his request; gave him some fruit and one or two other gifts; envelop'd and directed his letter, &c. Then went thoroughly through ward 6, observ'd every case in the ward, without, I think, missing one; gave perhaps from twenty to thirty persons, each one some little gift, such as oranges, apples, sweet crackers, figs, &c.

Thursday, Jan. 21.—Devoted the main part of the day to Armory-square hospital; went pretty thoroughly through wards F, G, H, and I; some fifty cases in each ward. In ward F supplied the men throughout with writing paper and stamp'd envelope each; distributed in small portions, to proper subjects, a large jar of first-rate preserv'd berries, which had been donated to me by a lady—her own cooking. Found several cases I thought good subjects for small sums of money, which I furnish'd. (The wounded men often come up broke, and it helps their spirits to have even the small sum I give them.) My paper and envelopes all gone, but distributed a good lot of amusing reading matter; also, as I thought judicious, tobacco, oranges, apples, &c. Interesting cases in ward I; Charles Miller, bed 19, company D, 53d Pennsylvania, is only sixteen years of age, very bright, courageous boy, left leg amputated below the knee; next bed to him, another young lad very sick; gave each appropriate gifts. In the bed above, also, amputation of the left leg; gave him a little jar of raspberries; bed I, this ward, gave a small sum; also to a soldier on crutches, sitting on his bed near . . . . (I am more and more surprised at the very great proportion of youngsters from fifteen to twenty-one in the army. I afterwards found a still greater proportion among the southerners.)

Evening, same day, went to see D.F.R., before alluded to; found him remarkably changed for the better; up and dress'd—quite a triumph; he afterwards got well, and went back to his regiment. Distributed in the wards a quantity of note-paper, and forty or fifty stamp'd envelopes, of which I had recruited my stock, and the men were much in need.

FIFTY HOURS LEFT WOUNDED ON THE FIELD.

Here is a case of a soldier I found among the crowded cots in the Patent-office. He likes to have some one to talk to, and we will listen to him. He got badly hit in his leg and side at Fredericksburgh that eventful Saturday, 13th of December. He lay the succeeding two days and nights helpless on the field, between the city and those grim terraces of batteries; his company and regiment had been compell'd to leave him to his fate. To make matters worse, it happen'd he lay with his head slightly down hill, and could not help himself. At the end of some fifty hours he was brought off, with other wounded, under a flag of truce. I ask him how the rebels treated him as he lay during those two days and nights within reach of them—whether they came to him—whether they abused him? He answers that several of the rebels, soldiers and others, came to him at one time and another. A couple of them, who were together, spoke roughly and sarcastically, but nothing worse. One middle-aged man, however, who seem'd to be moving around the field, among the dead and wounded, for benevolent purposes, came to him in a way he will never forget; treated our soldier kindly, bound up his wounds, cheer'd him, gave him a couple of biscuits and a drink of whiskey and water; asked him if he could eat some beef. This good secesh, however, did not change our soldier's position, for it might have caused the blood to burst from the wounds, clotted and stagnated. Our soldier is from Pennsylvania; has had a pretty severe time; the wounds proved to be bad ones. But he retains a good heart, and is at present on the gain. (It is not uncommon for the men to remain on the field this way, one, two, or even four or five days.)

HOSPITAL SCENES AND PERSONS.

Letter Writing.—When eligible, I encourage the men to write, and myself, when called upon, write all sorts of letters for them, (including love letters, very tender ones.) Almost as I reel off these memoranda, I write for a new patient to his wife, M. de F., of the 17th Connecticut, company H, has just come up (February

17th) from Windmill point, and is received in ward H Armory-square. He is an intelligent looking man, has a foreign accent, black-eyed and hair'd, a Hebraic appearance. Wants a telegraphic message sent to his wife, New Canaan, Conn. I agree to send the message—but to make things sure I also sit down and write the wife a letter, and despatch it to the post-office immediately, as he fears she will come on, and he does not wish her to, as he will surely get well.

Saturday, Janurary 30th.—Afternoon, visited Campbell hospital. Scene of cleaning up the ward, and giving the men all clean clothes—through the ward (6) the patients dressing or being dress'd—the naked upper half of the bodies—the good-humor and fun—the shirts, drawers, sheets of beds, &c., and the general fixing up for Sunday. Gave J.L. 50 cents.

Wednesday, February 4th.—Visited Armory-square hospital, went pretty thoroughly through wards E and D. Supplied paper and envelopes to all who wish'd—as usual, found plenty of men who needed those articles. Wrote letters. Saw and talk'd with two or three members of the Brooklyn 14th regt. A poor fellow in ward D, with a fearful wound in a fearful condition, was having some loose splinters of bone taken from the neighborhood of the wound. The operation was long, and one of great pain—yet, after it was well commenced, the soldier bore it in silence. He sat up, propp'd—was much wasted—had lain a long time quiet in one position (not for days only but weeks,) a bloodless, brown-skinn'd face, with eyes full of determination—belong'd to a New York regiment. There was an unusual cluster of surgeons, medical cadets, nurses, &c. around his bed—I thought the whole thing was done with tenderness, and done well. In one case, the wife sat by the side of her husband, his sickness typhoid fever, pretty bad. In another, by the side of her son, a mother—she told me she had seven children, and this was the youngest. (A fine, kind, healthy, gentle mother, good-looking, not very old, with a cap on her head, and dress'd like home—what a charm it gave to the whole ward.) I liked the woman nurse in ward E—I noticed how she sat a long time by a poor fellow who just had,

that morning, in addition to his other sickness, bad hemor-
rhage—she gently assisted him, reliev'd him of the blood, holding a cloth to his mouth, as he coughed it up—he was so weak
he could only just turn his head over on the pillow.

One young New York man, with a bright, handsome face, had
been lying several months from a most disagreeable wound,
receiv'd at Bull Run. A bullet had shot him right through the
bladder, hitting him front, low in the belly, and coming out back.
He had suffer'd much—the water came out of the wound, by
slow but steady quantities, for many weeks—so that he lay
almost constantly in a sort of puddle—and there were other disagreeable circumstances. He was of good heart, however. At
present comparatively comfortable, had a bad throat, was
delighted with a stick of horehound candy I gave him, with one
or two other trifles.

PATENT-OFFICE HOSPITAL.

February 23.—I must not let the great hospital at the Patent-
office pass away without some mention. A few weeks ago the
vast area of the second story of that noblest of Washington
buildings was crowded close with rows of sick, badly wounded
and dying soldiers. They were placed in three very large apartments. I went there many times. It was a strange, solemn, and,
with all its features of suffering and death, a sort of fascinating
sight. I go sometimes at night to soothe and relieve particular
cases. Two of the immense apartments are fill'd with high and
ponderous glass cases, crowded with models in miniature of
every kind of utensil, machine or invention, it ever enter'd into
the mind of man to conceive; and with curiosities and foreign
presents. Between these cases are lateral openings, perhaps eight
feet wide and quite deep, and in these were placed the sick,
besides a great long double row of them up and down through
the middle of the hall. Many of them were very bad cases,
wounds and amputations. Then there was a gallery running

above the hall in which there were beds also. It was, indeed, a curious scene, especially at night when lit up. The glass cases, the beds, the forms lying there, the gallery above, and the marble pavement under foot—the suffering, and the fortitude to bear it in various degrees—occasionally, from some, the groan that could not be repress'd—sometimes a poor fellow dying, with emaciated face and glassy eye, the nurse by his side, the doctor also there, but no friend, no relative—such were the sights but lately in the Patent-office. (The wounded have since been removed from there, and it is now vacant again.)

The White House by Moonlight.

February 24th.—A spell of fine soft weather. I wander about a good deal, sometimes at night under the moon. To-night took a long look at the President's house. The white portico—the pal-ace-like, tall, round columns, spotless as snow—the walls also—the tender and soft moonlight, flooding the pale marble, and making peculiar faint languishing shades, not shadows—every-where a soft transparent hazy, thin, blue moon-lace, hanging in the air—the brilliant and extra-plentiful clusters of gas, on and around the facade, columns, portico, &c.—everything so white, so marbly pure and dazzling, yet soft—the White House of future poems, and of dreams and dramas, there in the soft and copious moon—the gorgeous front, in the trees, under the lus-trous flooding moon, full of reality, full of illusion—the forms of the trees, leafless, silent, in trunk and myriad-angles of branches, under the stars and sky—the White House of the land, and of beauty and night—sentries at the gates, and by the portico, silent, pacing there in blue overcoats—stopping you not at all, but eyeing you with sharp eyes, whichever way you move.

from *The Education of Henry Adams*

HENRY ADAMS (1838–1918)

Henry Brooks Adams was born and raised in Boston and was educated at Harvard College. He first went to Washington at age twelve, accompanying his father on a visit to his grandmother, the widow of the country's sixth president. (Henry was also the great-grandson of John Adams, the second American president.) During the Civil War, Adams lived in England. Upon returning to America, he taught history at Harvard and then moved to Washington, D.C., where he published two novels, *Democracy* (1880) and *Esther* (1884), the first anonymously and the second under a pseudonym. He completed a nine-volume history of the administrations of Presidents Jefferson and Madison and then spent some time traveling in Europe. This trip put him in a more philosophical mindset, leading directly to his memoir *The Education of Henry Adams*. The book, composed in 1907, was posthumously published in 1918 and received the Pulitzer Prize the following year. Its combination of the highly personal and the historically accurate has led critic Alfred Kazin to call Adams "the Gibbons, the Voltaire, the Proust, and even, alas, the doom-filled Oswald Spengler of Washington society."

One lived in the atmosphere of the Stamp Act, the Tea Tax, and the Boston Massacre. Within Boston, a boy was first an eighteenth-century politician, and afterwards only a possibility; beyond Boston the first step led only further into politics. After February, 1848, but one slight tie remained of all those that, since 1776, had connected Quincy with the outer world. The Madam stayed in Washington, after her husband's death, and in her turn was struck by paralysis and bedridden. From time to time her son Charles, whose affection and sympathy for his mother in her many tribulations were always pronounced, went on to see her, and in May, 1850, he took with him his twelve-year-old son. The journey was meant as education, and as education it served the purpose of fixing in memory the stage of a boy's thought in 1850. He could not remember taking special interest in the railroad journey or in New York; with railways and cities he was familiar enough. His first impression was the novelty of crossing New York Bay and finding an English railway carriage on the Camden and Amboy Railroad. This was a new world; a suggestion of corruption in the simple habits of American life; a step to exclusiveness never approached in Boston; but it was amusing. The boy rather liked it. At Trenton the train set him on board a steamer which took him to Philadelphia where he smelt other varieties of town life; then again by boat to Chester, and by train to Havre de Grace; by boat to Baltimore and thence by rail to Washington. This was the journey he remembered. The actual journey may have been quite different, but the actual journey has no interest for education. The memory was all that mattered; and what struck him most, to remain fresh in his mind all his lifetime, was the sudden change that came over the world on entering a slave State. He took education politically. The mere raggedness of outline could not have seemed wholly new, for even Boston had its ragged edges, and the town of Quincy was far from being a vision of neatness or good-repair; in truth, he had never seen a finished landscape; but Maryland was raggedness of a new kind. The railway, about the size and character of a modern tram, rambled through unfenced fields and woods, or through village streets, among a haphazard variety of pigs, cows, and negro babies, who might all have used the cabins for pens and styes, had the Southern pig required styes, but who never showed a sign of care. This was the boy's impression of what slavery caused, and, for him, was all it taught. Coming down in the early morning from his bedroom in his grandmother's house—still called the Adams Building—in F Street and venturing outside into the air reeking with the thick odor of the catalpa trees, he found himself on an earth-road, or village street, with wheel-tracks meandering from the colonnade of the Treasury hard by, to the white marble columns and fronts of the Post Office and Patent Office which faced each other in the distance, like white Greek temples in the abandoned gravel-pits of a deserted Syrian city. Here and there low wooden houses were scattered along the streets, as in other Southern villages, but he was chiefly attracted by an unfinished square marble shaft, half-a-mile below, and he walked down to inspect it before breakfast. His aunt drily remarked that, at this rate, he would soon get through all the sights; but she could not guess—having lived always in Washington—how little the sights of Washington had to do with its interest.

The boy could not have told her; he was nowhere near an understanding of himself. The more he was educated, the less he understood. Slavery struck him in the face; it was a nightmare; a horror; a crime; the sum of all wickedness! Contact made it only more repulsive. He wanted to escape, like the negroes, to free soil. Slave States were dirty, unkempt, poverty-stricken, ignorant, vicious! He had not a thought but repulsion for it; and yet the picture had another side. The May sunshine and shadow had something to do with it; the thickness of foliage and the heavy smells had more; the sense of atmosphere, almost new, had perhaps as much again; and the brooding indolence of a warm climate and a negro population hung in the atmosphere heavier than the catalpas. The impression was not simple, but the boy liked it: distinctly it remained on his mind as an attraction, almost obscuring Quincy itself. The want of barriers, of pavements, of forms; the looseness, the laziness; the indolent Southern drawl; the pigs in the streets; the negro babies and their mothers with bandanas; the freedom, openness, swagger, of nature and man, soothed his Johnson blood. Most boys would have felt it in the same way, but with him the feeling caught on to an inheritance. The softness of his gentle old grandmother as she lay in bed and chatted with him, did not come from Boston. His aunt was anything rather than Bostonian. He did not wholly come from Boston himself. Though Washington belonged to a differ-

ent world, and the two worlds could not live together, he was
not sure that he enjoyed the Boston world most. Even at twelve
years old he could see his own nature no more clearly than he
would at twelve hundred, if by accident he should happen to live
so long.

His father took him to the Capitol and on the floor of the
Senate, which then, and long afterwards, until the era of tourists, was freely open to visitors. The old Senate Chamber resembled a pleasant political club. Standing behind the Vice-President's
chair, which is now the Chief Justice's, the boy was presented to
some of the men whose names were great in their day, and as
familiar to him as his own. Clay and Webster and Calhoun were
there still, but with them a Free Soil candidate for the Vice-
Presidency had little to do; what struck boys most was their
type. Senators were a species; they all wore an air, as they wore
a blue dress coat or brass buttons; they were Roman. The type
of Senator in 1850 was rather charming at its best, and the
Senate, when in good temper, was an agreeable body, numbering
only some sixty members, and affecting the airs of courtesy. Its
vice was not so much a vice of manners or temper as of attitude.
The statesman of all periods was apt to be pompous, but even
pomposity was less offensive than familiarity—on the platform
as in the pulpit—and Southern pomposity, when not arrogant,
was genial and sympathetic, almost quaint and childlike in its
simple-mindedness; quite a different thing from the Websterian
or Conklinian pomposity of the North. The boy felt at ease
there, more at home than he had ever felt in Boston State House,
though his acquaintance with the codfish in the House of
Representatives went back beyond distinct recollection. Senators
spoke kindly to him, and seemed to feel so, for they had known
his family socially; and, in spite of slavery, even J.Q. Adams in
his later years, after he ceased to stand in the way of rivals, had
few personal enemies. Decidedly the Senate, pro-slavery though
it were, seemed a friendly world.

This first step in national politics was a little like the walk
before breakfast; an easy, careless, genial, enlarging stride into a

fresh and amusing world, where nothing was finished, but where even the weeds grew rank. The second step was like the first, except that it led to the White House. He was taken to see President Taylor. Outside, in a paddock in front, "Old Whitey," the President's charger, was grazing, as they entered; and inside, the President was receiving callers as simply as if he were in the paddock too. The President was friendly, and the boy felt no sense of strangeness that he could ever recall. In fact, what strangeness should he feel? The families were intimate; so intimate that their friendliness outlived generations, civil war, and all sorts of rupture. President Taylor owed his election to Martin Van Buren and the Free Soil Party. To him, the Adamses might still be of use. As for the White House, all the boy's family had lived there, and, barring the eight years of Andrew Jackson's reign, had been more or less at home there ever since it was built. The boy half thought he owned it, and took for granted that he should some day live in it. He felt no sensation whatever before Presidents. A President was a matter of course in every respectable family; he had two in his own; three, if he counted old Nathaniel Gorham, who was the oldest and first in distinction. Revolutionary patriots, or perhaps a Colonial Governor, might be worth talking about, but any one could be President, and some very shady characters were likely to be. Presidents, Senators, Congressmen, and such things were swarming in every street.

Everyone thought alike whether they had ancestors or not. No sort of glory hedged Presidents as such, and, in the whole country, one could hardly have met with an admission of respect for any office or name, unless it were George Washington. That was—to all appearance sincerely—respected. People made pilgrimages to Mount Vernon and made even an effort to build Washington a monument. The effort had failed, but one still went to Mount Vernon, although it was no easy trip. Mr. Adams took the boy there in a carriage and pair, over a road that gave him a complete Virginia education for use ten years afterwards. To the New England mind, roads, schools, clothes, and a clean face were connected as part of the law of order or divine system. Bad roads meant bad morals. The moral of this Virginia road was clear, and the boy fully learned it. Slavery was wicked, and slavery was the cause of this road's badness which amounted to social crime—and yet, at the end of the road and product of the crime stood Mount Vernon and George Washington.

Luckily boys accept contradictions as readily as their elders do, or this boy might have become prematurely wise. He had only to repeat what he was told—that George Washington stood alone. Otherwise this third step in his Washington education would have been his last. On that line, the problem of progress was not soluble, whatever the optimists and orators might say—or, for that matter, whatever they might think. George Washington could not be reached on Boston lines. George Washington was a primary, or, if Virginians liked it better, an ultimate relation, like the Pole Star, and amid the endless restless motion of every other visible point in space, he alone remained steady, in the mind of Henry Adams, to the end. All the other points shifted their bearings; John Adams, Jefferson, Madison, Franklin, even John Marshall, took varied lights, and assumed new relations, but Mount Vernon always remained where it was, with no practicable road to reach it; and yet, when he got there, Mount Vernon was only Quincy in a Southern setting. No doubt it was much more charming, but it was the same eighteenth-century, the same old furniture, the same old patriot, and the same old President.

The boy took to it instinctively. The broad Potomac and the coons in the trees, the bandanas and the box-hedges, the bedrooms upstairs and the porch outside, even Martha Washington herself in memory, were as natural as the tides and the May sunshine; he had only enlarged his horizon a little; but he never thought to ask himself or his father how to deal with the moral problem that deduced George Washington from the sum of all wickedness. In practice, such trifles as contradictions in principle are easily set aside; the faculty of ignoring them makes the practical man; but any attempt to deal with them seriously as education is fatal. Luckily Charles Francis Adams never preached and was singularly free from cant. He may have had views of his own, but he let his son Henry satisfy himself with the simple elementary fact that George Washington stood alone.

Life was not yet complicated. Every problem had a solution, even the negro. The boy went back to Boston more political than ever, and his politics were no longer so modern as the eighteenth century, but took a strong tone of the seventeenth. Slavery drove the whole Puritan community back on its Puritanism. The boy thought as dogmatically as though he were one of his own ancestors. The Slave Power took the place of Stuart kings and Roman popes. Education could go no further in that course, and ran off into emotion; but, as the boy gradually found his surroundings change, and felt himself no longer an isolated atom in a hostile universe, but a sort of herring-fry in a shoal of moving fish, he began to learn the first and easier lessons of practical politics. Thus far he had seen nothing but eighteenth-century statesmanship. America and he began, at the same time, to become aware of a new force under the innocent surface of party machinery.

from *The American Scene*

HENRY JAMES (1843–1916)

New York City–born Henry James was the youngest son of noted theologian Henry James, and brother to psychologist and philosopher William James. James lived much of his life in Europe, particularly London and Paris, and became a naturalized British citizen. After completing his best-known novels, *Washington Square* (1881), *The Wings of the Dove* (1902), *The Ambassadors* (1903), and *The Golden Bowl* (1904), James made one of his infrequent visits to his homeland. This trip produced his most perceptive travel book, *The American Scene* (1907), an excerpt from which follows.

One might have been sure in advance that the character of a democracy would nowhere more sharply mark itself than in the democratic substitute for a court city, and Washington is cast in the mould that expresses most the absence of salient social landmarks and constituted features. Here it is that conversation, as the only invoked presence, betrays a little in its adequacy to the furnishing forth, all by itself, of an outward view. It tells us it must be there, since in all the wide empty vistas nothing else is, and the general elimination *can* but have left it. A pleading, touching effect, indeed, lurks in this sense of it as seated, at receipt of custom, by any decent door of any decent domicile and watching the vacancy for reminder and appeal. It is left to conversation alone to people the scene with accents; putting aside two or three objects to be specified, there is *never* an accent in it, up and down, far and wide, save such as fall rather on the ear of the mind: those projected by the social spirit starved for the sense of an occasional emphasis. The White House is an accent—one of the lightest, sharpest possible; and the Capitol, of course, immensely, another; though the latter falls on the exclusively political page, as to which I have been waiting to say a word. It should meanwhile be mentioned that we are promised these enhancements, these illustrations, of the great general text, on the most magnificent scale; a splendid projected and announced Washington of the future, with approaches even now grandly outlined and massively marked; in face of which one should perhaps confess to the futility of any current estimate. If I speak thus of the Capitol, however, let me not merely brush past the White House to get to it—any more than feel free to pass into it without some preliminary stare at that wondrous Library of Congress which glitters in fresh and almost unmannerly emulation, almost frivolous irrelevance of form, in the neighbourhood of the greater building. About the ingenuities and splendours of this last costly structure, a riot of rare material and rich ornament, there would doubtless be much to say— did not one everywhere, on all such ground, meet the open eye of criticism simply to establish with it a private intelligence, simply to respond to it by a deprecating wink. The guardian of that altar, I think, is but too willing, on such a hint, to let one pass without the sacrifice.

It is a case again here, as on fifty other occasions, of the tribute instantly paid by the revisiting spirit; but paid, all without question, to the general *kind* of presence for which the noisy air, over the land, feels so sensibly an inward ache—the presence that corresponds there, no matter how loosely, to that of the housing and harbouring European Church in the ages of great disorder. The Universities and the greater Libraries (the smaller, for a hundred good democratic reasons, are another question), repeat, in their manner, to the imagination, East and West, the note of the old thick-walled convents and quiet cloisters: they are large and charitable, they are sturdy, often proud and often rich, and they have the incalculable value that they represent the only intermission to inordinate rapacious traffic that the scene offers to view. With this suggestion of sacred ground they play even upon the most restless of analysts as they will, making him face about, with ecstasy, any way they seem to point; so that he feels it his business much less to count over their shortcomings than, to proclaim them places of enchantment. They are better at their worst than anything else at its best, and the comparatively sweet sounds that stir their theoretic stillness are for him as echoes of the lyre of Apollo. The Congressional Library is magnificent, and would become thus a supreme sanctuary even were it ten times more so: there would seem to be nothing then but to pronounce it a delight and have done with it—or let the appalled imagination, in other words, slink into it and stay there. But here is pressed precisely, with particular force, the spring of the question that takes but a touch to sound: is the case of this remarkable creation, by exception, a case in which the violent waving of the pecuniary wand *has* incontinently produced interest? The answer can only be, I feel, a shy assent—though shy indeed only till the logic of the matter is apparent. This logic is that, though money alone can gather in on such a scale the treasures of knowledge, these treasures, in the form of books and documents, themselves organize and furnish their world. They appoint and settle the proportions, they thicken the air, they people the space, they create and consecrate all their relations, and no one shall say that, where they scatter life, which they themselves in fact *are*, history does not promptly attend. Emphatically yes, therefore, the great domed and tiered, galleried and statued central hall of the Congressional, the last word of current constructional science and artistic resource, already crowns itself with that grace.

The graceful thing in Washington beyond any other, none the less, is the so happily placed and featured White House, the late excellent extensions and embellishments of which have of course represented expenditure—but only of the refined sort imposed by some mature portionless gentlewoman on relatives who have accepted the principle of making her, at a time of life, more honourably comfortable. The whole ample precinct and margin formed by the virtual continuity of its grounds with those expanses in which the effect of the fine Washington Obelisk rather spends or wastes itself (not a little as if some loud monosyllable had been uttered, in a preoccupied company, without a due production of sympathy or sense)—the fortunate isolation of the White House, I say, intensifies its power to appeal to that musing and mooning visitor whose perceptions alone, in all the conditions, I hold worthy of account. Hereabouts, beyond doubt, history had from of old seemed to me insistently seated, and I remember a short spring-time of years ago when Lafayette Square itself, contiguous to the Executive Mansion, could create a rich sense of the past by the use of scarce other witchcraft than its command of that pleasant perspective and its possession of the most prodigious of all Presidential effigies, Andrew Jackson, as archaic as a Ninevite king, prancing and rocking through the ages. If that atmosphere, moreover, in the fragrance of the Washington April, was even a quarter of a century since as a liquor of bitter-sweet taste, overflowing its cup, what was the ineffable mixture, now, with all the elements further distilled, all the life further sacrificed, to make it potent? One circled about the place as for meeting the ghosts, and one paused, under the same impulse, before the high palings of the White House drive, as if wondering at haunted ground. There the ghosts stood in their public array, spectral enough and clarified; yet scarce making it easier to "place" the strange, incongruous blood-drops, as one looked through the rails, on that revised and freshened page. But one fortunately has one's choice, in all these connections, as one turns away; the mixture, as I have called it, is really here so fine. General Jackson, in the centre of the Square, still rocks his hobby and the earth; but the fruit of the interval, to my actual eyes, hangs nowhere brighter than in the brilliant memorials lately erected to Lafayette and to Rochambeau. Artful, genial, expressive, the tribute of French talent, these happy images supply, on the spot, the note without which even the most fantasticating sense of our national past would feel itself rub forever against mere brown homespun. Everything else gives way, for me, I confess, as I again stand before them; everything, whether as historic fact, or present *agrément*, or future possibility, yields to this one high luxury of our old friendship with France.

The "artistic" Federal city already announced spreads itself then before us, in plans elaborated even to the finer details, a city of palaces and monuments and gardens, symmetries and circles and far radiations, with the big Potomac for water-power and water-effect and the recurrent Maryland spring, so prompt and so full-handed, for a perpetual benediction. This imagery has, above all, the value, for the considering mind, that it presents itself as under the wide-spread wings of the general Government, which fairly make it figure to the rapt vision as the object caught up in eagle claws and lifted into fields of air that even the high brows of the municipal boss fail to sweep. The wide-spread wings affect us, in the prospect, as great fans that, by their mere tremor, will blow the work, at all steps and stages, clean and clear, disinfect it quite ideally of any germ of the job, and pre-pare thereby for the American voter, on the spot and in the pride of possession, quite a new kind of civic consciousness. The scheme looms largest, surely, as a demonstration of the possi-bilities of that service to him, and nothing about it will he more interesting than to measure—though this may take time—the nature and degree of his alleviation. Will the new pride I speak of sufficiently inflame him? Will the taste of the new conscious-ness, finding him so fresh to it, prove the right medicine? One can only regret that we must still rather indefinitely wait to see—and regret it all the more that there is always, in America, yet another lively source of interest involved in the execution of such designs, and closely involved just in proportion as the high intention, the formal majesty, of the thing seems assured. It comes back to what we constantly feel, throughout the country, to what the American scene everywhere depends on for half its appeal or its effect; to the fact that the social conditions, the material, pressing and pervasive, make the particular experi-ment or demonstration, whatever it may pretend to, practically a new and incalculable thing. This general Americanism is often the one tag of character attaching to the case after every other appears to have abandoned it. The thing is happening, or will have to happen, in the American way—that American way which is more different from all other native ways, taking country with country, than any of these latter are different from each other; and the question is of how, each time, the American way will see it through.

The element of suspense—beguilement, ever, of the sincere observer—is provided for by the fact that, though this American way never fails to come up, he has to recognize as by no means equally true that it never fails to succeed. It is inveterately applied, but with consequences bewilderingly various; which means, however, for our present moral, but that the certainty of the *determined* American effect is an element to attend quite especially such a case as the employment of the arts of design, on an unprecedented scale, for public uses, the adoption on this scale of the whole aesthetic law. Encountered in America, phenomena of this order strike us mostly as occurring in the historic void, as having to present themselves in the hard light of that desert, and as needing to extort from it, so far as they can, something of the shading of their interest. Encountered in older countries, they show, on the contrary, as taking up the references, as consenting perforce to the relations, of which the air is already full, and as having thereby much rather to get themselves expressive by charm than to get themselves expressive by weight. The danger "in Europe" is of their having too many things to say, and too many others to distinguish these from; the danger in the States is of their not having things enough—with enough tone and resonance furthermore to give them. What therefore will the multitudinous and elaborate forms of the Washington to come have to "say," and what, above all, besides gold and silver, stone and marble and trees and flowers, will they be able to say it *with*? That is one of the questions in the mere phrasing of which the restless analyst finds a thrill. There is a thing called interest that has to be produced for him—positively as if he were a rabid usurer with a clutch of his imperilled bond. He has seen again and again how the most expensive effort often fails to lead up to interest, and he has seen how it may bloom in soil of no more worth than so many layers of dust and ashes. He has learnt in fact—he learns greatly in America—to mistrust any plea for it *directly* made by money, which operates too often as the great puffing motor-car framed for whirling him, in his dismay, quite away from it. And he has inevitably noted, at the same time, from how comparatively few other sources this rewarding dividend on his in vested attention may be drawn. He thinks of these sources as few, that is, because he sees the same ones, which are the references by which interest is fed, used again and again, with a desperate economy; sees the same ones, even as the human heroes, celebrities, extemporized lions or scapegoats, required social and educational figure-heads and "values," having to serve in *all* the connections and adorn all the tales. That is one of the liveliest of his American impressions. He has at moments his sense that, in presence of such vast populations, and instilled, emulous demands, there is not, outside the mere economic, enough native history, recorded or current, to go round.

It seemed to me on the spot, moreover, that such reflections were rather more than less pertinent in face of the fact that I was again to find the Capitol, whenever I approached, and above all whenever I entered it, a vast and many-voiced creation. The thing depends of course somewhat on the visitor, who will be the more responsive, I think, the further back into the "origins" of the whole American spectacle his personal vision shall carry him; but this hugest, as I suppose it, of all the homes of debate only asks to put forth, on opportunity, an incongruous, a various, an inexhaustible charm. I may as well say at once that I had found myself from the first adoring the Capitol, though I may not pretend here to dot all the i's of all my reasons—since some of these might appear below the dignity of the subject and others alien to its simplicity. The ark of the American covenant may strike one thus, at any rate, as a compendium of all the national ideals, a museum, crammed full, even to overflowing, of all the national terms and standards, weights and measures and emblems of greatness and glory, and indeed as a builded record of half the collective vibrations of a people; their conscious spirit, their public faith, their bewildered taste, their ceaseless curiosity, their arduous and interrupted education. Such were to my vision at least some of its aspects, but the place had a hundred sides, and if I had had time to look for others still I felt I should have found them. What it comes to—whereby the "pull," in America, is of the greatest—is that association really reigns there, and in the richest, and even again and again in the drollest, forms; it is thick and vivid and almost gross, it assaults the wondering mind. The labyrinthine pile becomes thus inordinately *amusing*—taking the term in its finer modern sense. The analogy may seem forced, but it affected me as playing in Washington life very much the part that St. Peter's, of old, had seemed to me to play in Roman: it offered afternoon entertainment, at the end of a longish walk, to any spirit in the humour for the uplifted and flattered vision—and this without suggesting that the sublimities in the two cases, even as measured by the profanest mind, tend at all to be equal. The Washington dome is indeed, capable, in the Washington air, of admirable, of sublime effects; and there are cases in which, seen at a distance above its yellow Potomac, it varies but by a shade from the sense—yes, absolutely the divine Campagna-sense—of St. Peter's and the like-coloured Tiber.

But the question is positively of the impressiveness of the great terraced Capitol hill, with its stages and slopes, staircases and fountains, its general presentation of its charge. And if the whole mass and prospect "amuse," as I say, from the moment they are embraced, the visitor curious of the *democratic assimilation* of the greater dignities and majesties will least miss the general logic. That is the light in which the whole thing is supremely interesting; the light of the fact, illustrated at every turn, that the populations maintaining it deal with it so directly and intimately, so sociably and humorously. We promptly take in that, if ever we are to commune in a concentrated way with the sovereign people and see their exercised power raise a side-wind of irony for forms and arrangements other than theirs, the occasion here will amply serve. Indubitably, moreover, at a hundred points, the irony operates, and all the more markedly under such possible interference; interference of the monumental spittoons, that of the immense amount of vulgar, of barbaric, decoration, that of the terrible artistic tributes from, and scarce less to, the different States—the unassorted marble mannikins in particular each a portrayal by one of the commonwealths of her highest worthy, which make the great Rotunda, the intended Valhalla, resemble a stonecutter's collection of priced sorts and sizes. Discretion exists, throughout, only as a flower of the very first or of these very latest years; the large middle time, corresponding, and even that unequally, with the English Victorian, of sinister memory, was unacquainted with the name, and waits there now, in its fruits, but for a huge sacrificial fire, some far-flaring act-of-faith of the future: a tribute to the aesthetic law which one already feels stirring the air, so that it may arrive, I think, with an unexampled stride. Nothing will have been more interesting, surely, than so public a wiping-over of the aesthetic slate, with all the involved collective compunctions and repudiations, the general exhibition of a colossal conscience, a conscience proportionate to the size and wealth of the country. To such grand gestures does the American scene lend itself!

The elements in question are meanwhile there, in any case, just as the sovereign people are there, "going over" their property; but we are aware none the less of impressions—that of the ponderous proud Senate, for instance, so sensibly massive; that of the Supreme Court, so simply, one almost says so chastely, yet, while it breathes supremacy, so elegantly, so all intellectually, in session—under which the view, taking one extravagance with another, recurs rather ruefully to glimpses elsewhere caught, glimpses of authority emblazoned, bewigged, bemantled, bemarshalled, in almost direct defeat of its intention of gravity. For the reinstated absentee, in these presences, the mere recovery of native privilege was at all events a balm—after too many challenged appeals and abused patiences, too many hushed circuitous creepings, among the downtrodden, in other and more bristling halls of state. The sense of a certain large, final benignity in the Capitol comes then, I think, from this impression that

the national relation to it is that of a huge flourishing Family to
the place of business, the estate-office, where, in a myriad open
ledgers, which offer no obscurity to the hereditary head for figures, the account of their colossal revenue is kept. They meet
there in safe sociability, as all equally initiated and interested—
not as in a temple or a citadel, but by the warm domestic hearth
of Columbia herself; a motherly, chatty, clear-spectacled
Columbia, who reads all the newspapers, knows, to the last
man, every one of her sons by name, and, to the last boy, even
her grandsons, and is fenced off, at the worst, but by concentric
circles of rocking-chairs. It is impossible, as I say, not to he
fondly conscious of her welcome—unless again, and yet again, I
read into the general air, confusedly too much of the happy accident of the basis of my introduction. But if my sensibility
responds with intensity to this, so much the better; for what
were such felt personal aids and influences, after all, but cases
and examples, embodied expressions of character, type, distinction, products of the *working* of the whole thing?—specimens,
indeed, highly concentrated and refined, and made thereby, I
admit, more charming and insidious.

It must also be admitted that to exchange the inner aspects of
the vast monument for the outer is to be reminded with some
sharpness of a Washington in which half the sides that have held
our attention drop, as if rather abashed, out of sight. Not its
pleasant brightness as of a winter watering-place, not its connections, however indirect, with the older, but those with the newer,
the newest, civilization, seem matter of recognition for its various marble fronts; it rakes the prospect, it rakes the continent, to
a much more sweeping purpose, and is visibly concerned but in
immeasurable schemes of which it can consciously remain the
centre. Here, in the vast spaces—mere empty light and air,
though such pleasant air and such pretty light as yet—the great
Federal future seems, under vague bright forms, to hover and to
stalk, making the horizon recede to take it in, making the terraces too, below the long colonnades, the admirable standpoints,
the sheltering porches, of political philosophy. The compara-

tively new wings of the building filled me, whenever I walked here, with thanksgiving for their large and perfect elegance: so, in Paris, might the wide mated fronts that are of such a noble effect on either side of the Rue Royale shine in multiplied majesty and recovered youth over an infinite Place de la Concorde. These parts of the Capitol, on their Acropolis height, are ideally constructed for "raking," and for this suggestion of their dominating the American scene in playhouse gallery fashion. You are somehow possessed of it *all* while you tread them—their marble embrace appears to the complement of the vast democratic lap. Though I had them in general, for contemplation, quite to myself, I met one morning a trio of Indian braves, braves dispossessed of forest and prairie, but as free of the builded labyrinth as they had ever been of these; also arrayed in neat pot-hats, shoddy suits and light overcoats, with their pockets, I am sure, full of photographs and cigarettes: circumstances all that quickened their resemblance, on the much bigger scale, to Japanese celebrities, or to specimens, on show, of what the Government can do with people with whom it is supposed able to do nothing. They seemed just then and there, for a mind fed betimes on the *Leatherstocking Tales,* to project as in a flash an image in itself immense, but foreshortened and simplified—-reducing to a single smooth stride the bloody footsteps of time. One rubbed one's eyes, but there, at its highest polish, shining in the beautiful day, was the brazen face of history, and there, all about one, immaculate, the printless pavements of the State.

from *Cane*

JEAN TOOMER (1894–1967)

Jean Toomer was born Nathan Eugene Toomer in Washington, D.C., where he spent most of his early years. He came from a racially mixed family, and his life was consumed by an often futile search for racial and personal identity. His father disappeared before he was born, and his mother died when he was a teenager, so he grew up primarily under the care and financial backing of his maternal grandparents. Toomer went to M Street High School. Between 1914 and 1919, he attended six colleges and traveled sporadically throughout the Northeast and Midwest, but Washington remained for him an anchor. He decided to become a writer in 1919 but made little progress until 1921, when a trip to Sparta, Georgia, changed his life forever. As an elementary school teacher he was exposed to the rural black culture of the Deep South, and his appreciation of his racial roots grew. This sojourn inspired *Cane* (1923), a groundbreaking collection of prose, poetry, and drama. That same year, he adopted the philosophical system of Georges Ivanovitch Gurdjieff, the first of many attempts at finding the inner harmony that constantly eluded him. His later published work includes *Balo* (1927), a one-act play; *Essentials* (1931), a book of aphorisms; and several essays and stories. Most of his writing, however, remained unpublished at the time of his death. The following excerpt from *Cane* is a piece of poetic prose in which the narrator attempts to understand a mysteriously difficult girl from Washington named Avey.

For a long while she was nothing more to me than one of those skirted beings whom boys at a certain age disdain to play with. Just how I came to love her, timidly, and with secret blushes, I do not know. But that I did was brought home to me one night, the first night that Ned wore his long pants. Us fellers were seated on the curb before an apartment house where she had gone in.

The young trees had not outgrown their boxes then. V Street was lined with them. When our legs grew cramped and stiff from the cold of the stone, we'd stand around a box and whittle it. I like to think now that there was a hidden purpose in the way we hacked them with our knives. I like to feel that something deep in me responded to the trees, the young trees that whinnied like colts impatient to be let free . . . On the particular night I have in mind, we were waiting for the top-floor light to go out. We wanted to see Avey leave the flat. This night she stayed longer than usual and gave us a chance to complete the plans of how we were going to stone and beat that feller on the top floor out of town. Ned especially had it in for him. He was about to throw a brick up at the window when at last the room went dark. Some minutes passed. Then Avey, as unconcerned as if she had been paying an old-maid aunt a visit, came out. I don't remember what she had on, and all that sort of thing. But I do know that I turned hot as bare pavements in the summertime at Ned's boast: "Hell, bet I could get her too if you little niggers weren't always spying and crabbing everything." I didn't say a word to him. It wasn't my way then. I just stood there like the others, and something like a fuse burned up inside of me. She never noticed us, but swung along lazy and easy as anything. We sauntered to the corner and watched her till her door banged to. Ned repeated what he'd said. I didn't seem to care. Sitting around old Mush-Head's bread box, the discussion began. "Hang if I can see how she gets away with it," Doc started. Ned knew, of course. There was nothing he didn't know when it came to women. He dilated on the emotional needs of girls. Said they weren't much different from men in that respect. And concluded with the solemn avowal: "It does 'em good." None of us liked Ned much. We all talked dirt; but it was the way he said it. And then too, a couple of the fellers had sisters and had caught Ned playing with them. But there was no disputing the superiority of his smutty wisdom. Bubs Sanborn, whose mother was friendly with Avey's, had overheard the old ladies talking. "Avey's mother's ont her," he said. We thought that only natural and began to guess at what would happen. Someone said she'd marry that feller on the top floor. Ned called that a lie because Avey was going to marry nobody but him. We had our doubts about that, but we did agree that she'd soon leave school and marry someone. The gang broke up, and I went home, picturing myself as married.

Nothing I did seemed able to change Avey's indifference to me. I played basketball, and when I'd make a long clean shot she'd clap with the others, louder than they, I thought. I'd meet her on the street, and there'd be no difference in the way she said hello. She never took the trouble to call me by my name. On the days for drill, I'd let my voice down a tone and call for a complicated maneuver when I saw her coming. She'd smile appreciation, but it was an impersonal smile, never for me. It was on a summer excursion down to Riverview that she first seemed to take me into account. The day had been spent riding merry-gorounds, scenic railways, and shoot-the-chutes. We had been in swimming and we had danced. I was a crack swimmer then. She didn't know how. I held her up and showed her how to kick her legs and draw her arms. Of course she didn't learn in one day, but she thanked me for bothering with her. I was also somewhat of a dancer. And I had already noticed that love can start on a dance floor. We danced. But though I held her tightly in my arms, she was way away. That college feller who lived on the top floor was somewhere making money for the next year. I imagined that she was thinking, wishing for him. Ned was along. He treated her until his money gave out. She went with another feller. Ned got sore. One by one the boys' money gave out. She left them. And they got sore. Every one of them but me got sore. This is the reason, I guess, why I had her to myself on the top deck of the *Jane Mosely* that night as we puffed up the Potomac, coming home. The moon was brilliant. The air was sweet like clover. And every now and then, a salt tang, a stale drift of seaweed. It was not my mind's fault if it went romancing. I should have taken her in my arms the minute we were stowed in that old lifeboat. I dallied, dreaming. She took me in hers. And I could feel by the touch of it that it wasn't a man-to-woman love. It made me restless. I felt chagrined. I didn't know what it was, but I did know that I couldn't handle it. She ran her fingers through my hair and kissed my forehead. I itched to break through her tenderness to passion. I wanted her to take me in her arms as I knew she had that college feller. I wanted her to love me passionately as she did him. I gave her one burning kiss. Then she laid me in her lap as if I were a child. Helpless. I got sore when she started to hum a lullaby. She wouldn't let me go. I talked. I knew damned well that I could beat her at that. Her eyes were soft and misty, the curves of her lips were wistful, and her smile seemed indulgent of the irrelevance of my remarks. I gave up at last and let her love me, silently, in her own way. The moon was brilliant. The air was sweet like clover, and every now and then, a salt tang, a stale drift of sea-weed . . .

   The next time I came close to her was the following summer at Harper's Ferry. We were sitting on a flat projecting rock they give the name of Lover's Leap. Someone is supposed to have jumped off it. The river is about six hundred feet beneath. A railroad track runs up the valley and curves out of sight where part of the mountain rock had to be blasted away to make room for it. The engines of this valley have a whistle, the echoes of which sound like iterated gasps and sobs. I always think of them as crude music from the soul of Avey. We sat there holding hands. Our palms were soft and warm against each other. Our fingers were not tight. She would not let them be. She would not let me twist them. I wanted to talk. To explain what I meant to her. Avery was as silent as those great trees whose tops we looked down upon. She has always been like that. At least, to me. I had the notion that if I really wanted to, I could do with her just what I pleased. Like one can strip a tree. I did kiss her. I even let my hands cup her breasts. When I was through, she'd seek my hand and hold it till my pulse cooled down. Evening after evening we sat there. I tried to get her to talk about that college feller. She never would. There was no set time to go home. None of my family had come down. And as for hers, she didn't give a hang about them. The general gossips could hardly say more than they had. The boarding-house porch was always deserted when we returned. No one saw us enter, so the time was set conveniently for scandal. This worried me a little, for I thought it might keep Avey from getting an appointment in the schools. She didn't care. She had finished normal school. They could give her a job if they wanted to. As time went on, her indifference to things began to pique me; I was ambitious. I left the Ferry earlier than she did. I was going off to college. The more I thought of it, the more I resented, yes, hell, that's what it was, her downright laziness. Sloppy indolence. There was no excuse for a healthy girl taking life so easy. Hell! She was no better than a cow. I was certain that she was a cow when I felt an udder in a Wisconsin stock-judging class. Among those energetic Swedes, or whatever they are, I decided to forget her. For two years I thought I did.

When I'd come home for the summer she'd be away. And before she returned, I'd be gone. We never wrote; she was too damned lazy for that. But what a bluff I put up about forgetting her. The girls up that way, at least the ones I knew, haven't got the stuff: they don't know how to love. Giving themselves completely was tame beside just the holding of Avey's hand. One day I received a note from her. The writing, I decided, was slovenly. She wrote on a torn bit of note-book paper. The envelope had a faint perfume that I remembered. A single line told me she had lost her school and was going away. I comforted myself with the reflection that shame held no pain for one so indolent as she. Nevertheless, I left Wisconsin that year for good. Washington had seemingly forgotten her. I hunted Ned. Between curses, I caught his opinion of her. She was no better than a whore. I saw her mother on the street. The same old pinch-beck, jerky-gaited creature that I'd always known.

Perhaps five years passed. The business of hunting a job or something or other had bruised my vanity so that I could recognize it. I felt old. Avey and my real relation to her, I thought I came to know. I wanted to see her. I had been told that she was in New York. As I had no money, I hiked and bummed my way there. I got work in a ship-yard and walked the streets at night, hoping to meet her. Failing in this, I saved enough to pay my fare back home. One evening in early June, just at the time when dusk is most lovely on the eastern horizon, I saw Avey, indolent as ever, leaning on the arm of a man, strolling under the recently lit arclights of U Street. She had almost passed before she recognized me. She showed no surprise. The puff over her eyes had grown heavier. The eyes themselves were still sleepy-large, and beautiful. I had almost concluded—indifferent. "You look older," was what she said. I wanted to convince her that I was, so I asked her to walk with me. The man whom she was with, and whom she never took the trouble to introduce, at a nod from her, hailed a taxi, and drove away. That gave me a notion of what she had been used to. Her dress was of some fine, costly stuff. I suggested the park, and then added that the grass might stain her skirt. Let it get stained, she said, for where it came from there are others.

I have a spot in Soldier's Home to which I always go when I want the simple beauty of another's soul. Robins spring about the lawn all day. They leave their footprints in the grass. I imagine that the grass at night smells sweet and fresh because of them. The ground is high. Washington lies below. Its light spreads like a blush against the darkened sky. Against the soft dusk sky of Washington. And when the wind is from the South, soil of my homeland falls like a fertile shower upon the lean streets of the city. Upon my hill in Soldier's Home, I know the policeman who watches the place of nights. When I go there alone, I talk to him. I tell him I come there to find the truth that people bury in their hearts. I tell him that I do not come there with a girl to do the thing he's paid to watch out for. I look deep in his eyes when I say these things, and he believes me. He comes over to see who it is on the grass. I say hello to him. He greets me in the same way and goes off searching for other black splotches upon the lawn. Avey and I went there. A band in one of the buildings a fair distance off was playing a march. I wished they would stop. Their playing was like a tin spoon in one's mouth. I wanted the Howard Glee Club to sing "Deep River," from the road. To sing "Deep River, Deep River," from the road . . . Other than the first comments, Avey had been silent. I started to hum a folk-tune. She slipped her hand in mine. Pillowed her head as best she could upon my arm. Kissed the hand that she was holding and listened, or so I thought, to what I had to say. I traced my development from the early days up to the present time, the phase in which I could understand her. I described her own nature and temperament. Told how they needed a larger life for their expression. How incapable Washington was of understanding that need. How it could not meet it. I pointed out that in lieu of proper channels, her emotions had overflowed into paths that dissipated them. I talked, beautifully I thought, about an art that would be born, an art that would open the way for women the likes of her. I asked her to hope, and build up an inner life against the coming of that day. I recited some of my own things to her. I sang, with a strange quiver in my voice, a promise-song. And then I began to wonder why her hand had not once returned a single pressure. My old-time feeling about her laziness came back. I spoke sharply. My policeman friend passed by. I said hello to him. As he went away, I began to visualize certain possibilities. An immediate and urgent passion swept over me. Then I looked at Avey. Her heavy eyes were closed. Her breathing was as faint and regular as a child's in slumber. My passion died. I was afraid to move lest I disturb her. Hours and hours, I guess it was, she lay there. My body grew numb. I shivered. I coughed. I wanted to get up and whittle at the boxes of young trees. I withdrew my hand. I raised her head to waken her. She did not stir. I got up and walked around. I found my policeman friend and talked to him. We both came up, and bent over her. He said it would be all right for her to stay there just so long as she got away before the workmen came at dawn. A blanket was borrowed from a neighbor house. I sat beside her through the night. I saw the

dawn steal over Washington. The Capitol dome looked like a
gray ghost ship drifting in from sea. Avey's face was pale, and
her eyes were heavy. She did not have the gray crimson-splashed
beauty of the dawn. I hated to wake her. Orphan-woman . . .

"The Capital of a Great Republic"

H. L. MENCKEN (1880–1956)

A newspaperman since age nineteen, Baltimore-born Henry Louis Mencken joined the staff of the *Baltimore Sun* in 1906 and worked at that newspaper in various capacities for the remainder of his life. He became literary editor of *Smart Set* in 1908 and served as coeditor (with George Jean Nathan) of the magazine until leaving to found the *American Mercury* in 1924 with the backing of Alfred A. Knopf. The prolific Mencken tried his hand at virtually every genre of belles lettres and journalism and at the height of his literary activity wrote an average of 10,000 words a week for publication. He was one of the most influential literary critics of his time and helped establish the reputations of Theodore Dreiser, Eugene O'Neill, F. Scott Fitzgerald, and Sinclair Lewis. He wrote in an article for the *Chicago Tribune* in 1925 that "novelists [have always] made the mistake of assuming that the essential conflict in Washington is between ideas. This is not true. The essential conflict there, as in Summit, N.J., and in Vladivostock, is between desires." Mencken is best remembered, if not for his coinage of the phrase "the Bible Belt," for his classic of philology, *The American Language* (first published in 1919); his collected essays on social philosophy, including *Treatise on the Gods* (1930) and *Treatise on Right and Wrong* (1934); and his reminiscences, *The Days of H. L. Mencken: Happy Days, Newspaper Days* and *Heathen Days* (1941–1947). Mencken included the following in the 1924 *Prejudices*, part of his 1919–1927 annual collection of what he considered his best articles.

The fourth secretary of the Paraguayan delegation. . . . The chief clerk to the House committee on industrial arts and expositions. . . . The secretary to the secretary to the Secretary of Labor. . . .

The brother to the former Congressman from the third Idaho district. . . . The messenger to the chief of the Senate folding-room. . . . The door keeper outside the committee-room of the House committee on the disposition of useless executive papers. . . . The chief correspondent of the Toomsboro, Ga., *Banner* in the Senate press-gallery. . . . The stenographer to the assistant chief entomologist of the Bureau of Animal Industry. . . . The third assistant chief computor in the office of the Naval Almanac. . . . The assistant Attorney General in charge of the investigation of postal frauds in the South Central States. . . . The former wife of the former secretary to the former member of the Interstate Commerce Commission. . . . The brother to the wife of the *chargé d'affaires* of Czecho-Slovakia. . . . The bootlegger to the ranking Democratic member of the committee on the election of President, Vice-President, and representatives in Congress. . . . The acting assistant doorkeeper of the House visitors' gallery. . . . The junior Senator from Delaware. . . . The assistant to the secretary to the chief clerk of the Division of Audits and Disbursements, Bureau of Stationary and Supplies, Post Office Department. . . . The press-agent to the chaplain of the House. . . . The commercial attaché to the American delegation at Quito. . . . The chauffeur to the fourth assistant Postmaster-General. . . . The acting substitute elevator-man in the Washington monument. . . . The brother to the wife of the brother-in-law of the Vice-President. . . . The aunt to the sister of the wife of the officer in charge of ceremonials, State Department. . . . The neighbor of the cousin of the stepfather of the sister-in-law of the President's pastor. . . . The superintendent of charwomen in Temporary Storehouse B7, Bureau of Navy Yards and Docks. . . . The assistant confidential clerk to the chief clerk to the acting chief examiner of the Patent Office. . . . The valet to the Chief Justice.

"Glory, Glory"

STERLING A. BROWN (1901–1989)

Sterling A. Brown attended Dunbar High School in his home town of Washington, D.C., before attending Williams College. He earned a master's degree from Harvard University and worked as a teacher at the Virginia Seminary and College in Lynchburg until 1926. Three years later, Brown took a position on the faculty of Howard University. *Southern Road*, his first collection of poetry, was published in 1932. With the onset of the Depression, he could not find a publisher for his second collection of verse and instead focused on the essay and his teaching. His prose includes *Outline for the Study of Poetry of American Negroes* (1931), *The Negro in American Fiction* (1937), *Negro Poetry and Drama* (1937), and *A Son's Return: Selected Essays of Sterling A. Brown* (1996). The second collection of poetry, *The Last Ride of Wild Bill*, found a publisher in 1975, six years after Brown's retirement from Howard. His *Collected Poems* appeared in 1980. Brown died in Takoma Park, Maryland. The following poem first appeared in *Esquire* in 1932.

When Annie Mae Johnson condescends to take the air,
Give up all your business, make haste to get there,
Glory oh glory, get there, be there.

The last time I saw Annie on the avenue,
She held up traffic for an hour or two.
The green light refused, absolutely, to go off at all;
And the red light and the amber nearly popped the glass,
When Annie walked by, they came on so fast,
Then stayed on together twenty minutes after she went past;
And it took three days for to get them duly timed again.
Even so, they palpitated every now and then,

A driver of a coal truck turned his head around,
Watching her walk and knocked an old man down,

Old man's weak eyes had been dazzled by the gorgeous sight;
Po' man collapsed and he heaved a sigh,
Said, "Lord, I'm willin' at the last to die,
Cause my state is blessed, everything's all right,
Happy, Lord, happy, yes happy am I."

Saw a Rock Creek Bridge car jump off the track,
Do the shim-sham and come reeling back;
Saw a big steam roller knocked clean off its base,
When it got together, the little Austin had its place.

Ambulance came a-clanging, the fire truck banging,
Police patrol a-sailing, the sirens all wailing,
Parked any whichaway and turned their headlights high,
With their engines just a-purring, till Annie Mae tipped on by.

Folks gathered from the manors, swarmed in from the alleys,
Deserted their pool-rooms, rushed out of their lodges,
Some took taxis to get them to the place on time;
Way the preachers left their congregations was a holy crime.
Twixt Uncle Ham's sonny boys and Aunt Hagar's daughters
Just like Daddy Moses through the Red Sea Waters,
Annie Johnson made a path, as she laid it on the frazzling line;
The dark waves parted, and then they closed in behind.

Aaanh, Lord, when Annie Mae lays it down,
If you want to take the census proper, better come around.

from *The Big Sea*

LANGSTON HUGHES (1902–1967)

Joplin, Missouri–born Langston Hughes was raised by his grandmother in Kansas after his parents separated. His first major publication came in the National Association for the Advancement of Colored People publication *Crisis* in 1920, a year before he entered Columbia University. That poem, "The Negro Dreams of Rivers" has become one of the prolific poet's best known. He attended Columbia University for one year and then led a vagabond existence for several years. He worked odd jobs in New York City and served as a ship's mess boy, which allowed him to travel to Europe and Africa. While working as a busboy at the Wardman Hotel in Washington, he met Vachel Lindsay, who encouraged him in his writing and brought him to the attention of the media, calling him "the bus boy poet." After a short residency in Europe, Hughes returned to his university studies and to a volume of poetry, *The Weary Blues*, which launched his successful career as a poet upon its publication in 1926. Hughes went on to become one of the most influential members of the Harlem Renaissance. His best-known prose fiction is the 1950 *Simple Speaks His Mind*, featuring the shrewdly plainspoken character Jesse B. Simple. "Washington Society," the following selection from Hughes's 1940 autobiography, relates his arrival to Washington from New York with twenty-five cents in his pocket.

Besides the quarter, I landed with a few poems. I took them that afternoon to show to Countee Cullen, whose work I admired. Cullen told me the National Association for the Advancement of Colored People was having a benefit cabaret party that night at Happy Rhone's Club on Lenox Avenue. So I went—and got in free, being a writer for the *Crisis*. It was a very gay and very crowded party, sprinkled with celebrities. Alberta Hunter was singing a song about, "Everybody loves my baby, but my baby don't love nobody but me."

At the door I met Walter White and he introduced me to Mary White Ovington, James Weldon Johnson and Carl Van Vechten. I sat at a table with Walter's charming and very beautiful wife, and I was properly dazed. She looked like a Moorish princess.

I wanted to ask her for a dance, but I still had my sea legs on. Besides, I was bashful.

All the *Crisis* people were at the party and I asked if they had liked my article and they said: "Yes." They told me their office had cabled me twenty dollars to Genoa. But the cable came back. The next day they showed me the cable receipt, and the date indicated that it reached the Albergo Populare the day after I sailed. I was glad it had missed me, because now I had twenty dollars to start life anew in my New World, like an immigrant from Europe. So I went to see Jeanne Eagels in *Rain*, and then *What Price Glory*, before I went home.

My mother and kid brother were in Washington. This time, she wrote, she and my step-father had separated for good, and she had decided to come to Washington to live with our cousins there, who belonged to the more intellectual and high-class branch of our family, being direct descendants of Congressman John M. Langston. She asked me to join her. It all sounded risky to me, but I decided to try it. My cousins extended a cordial invitation to come and share their life with them. They were proud of my poems, they said, and would be pleased to have a writer in the house.

By now, I wanted to go back to college, anyhow. And I thought that Howard, in Washington, would be a good place to start, if I could manage to get together the tuition. So I bought a ticket to Washington. The twenty dollars from the *Crisis* would not cover both a ticket and an overcoat, which I needed, so I arrived in Washington with only a sailor's peajacket protecting me from the winter winds. All my shirts were ragged and my trousers frayed. I am sure I did not look like a distinguished poet, when I walked up to my cousin's porch in Washington's Negro society section, LeDroit Park, next door to the famous colored surgeon and heart specialist, Dr. Carson.

Listen, everybody! Never go to live with relatives if you're broke! That is an error. My cousins introduced me as just back from Europe, but they didn't say I came by chipping decks on a freight ship—which seemed to me an essential explanation.

The nice, cultured colored people I met in Washington seemed to think that by just being a poet I could get a dignified job, such as a page boy in the Library of Congress. I thought such a job would be nice, too, so they sent me to see Mary Church Terrell and some other famous Negro leaders who had political influence. But to be a page boy in the Library of Congress seems to require a tremendous list of qualifications and influential connections, and a great capacity for calling on politicians and race leaders, as well as a vast patience for waiting and waiting. So, being broke, I finally got a job in a wet wash laundry instead.

I had to help unload the wagons, and open the big bags of dirty clothes people send to wet wash laundries. Then I had to sort out and pin the clothes together with numbered pins so that, once washed, they could be reassembled again. I never dreamed human beings sent *such* dirty clothes to a laundry. But I knew that, as a rule, only very poor people use wet wash laundries. And very poor people cannot afford to be changing clothes every day. Nor every week, either, I guess, from the look of those I handled.

Cultured Washington, I mean cultured colored Washington, who read my poems in the *Crisis,* did not find it fitting and proper that a poet should work in a wet wash laundry. Still, they did nothing much about it. And since none of them had any better jobs to offer me, I stayed there. The laundry at least paid twelve dollars a week.

I spoke with Dean Kelly Miller at Howard University about the possibility of trying for a scholarship at the college. And he spoke grandiloquently about my grand-uncle, who had been the first Dean of the Howard Law School, and what a fine man he was. But it seems that there were no scholarships forthcoming. I spoke with Dr. Alain Locke, who said my poems were about to appear in the New Negro Issue of the *Survey Graphic,* and who declared I was the most racial of the New Negro poets. But he didn't have any scholarship up his sleeve, either.

So I began to try to save a dollar a week toward entering college. But if you ever started out with nothing, maybe you know how hard it is to work up even to an overcoat.

I wanted to return to college mostly in order to get a better background for writing and for understanding the world. I wanted to study sociology and history and psychology, and find out why countries and people were the kind of countries and people they are. Somebody lent me *This Believing World,* which I put on the sorting table at the laundry and read between bundles of wet wash. Comparative religions interested me, but I didn't believe the end of *This Believing World* was necessarily true.

One day my mother came to the laundry, crying. She said she couldn't stay at our cousin's house a minute longer, not one minute! It seems that in some way they had hurt both her pride and her feelings. So I took my lunch hour off to help her find a new place to stay. We located two small rooms on the second floor in an old brick house not far from where I worked. The rooms were furnished, but they had no heat in them, so we bought a second-hand oil stove, which we had to take turns using, carrying it back and forth between my room and my mother's room, since we couldn't afford two oil stoves that winter.

My little brother, Kit, was in school then and could kick out a pair of shoes as fast as any boy his age in America. My mother worked in service, but wages were very low in Washington. So, together, we made barely enough to get along. Hard as I tried, I could not save a dollar a week to go to college. I could not even save enough to buy a heavy coat.

Folks! Start out with nothing sometime and see how long it takes to work up to something.

I felt very bad in Washington that winter, so I wrote a great many poems. (I wrote only a few poems in Paris, because I had had such a good time there.) But in Washington I didn't have a good time. I didn't like my job, and I didn't know what was going to happen to me, and I was cold and half-hungry, so I wrote a great many poems. I began to write poems in the manner of the Negro blues and the spirituals.

Seventh Street in Washington was the nearest thing I had known to the South up to that time, never having been in Dixie proper. But Washington is like the South. It has all the prejudices and Jim Crow customs of any Southern town, except that there are no Jim Crow sections on the street cars.

Negro life in Washington is definitely a ghetto life and only in the Negro sections of the city may colored people attend theaters, eat a meal, or drink a Coca-Cola. Strangely undemocratic doings take place in the shadow of "the world's greatest democracy."

In Europe and in Mexico I have lived with white people, worked and eaten and slept with white people, and no one seemed any the worse for it. In New York I have sat beside white people in theaters and movie houses and neither they nor I appeared to suffer. But in Washington I could not see a legitimate stage show, because the theaters would not sell Negroes a ticket. I could not get a cup of coffee on a cold day anywhere within sight of the Capitol, because no "white" restaurant would serve a Negro. I could not see the new motion pictures, because they did not play in the Negro houses.

I asked some of the leading Washington Negroes about this, and they loftily said that they had their own society and their own culture—so I looked around to see what that was like.

To me it did not seem good, for the "better class" Washington colored people, as they called themselves, drew rigid class and color lines within the race against Negroes who worked with their hands, or who were dark in complexion and had no degrees from colleges. These upper class colored people consisted largely of government workers, professors and teachers, doctors, lawyers, and resident politicians. They were on the whole as unbearable and snobbish a group of people as I have ever come in contact with anywhere. They lived in comfortable homes, had fine cars, played bridge, drank Scotch, gave exclusive "formal" parties, and dressed well, but seemed to me altogether lacking in real culture, kindness, or good common sense.

Lots of them held degrees from colleges like Harvard and Dartmouth and Columbia and Radcliffe and Smith, but God knows what they had learned there. They had all the manners and airs of reactionary, ill-bred *nouveaux riches*—except that they were not really rich. Just middle class. And many of them had less fortunate brothers or cousins working as red-caps and porters—so near was their society standing to that of the poorest Negro. (Their snobbishness was so precarious, that I suppose for that very reason it had to be doubly reinforced.)

To seem people of culture, they performed in an amazing fashion. Perhaps, because I was very young and easily hurt, I remember so well some of the things that happened to me. When Dr. Locke's fine collection of articles, stories, pictures, and poems by and about Negroes was published, *The New Negro*, Washington's leading colored literary club, decided to honor the "New Negro" writers by inviting them to their annual dinner, a very "formal" event in the city. To represent the younger poets, they invited Countee Cullen and me. Mr. Cullen wrote from New York that he accepted the invitation.

I dropped them a note saying that I could not come, because, among other reasons, I had no dinner clothes to wear to a formal dinner. They assured me that in such a case I could attend their dinner without dinner clothes—just so I would read some of my poems. They also stated that their invitation included my mother, who, they knew, would be proud to see me honored.

I did not want to go to the dinner, but finally I agreed. On the evening of the dinner, however, I came home from work to find my mother in tears. She had left her job early to get ready to go with me. But about five o'clock, one of the ladies of the committee had telephoned her to say that, after all, she didn't feel it wise for her to come—since it was to be a formal dinner, and perhaps my mother did not possess an evening gown.

We didn't go.

Again, some months later, at the home of a prominent hostess, at a supper for Roland Hayes after his first big Washington concert, I was placed near the end of the table.

The lady next to me kept her back turned all the time, talking up the table in the direction of Mr. Hayes. A few days later, however, (amusingly enough) I got a note from this lady, saying she was extremely sorry she hadn't known she was sitting next to Langston Hughes, the poet, because we could have talked together!

One of the things that amused me in Washington, though, was that with all their conventional-mindedness, a number of the families in the best colored society made proud boast of being directly descended from the leading Southern white families, "on the colored side"—which, of course, meant the *illegitimate* side. One prominent Negro family tree went straight back to George Washington and his various slave mistresses.

From all this pretentiousness Seventh Street was a sweet relief. Seventh Street is the long, old, dirty street, where the ordinary Negroes hang out, folks with practically no family tree at all, folks who draw no color line between mulattoes and deep dark-browns, folks who work hard for a living with their hands. On Seventh Street in 1924 they played the blues, ate watermelon, barbecue, and fish sandwiches, shot pool, told tall tales, looked at the dome of the Capitol and laughed out loud. I listened to their blues:

> *Did you ever dream lucky—*
> *Wake up cold in hand?*

And I went to their churches and heard the tambourines play and the little tinkling bells of the triangles adorn the gay shouting tunes that sent sisters dancing down the aisles for joy.

I tried to write poems like the songs they sang on Seventh Street—gay songs, because you had to be gay or die; sad songs, because you couldn't help being sad sometimes. But gay or sad, you kept on living and you kept on going. Their songs—those of Seventh Street—had the pulse beat of the people who keep on going.

Like the waves of the sea coming one after another, always one

after another, like the earth moving around the sun, night, day—
night, day—night, day—forever, so is the undertow of black
music with its rhythm that never betrays you, its strength like the
beat of the human heart, its humor, and its rooted power.

> *I'm goin' down to de railroad, baby,*
> *Lay ma head on de track.*
> *I'm goin' down to de railroad, babe,*
> *Lay ma head on de track—*
> *But if I see de train a-comin'*
> *I'm gonna jerk it back.*

I liked the barrel houses of Seventh Street, the shouting
churches, and the songs. They were warm and kind and didn't
care whether you had an overcoat or not.

In one of the little churches one night I saw something that
reminded me of my own unfortunate "conversion." A revival
had been going full swing since early evening. It was now nearing
one o'clock. A sinner, overcome by his guilt, had passed out in
front of the mourners' bench and was lying prone on the floor.
All the other sinners by now had been brought to Jesus, but this
fellow looked distinctly as if he had fallen asleep.

It was a Sanctified Church, so the Saints came and gathered
around the prostrate soul in prayer. They prayed and prayed and
they sang and sang. But some of the less devout, as the hour
grew late, had to get up and go home, leaving the unsaved soul
for another day. Others prayed on. Still the man did not rise. He
was resting easy. Neither prayer nor song moved him until,
finally, one old lady bent down, shook him, and said sternly:
"Brother! You get up—'cause de Saints is gettin' tired!"

"A Poet Speaks from the Visitors' Gallery"

ARCHIBALD MACLEISH (1892–1982)

Archibald MacLeish was born in Glencoe, Illinois. He attended Yale University, where he wrote articles, poetry, and editorials for the school newspaper, and later graduated from Harvard Law School. He was offered a partnership in a Boston law firm on the same day that he had decided to quit law and return to his first love—poetry. From 1928 until 1938, he served as an editor of *Fortune* magazine, where he wrote on the past and future of America. In 1938 he became the curator of the Nieman Foundation of Journalism at Harvard. In 1939, he moved to Washington, D.C., to become Librarian of Congress, a position he held until 1944. During this appointment, MacLeish also served as director of the U.S. Office of Facts and Figures (1941–42), assistant director of the U.S. Office of War Information (1942–43), and assistant secretary of state (1944–45). MacLeish was perhaps the most active among the group of American intellectuals who argued for the release of Ezra Pound from Washington's St. Elizabeth's Hospital after World War II. He left D.C. to teach at Amherst College and Harvard. MacLeish published over forty books of poetry, essays, and plays and received his first Pulitzer Prize for *Conquistador* in 1933, his second in 1953 for his *Collected Poems: 1917–1952,* and his third in 1959 for his play *J.B.: A Play in Verse.* The following poem dates from 1943.

Have Gentlemen perhaps forgotten this?—
We write the histories.

Do gentlemen who snigger at the poets,
Who speak the word *professor* with guffaws—

Do Gentlemen expect their fame to flourish
When we, not they, distribute the applause?

Or do they trust their hope of long remembrance
To those they name with such respectful care—
To those who write the title in the papers,
To those who tell the tattle on the air?

Do Gentlemen expect the generation
That counts the losers out when tolls the bell
To take some gossip-caster's estimation,
Some junior voice of fame with fish to sell?

Do Gentlemen believe time's hard-boiled jury,
Judging the sober truth, will trust again
The words some copperhead who owned a paper
Ordered one Friday from the hired man?

Have Gentlemen forgotten Mr. Lincoln?

A poet wrote that story, not a newspaper,
Not the New Yorker of the nameless name
Who spat with hatred like some others later
And left, as they will, in his hate his shame.

History's not written in the kind of ink
The richest man of most ambitious mind
Who hates a president enough to print
A daily paper can afford or find.

Gentlemen have power now and know it,
But even the greatest and most famous kings
Feared and with reason to offend the poets
Whose songs are marble
                                    and whose marble sings.

"View of the Capitol from the Library of Congress"

ELIZABETH BISHOP (1911–1979)

Elizabeth Bishop was born in Worcester, Massachusetts, but after the death of her father and the institutionalizing of her mother, she was raised primarily by her grandparents in Canada. She founded a literary magazine at Vassar College called *Con Spirito* with Eleanor Clark, Mary McCarthy, and Muriel Rukeyser before graduating from the school in 1934. Bishop was a world traveler, venturing throughout Europe, Mexico, and South America and living in New York City; Washington, D.C.; Key West; and Brazil. Her work won her virtually every major poetry award, including the Pulitzer Prize for *Poems: North and South–A Cold Spring* (1955) and the National Book Award for *Questions of Travel* (1965). The first American and the first woman to win the Books Abroad/ Neustadt Prize for Literature, Bishop was also the recipient of two Guggenheim fellowships and numerous honorary degrees. She served as poetry consultant to the Library of Congress in 1949–50. She taught at the University of Washington, Harvard University, New York University, and the Massachusetts Institute of Technology. The following poem, from 1951, "View of the Capitol from the Library of Congress," was collected in her *Complete Poems* (1969).

Moving from left to left, the light
is heavy on the Dome, and coarse.
One small lunette turns it aside
and blankly stares off to the side
like a big white old wall-eyed horse.

On the east steps the Air Force Band
in uniforms of Air Force blue

is playing hard and loud, but—queer—
the music doesn't quite come through.

It comes in snatches, dim then keen,
then mute, and yet there is no breeze.
The giant trees stand in between.
I think the trees must intervene,

catching the music in their leaves
like gold-dust, till each big leaf sags.
Unceasingly the little flags
feed their limp stripes into air,
and the band's effort vanish there.

Great shades, edge over,
give the music room.
The gathered brasses want to go
boom—boom.

from *Advise and Consent*

ALLEN DRURY (1918–)

Houston-born Allen Drury spent twenty years covering Washington, D.C., as a newspaper correspondent for United Press International, *Pathfinder* magazine, the *Washington Evening Star,* and the *New York Times*. Following his experiences in Washington, mostly covering the U.S. Senate, Drury wrote his first novel, *Advise and Consent* (1959), about political and sexual scandal. The book received the Pulitzer Prize for fiction in 1960 and was later a Book-of-the-Month Club selection and a feature film. Among Drury's other novels are *Public Men* (1998), *Decision* (1983), *Anna Hastings: The Story of a Washington Newspaperperson* (1977), and *Preserve and Protect* (1968).

Like a city in dreams, the great white capital stretches along the placid river from Georgetown on the west to Anacostia on the east. It is a city of temporaries, a city of just-arriveds and only-visitings, built on the shifting sands of politics, filled with people passing through. They may stay fifty years, they may love, marry, settle down, build homes, raise families, and die beside the Potomac, but they usually feel, and frequently they will tell you, that they are just here for a little while. Someday soon they will be going home. They do go home, but it is only for visits, or for a brief span of staying-away; and once the visits or the brief spans are over ("It's so nice to get away from Washington, it's so inbred; so nice to get out in the country and find out what people are really thinking") they hurry back to their lodestone and their star, their self-hypnotized, self-mesmerized, self-enamored, self-propelling, wonderful city they cannot live away from or, once it has claimed them, live without. Washington takes them like a lover and they are lost. Some are big names, some are little, but once they succumb it makes no difference; they always return, spoiled for the Main Streets without which Washington could not live, knowing instinctively that this is the biggest Main Street of them all, the granddaddy and grandchild of Main Streets rolled into one. They come, they stay, they make their mark, writing big or little on their times, in the strange, fantastic, fascinating city that mirrors so faithfully their strange, fantastic, fascinating land in which there are few absolute wrongs or absolute rights, few all-blacks or all-whites, few dead-certain positives that won't be changed tomorrow; their wonderful, mixed-up, blundering, stumbling, hopeful land in which evil men do good things and good men do evil in a way of life and government so complex and delicately balanced that only Americans can understand it and often they are baffled.

In this bloodshot hour, when Bob Munson is assessing anew the endless problems of being Majority Leader and Washington around him is preparing with varying degrees of unenthusiasm to go to work, various things are happening to various people, all of whom sooner or later will be swept up, in ways they may not now suspect, in the political vortex created by the nomination of Robert A. Leffingwell.

At the Sheraton-Park Hotel the Senator himself completes his dressing and starts downstairs to breakfast, stopping on his way at the apartment of Victor Ennis of California to see whether he wants to share a cab later to the Hill. Vic and Hazel Ennis invite him in for coffee, which soon expands to breakfast, and before long Bob Munson has discovered that both Vic and his junior colleague, Raymond Robert Smith, a child of television out of M-G-M who progressed easily from Glamour Boy No. 3 to TV Commentator No. 1 and from there to the House and then to the Senate, will vote for Bob Leffingwell. They have already talked it over, Senator Ennis explains—-Ray called from the Coast as soon as he got in last night from the Academy Awards dinner, "and of course you know Hollywood will be behind him, and Ray thinks he'd better be, and so do I. This is entirely aside from the merits of the nominee, but Bob Munson, who knows his two Californians thoroughly, is quite content to accept their votes without quibbling over motives, the first and most valuable les-

son he learned in Washington and one he never forgets. Senator
Ennis volunteers the information that he called Arly Richardson,
just for the hell of it, and the Majority Leader asks quizzically:
"And what did that sardonic son of Arkansas have to say?"

"He said, 'I guess this will make Bobby sweat a little,'" Senator
Ennis reports, and Senator Munson laughs.

"I think I'll put him down as doubtful, but probably leaning
to Leffingwell," he says, and Victor Ennis nods.

"If you can ever expect Arly to stand hitched," he says, "that's
where I'd hitch him."

And as Hazel comes in briskly with the firm intention of
diverting the conversation from politics for at least ten minutes,
they turn to her excellent meal and start talking baseball.

While the Ennises and the Majority Leader are thus occupied
they do not know—although they would hardly be surprised if
they did—that at this very moment, out Sixteenth Street in an
apartment high in the Woodner, the Honorable Lafe W. Smith,
junior Senator from the state of Iowa, is engaged in a most intimate form of activity with a young lady. This is the fourth time
in eight hours that this has occurred, and Lafe Smith is getting a
little tired of it. The young lady, however, a minor clerk on a
House committee and new to the attractions of living in her
Nation's Capital, is still filled with a carefree enthusiasm, and so
the Senator, somewhat against his better judgment, is doing his
best to oblige. After the standard processes have produced the
standard result, the young lady will shower, dress, and amid
many tremulous farewells and mutual pledges will peek nervously out the door and then hurry away down the corridor,
hoping she has not been seen. The Senator, who thinks he knows
something the young lady does not know, which is that he will
never see her again, will also shower, shave, examine himself
critically in the mirror, be amazed as always at how his unlined
and engagingly boyish visage manages to stand the gaff, and
then will depart by cab for the Hill, where he is scheduled to
meet two elderly constituents from Council Bluffs for breakfast.
These kindly folk will be suitably impressed by his air of All-

American Boy, and they will go away bemused and bedazzled by their meeting, never dreaming that their All-American Boy, like many another All-American Boy is one hell of a man with the old razzmatazz. As this tender scene, so typical of life in the world's greatest democracy, is unfolding at the Woodner, Walter F. Calloway, the junior Senator from Utah, is also standing before the mirror in the bathroom of his house near Chevy Chase Circle just inside the District-Maryland Line, muttering and whistling through his teeth in his reedy voice just as he does on the floor of the Senate. "It iss my opinion," he is saying (downstairs Emma Calloway, preparing the usual eggs and bacon, hears the faint droning buzz and wonders tiredly what Walter is practicing this time), "that the confirmation of Mr. Leffingwell to thiss vitally important posst would seriously endanger the welfare of the United Statess in this most critical time. . ." None of Walter's colleagues would be surprised to hear this, and later in the day, when he issues the statement to the press and takes the time of the Senate to read it into the Congressional Record, they will shrug and look at one another as much as to say, "What did you expect?" They will be convinced then, prematurely as it turns out, that it is not among the Walter Calloways of the Senate that the fate of Robert A. Leffingwell will be decided, and they will promptly dismiss the opinion of the junior Senator from Utah, who is likable as a person, mediocre as a legislator, and generally ineffective as a United States Senator.

Also practicing, although unlike Walter Calloway not on his own superb voice, is Powell Hanson, the junior Senator from North Dakota. Powell is sitting in his study in Georgetown surrounded by Powell, Jr., twelve; Ruth, seven; and Stanley, four; and he is practicing the violin, an instrument he played in high school and hadn't touched since until about six months ago when Powell, Jr., began to play. Now by popular demand of the younger generation, he has resumed it; and since he never manages to get home from the Senate Office Building much before seven or eight, and then only for a brief meal before either going

out again socially or locking himself up with legislation, it is
only in the half hour before breakfast that he can manage to
really see the children. The violin was Powell, Jr.'s own idea,
which the Senator feels should be encouraged; under the impetus
of their joint scratching Ruth now thinks she may want to start
piano, and Stanley bangs a mean drum, purchased for his recent
birthday. Elizabeth Hanson, who gave up a promising future as
a research chemist to marry the young lawyer in whom she saw
the same possibilities he saw in himself, is quite content with the
uproar created by the maestro and his crew, even though it
makes breakfast a rather catch-as-catch-can meal. The price
exacted by public office sometimes seems more to the Hansons
than they are willing to pay; but since they know perfectly well
that they will go right on paying it just as long as Powell can get
re-elected, they are doing what they can to protect their children
and their home. As long as the half hour is set aside as a special
time, they feel, as long as it comes regularly every day, it forms a
small but unbreachable wall around the family; not much, but
enough to do the trick. Also living in Georgetown in houses of
varying quaintness and antiquity whose price increases in direct
proportion to their degree of charming inconvenience are some
twenty-one Senators whom Bob Munson refers to for easy reference in his own mind as the "Georgetown Group." The quietest
of these domiciles on this morning of Robert A. Leffingwell's
nomination is probably that of the senior Senator from Kansas,
Elizabeth Ames Adams, eating breakfast alone overlooking her
tiny back garden; the noisiest is probably that of the junior
Senator from Wisconsin, Kenneth Hackett, with his hurly-burly
seven. Somewhere in between, in terms of decibels and general
activity, come such homes as the gracious residence of John Able
Winthrop of Massachusetts, the aunt-run ménage of Rowlett
Clark of Alabama, and the parakeet and fish-filled home of
ancient John J. McCafferty of Arkansas and his sole surviving
sister, Jane.

Far from the Georgetown Group along their delightfully tree-
shaded and quaintly impassable streets, certain other colleagues

are also greeting the new day in their separate fashions. Twenty-two Senators are out of town, taking advantage of the lull which has come about during the debate on the pending bill to revise some of the more obscure regulations of the Federal Reserve Board. Some people, like Murfee Andrews of Kentucky, Rhett Jackson of North Carolina, Taylor Ryan of New York, and Julius Welch of Washington, can throw themselves into this sort of abstruse economic discussion with all the passion of Lafe Smith on the trail of a new conquest but most of the Senate is quite willing to leave such topics to the experts, voting finally on the basis of the advice of whichever of the experts happens to be considered most reliable.

Consequently the experts, aware of their responsibility, are leaving no cliché unturned. All but Taylor Ryan, in fact, are already up and going busily over the economic theories they will hurl triumphantly at one another in a near-empty Senate chamber this afternoon. The small, chunky body of Murfee Andrews is already in imagination swiveling around scornfully as some scathing point sinks home in the unperturbed hide of Rhett Jackson, who in turn is contemplating the delicate sarcasms with which he will show up the ignorance of Murfee Andrews. Julius Welch, who has never gotten over having been a college president, is readying another of his typical fifty-five-minute lectures with the five little jokes and their necessary pauses to permit the conscientious titters to flutter over the classroom. Taylor Ryan, a man who likes his comfort, is still abed, but his mind is busy, and no one need think it isn't. He has no doubts whatever that he will be able to bull his way right through the flypaper arguments of Jay Welch and Murfee Andrews with the sort of "God damn it, let's be sensible about this" approach befitting a man who made his millions on the Stock Exchange and so knows exactly what he's talking about in a way these damned college professors never could.

Among the absentees, there are as many interests on this morning of the Leffingwell nomination as there are geographic locations in the great West, Royce Blair of Oregon, that ineffable combination of arrogance, pomposity, intelligence and good humor, is up very early preparing an address to the Portland Kiwanis Club luncheon on the topic, "The Crisis of Our Times." He has selected this title, with his small, private smile-to-himself, as being a sufficient tent to cover all the camels he wants to crowd under it; and the news of the nomination of Robert A. Leffingwell, provoking from him, as it did from the Majority Leader, a startled, "Oh, God damn!" provides the biggest camel of them all. Royce Blair does not like this nomination and Royce Blair, polishing sledgehammer phrase after sledgehammer phrase, is going to say so in terms that will take wings from the Portland Kiwanis Club and echo across the nation by nightfall. Already he has tried, in vain, to reach Tom August and tell him what to do, but the chairman of the Foreign Relations Committee, as usual in moments of crisis, is nowhere to be found.

Actually, by one of those happy coincidences which have characterized his turtle-like progress through three terms as Senator from Minnesota, Tom August at this moment just happens to be completely out of touch with almost everyone at a plantation in South Carolina. This is just as well from his point of view, because he knows that a lot of people are just as anxious as Royce Blair to tell him what to do and in his vague and gentle, otherworldly way, Tom August doesn't like to be told. So he is quite happy to be out of touch, and if his host should ask him to stay another day or two—-there won't be a vote on the Federal Reserve bill until next week, so there's no rush-—Tom August would be quite delighted to remain. The time for departure is nearing, however, and the Senator is beginning to perceive that the invitation will not be extended, and so with his usual philosophical and faintly resentful air of being buffeted unjustly by an unkind fate, he is getting ready to go back and face the music. His calm is not enhanced by the fact that for some strange reason known only to their host, his fellow house-guest and fellow voyager on the flight back to Washington is Harley M. Hudson, the Vice President of the United States. "What this country needs," Arly Richardson once remarked, "is a good five-cent

Vice President," and Harley has never gotten over it. He has been fretting about the Leffingwell nomination ever since the news came over the radio, dropping all pretense that he had been informed of it in advance and professing freely a worry as deep as it is voluble. Harley always means well, but Tom August can't stand him when he gets in a fussing mood, and the prospect of six hundred miles of this is almost more than the soft-voiced and wistfully willful senior Senator from Minnesota thinks he can stand.

In Albuquerque at this moment the first Senator to give a comment to the press has been waylaid by reporters on his way to the plane for Washington. Hugh B. Root of New Mexico, chewing his cellophane-wrapped cigar and giving the whistling, wheezing, mushlike wail that passes for his particular version of the English language, is blurting some thing that the wire-service reporters hear as, "—mushn't shpend our time on sucsh shtupid—sucsh shtupid—mushn't—I'm opposhed—opposhed—we shimply mushn't—" which they agree among them must mean, "The Senate must not spend its time and energies on such stupid nominations. I am unalterably opposed to the nomination of Robert A. Leffingwell to be Secretary of State." When they read this back to Hugh Root for confirmation he gestures with his dripping cigar, looks at them with sudden sharpness like an old badger unearthed in the sunlight, nods, waves, and clambers aboard, shaking his head indignantly. Then he takes the wings of the morning and is gone into the cold bright wind of the desert dawn. In something of the same vein, though more quietly and cogently, the senior Senator from New Jersey, James H. La Rue, bravely fighting the palsy which always afflicts him, says in his quavering voice in St. Louis that "the Senate must and will reject the nomination of Mr. Leffingwell. Mr. Leffingwell's views on world affairs do not agree with those of many patriotic and intelligent Americans. It would not be safe to have him in the office of Secretary of State." It is not an opinion Bob Munson will like to hear about, but Jim La Rue, a good weather vane, has indicated the ground on which the nomination battle will really be fought. It is ground to which Seab Cooley will presently repair along with the rest, and it will make of the matter something much more serious than a thirteen-year grudge. It is ground which is already concerning not only the capital of the United States and its Senate but London, Paris, Moscow, and the whole wide world, which is now beginning to get the news. The fight to confirm Bob Leffingwell is not going to be a simple thing, as Jim La Rue, with customary prescience, foresees.

"The Woman at
the Washington Zoo"

RANDALL JARRELL (1914–1965)

Randall Jarrell was born in Nashville, Tennessee, on May 6, and shared a birthday with Sigmund Freud, a coincidence that delighted the poet, who was intensely interested in psychoanalysis. During his undergraduate years at Vanderbilt University, he studied with John Crowe Ransom and was acquainted with Donald Davidson, Allen Tate, Peter Taylor, and Robert Penn Warren. His first book of poems, *Blood for a Stranger*, was issued in 1942. Upon his release from the Army Air Force in 1946, Jarrell took an instructor's position at Sarah Lawrence College, an experience he later satirized in his only novel, *Pictures at an Institution* (1954), and was named poetry editor of the *Nation*. In 1947, he began teaching at the University of North Carolina at Greensboro, a position he retained until his death in a car accident in Chapel Hill, North Carolina, in 1965. Jarrell's poetry includes *Little Friend, Little Friend* (1945) and *Selected Poems* (1955). His criticism includes *Poetry and the Age* (1953) and *A Sad Heart at the Supermarket* (1962). Jarrell served as consultant in poetry at the Library of Congress from 1956 to 1958. *The Woman at the Washington Zoo*, the title poem from which follows, won Jarrell the National Book Award in poetry in 1960.

The saris go by me from the embassies.

Cloth from the moon. Cloth from another planet.
They look back at the leopard like the leopard.

And I. . . .
                    this print of mine, that has kept its color
Alive through so many cleanings; this dull null

Navy I wear to work, and wear from work, and so
To my bed, so to my grave, with no
Complaints, no comment: neither from my chief,
The Deputy Chief Assistant, nor his chief—
Only I complain. . . . this serviceable
Body that no sunlight dyes, no hand suffuses
But, dome-shadowed, withering among columns,
Wavy beneath fountains—small, far-off, shining
In the eyes of animals, these beings trapped
As I am trapped but not, themselves, the trap,
Again, but without knowledge of their age,
Kept safe here, knowing not of death, for death—
Oh, bars of my own body, open, open!

The world goes by my cage and never sees me.
And there come not to me, as come to these,
The wild beasts, sparrows pecking the llamas' grain,
Pigeons settling on the bears' bread, buzzards
Tearing the meat the flies have clouded. . . .
                                    Vulture,
When you come from the white rate that the foxes left,
Take off the red helmet of your head, the black
Wings that have shadowed me, and step to me as man:
The wild brother at whose feet the white wolves fawn,
To whose hand of power the great lioness
Stalks, purring. . . .
                        You know what I was,
You see what I am: change me, change me!

"The Congressman Who Loved Flaubert"

WARD JUST (1935–   )

> Born in Michigan City, Indiana, the son and grandson of news-
> paper publishers, Ward Just has been a political reporter and
> war correspondent in the United States and abroad for *Reporter*
> and *Newsweek* magazines and the *Washington Post,* among
> other publications. Just's stories frequently appear in the *Atlantic
> Monthly, Antaeus, Virginia Quarterly Review,* and *Gentleman's
> Quarterly.* His nonfiction, short stories, and novels include
> *The American Ambassador* (1987), *Echo House* (1997), and *A
> Dangerous Friend* (1999). Just and his wife live in Paris and
> Vineyard Haven, Massachusetts. He received the *Washington
> Monthly* political book award in 1973 for *The Congressman
> Who Loved Flaubert and Other Washington Stories.* In the title
> story, which first appeared in the *Atlantic Monthly,* Representative
> LaRuth has been approached by Dr. Wein to sign a congres-
> sional resolution to oppose the Vietnam War. LaRuth himself is
> trying to pass an omnibus educational bill, the biggest of his
> twelve years in the U.S. House.

LaRuth was forty; he had been in the House since the age of
twenty-eight. Some of his colleagues had been there before he
was born, moving now around the halls and the committee
rooms as if they were extensions of antebellum county court-
houses. They smelled of tobacco and whiskey and old wool,
their faces dry as parchment. LaRuth was amused to watch them
on the floor; they behaved as they would at a board meeting of
a family business, attentive if they felt like it, disruptive if their
mood was playful. They were forgiven; it was a question of age.
The House was filled with old men, and its atmosphere was one
of very great age. Deference was a way of life. LaRuth recalled a
friend who aspired to a position of leadership. They put him

through his paces, and for some reason he did not measure up; the friend was told he'd have to wait, it was not yet time. He'd been there eighteen years and was only fifty-two. Fifty-two! Jack Kennedy was President at forty-three, and Thomas Jefferson had written the preamble when under thirty-five. But then, as one of the senior men put it, this particular fifty-two-year-old man had none of the durable qualities of Kennedy or Jefferson. That is, he did not have Kennedy's money or Jefferson's brains. Not that money counted for very much in the House of Representatives; plutocrats belonged in the other body.

It was not a place for lost causes. There were too many conflicting interests, too much confusion, too many turns to the labyrinth. Too many *people*: four hundred and thirty-five representatives and about a quarter of them quite bright. Quite bright enough and knowledgeable enough to strangle embarrassing proposals and take revenge as well. Everyone was threatened if the eccentrics got out of hand. The political coloration of the eccentric didn't matter. This was one reason why it was so difficult to build an ideological record in the House. A man with ideology was wise to leave it before reaching a position of influence, because by then he'd mastered the art of compromise, which had nothing to do with dogma or public acts of conscience, it had to do with simple effectiveness, the tact and strength with which a man dealt with legislation, inside committees, behind closed doors. That was where the work got done, and the credit passed around.

LaRuth, at forty, was on a knife's edge. Another two years and he'd be a man of influence, and therefore ineligible for any politics outside the House—or not ineligible, but shopworn, no longer new, no longer fresh. He would be ill-suited, and there were other practical considerations as well, because who wanted to be a servant for twelve or fourteen years and then surrender an opportunity to be master? Not LaRuth. So the time for temporizing was nearly past. If he was going to forsake the House and reach for the Senate (a glamorous possibility), he had to do it soon.

LaRuth's closest friend in Congress was a man about his own age from a neighboring state. They'd come to the Hill in the same year, and for a time enjoyed publicity in the national press, where they could least afford it. *Two Young Liberals from the South*, that sort of thing. Winston was then a bachelor, too, and for the first few years they shared a house in Cleveland Park. But it was awkward, there were too many women in and out of the place, and one groggy morning Winston had come upon LaRuth and a friend taking a shower together and that had torn it. They flipped for the house and LaRuth won, and Winston moved to grander quarters in Georgetown. They saw each other frequently and laughed together about the curiosities of the American political system; Winston, a gentleman farmer from the plantation South, was a ranking member of the House Foreign Affairs Committee. The friendship was complicated because they were occasional rivals: Who would represent the New South? They took to kidding each other's press notices: LaRuth was the "attractive liberal," Winston the "wealthy liberal." Thus, LaRuth became Liberal Lou and Winston was Wealthy Warren. To the extent that either of them had a national reputation, they were in the same category: they voted their consciences, but were not incautious.

It was natural for Wein and his committee of scientists to go directly to Winston after leaving LaRuth. The inevitable telephone call came the next day, Winston inviting LaRuth by for a drink around six; "small problem to discuss." Since leaving Cleveland Park, Warren Winston's life had become plump and graceful. Politically secure now, he had sold his big house back home and bought a small jewel of a place on Dumbarton Avenue, three bedrooms and a patio in back, a mirrored bar, and a sauna in the basement. Winston was drinking a gin and tonic by the pool when LaRuth walked in. The place was more elegant than he'd remembered; the patio was now decorated with tiny boxbushes, and a magnolia tree was in full cry.

They joked a bit, laughing over the new Southern manifesto floating around the floor of the House. They were trying to find a way to spike it without seeming to spike it. Winston mentioned the "small problem" after about thirty minutes of small talk.

"Lou, do you know a guy named Wein?"

"He's a friend of Annette's."

"He was in to see you, then."

"Yeah."

"And?"

"We didn't see eye to eye."

"You're being tight-lipped, Liberal Lou."

"I told him to piss off," LaRuth said. "He called me a war criminal, and then he called me a cynic. A pessimist, a cynic, and a war criminal. All this for some cream-puff resolution that will keep them damp in Cambridge and won't change a goddamned thing."

"You think it's *that* bad."

"Worse, maybe."

"I'm not sure. Not sure at all."

"Warren, *Christ.*"

"Look, doesn't it make any sense at all to get the position of the House on the record? That can't fail to have some effect downtown, and it can't fail to have an effect in the country. It probably doesn't stand a chance of being passed, but the effort will cause some commotion. The coon'll be treed. Some attention paid. It's a good thing to get on the record, and I can see some points being made."

"What points? Where?"

"The newspapers, the box. Other places. It'd show that at least some of us are not content with things as they are. That we want to change . . ."

LaRuth listened carefully. It was obvious to him that Winston was trying out a speech, like a new suit of clothes; he took it out and tried it on, asking his friend about the color, the fit, the cut of it.

". . . the idea that change can come from within the system . . ."

"Aaaaaah," LaRuth groaned.

"No?" Innocently.

"How about, *and so, my fellow Americans, ask not what you can do for Wein, but what Wein can do for you.* That thing is loose as a hound dog's tongue. Now tell me the true gen."

"Bettger's retiring."

"You don't say." LaRuth was surprised. Bettger was the senior senator from Winston's state, a living Southern legend.

"Cancer. No one knows about it. He'll announce retirement at the end of the month. It's my only chance for the next four years, maybe *ever*. There'll be half a dozen guys in the primary, but my chances are good. If I'm going to go for the Senate, it's got to be now. This thing of Wein's is a possible vehicle. I say possible. One way in. People want a national politician as a senator. It's not enough to've been a good congressman, or even a good governor. You need something more: when people see your face on the box they want to think *senatorial*, somehow. You don't agree?"

LaRuth was careful now. Winston was saying many of the things he himself had said. Of course he was right: a senator needed a national gloss. The old bulls didn't need it, but they were operating from a different tradition, pushing different buttons. But if you were a young man running statewide for the first time, you needed a different base. Out there in television land were all those followers without leaders. People were pulled by different strings now. The point was to identify which strings pulled strongest.

"I think Wein's crowd is a mistake. That resolution is a mistake. They'll kill you at home if you put your name to that thing."

"No, Lou. You do it a different way. With a little rewording, that resolution becomes a whole lot less scary; it becomes something straight out of Robert A. Taft. You e-*liminate* the fancy words and phrases. You steer *clear* of words like 'corrupt' and 'genocide' and 'violence.' You and I, Lou, we know: our people *like* violence, it's part of our way of life. So you don't talk about violence, you talk about American traditions, like 'the American tradition of independence and individuality. Noninterference!' Now you are saying a couple of *other* things when you're saying that, Lou. You dig? That's the way you get at imperialism. You don't call it imperialism, because that word's got a bad sound. A foreign sound."

LaRuth laughed. Winston had it figured out. He had to get Wein to agree to the changes, but that should present no problem. Wealthy Warren was a persuasive man.

"Point is, I've got to look to people down there like I can make a difference . . ."

I think you've just said the magic words."

"Like it?"

"I think so. Yeah, I think I do."

"*To make the difference. Winston for Senator.* A double line on the billboards, like this." Winston described two lines with his finger and mulled the slogan again. "*To make the difference. Winston for Senator.* See, it doesn't matter what kind of difference. All people know is that they're fed up to the teeth. *Fed up and mad at the way things are.* And they've got to believe that if they vote for you, in some unspecified way things will get better. Now I think the line about interference can do double duty. People are tired of being hassled, in all ways, Indochina, down home." Winston was a gifted mimic, and now he adopted a toothless expression and hooked his thumbs into imaginary galluses. "Ah think Ah'll vote for that-there Winston. Prob'ly won't do any harm. Mot do some good. Mot mek a diff'rence."

"Shit, Warren."

"You give me a little help?"

"Sure."

"Sign the Wein thing?"

LaRuth thought a moment. "No," he said.

"What the hell, Lou? Why not? If it's rearranged the way I said. Look, Wein will be out of it. It'll be strictly a congressional thing."

"It doesn't mean anything."

"Means a whole lot to me."

"Well, that's different. That's political."

"If you went in too, it'd look a safer bet."

"All there'd be out of that is more Gold Dust Twins copy. You don't want that."

"No, it'd be made clear that I'm managing it. I'm out front. I make all the statements, you're back in the woodwork. Far from harm's way, Lou." Winston took his glass and refilled it with gin and tonic. He carefully cut a lime and squeezed it into the glass. Winston looked the part, no doubt about that. Athlete's build, big, with sandy hair beginning to thin; he could pass for an astronaut.

"You've got to find some new names for the statement."

"Right on, brother. Too many Jews, too many foreigners. Why are there no scientists named Robert E. Lee or Thomas Jefferson? Talmadge, Bilbo." Winston sighed and answered his own question. "The decline of the WASP. Look, Lou. The statement will be forgotten in six weeks, and that's fine with me. I just need it for a little national coverage at the beginning. Hell, it's not decisive. But it could make a difference."

"You're going to *open* the campaign with the statement?"

"You bet. Considerably revised. It'd be a help, Lou, if you'd go along. It would give them a chance to crank out some updated New South pieces. The networks would be giving that a run just as I announce for the Senate and my campaign begins. See, it's a natural. Bettger is Old South, I'm New. But we're friends and neighbors, and that's a fact. It gives them a dozen pegs to hang it on, and those bastards love *you*, with the black suits and the beard and that cracker accent. It's a natural, and it would mean a hell of a lot, a couple of minutes on national right at the beginning. I wouldn't forget it. I'd owe you a favor."

LaRuth was always startled by Winston's extensive knowledge of the press. He spoke of "pieces" and "pegs," A.M. and P.M. cycles, facts "cranked out" or "folded in," who was up and who was down at CBS, who was analyzing Congress for the editorial board of the *Washington Post*. Warren Winston was always accessible, good for a quote, day or night; and he was visible in Georgetown.

"Can you think about it by the end of the week?"

"Sure," LaRuth said.

He returned to the Hill, knowing that he thought better in his office. When there was any serious thinking to be done, he did it there, and often stayed late, after midnight. He'd mix a drink at the small bar in his office and work. Sometimes Annette stayed with him, sometimes not. When LaRuth walked into his office she was still there, catching up, she said; but she knew he'd been with Winston.

"He's going to run for the Senate," LaRuth said.

"Warren?"

"That's what he says. He's going to front for Wein as well. That statement of Wein's—Warren's going to sign it. Wants me to sign it, too."

"Why you?"

"United front. It would help him out. No doubt about that. But it's a bad statement. Something tells me not to do it."

"Are you as mad as you look?"

He glanced at her and laughed. "Does it show?"

"To me it shows."

It was true; there was no way to avoid competition in politics. Politics was a matter of measurements, luck, and ambition, and he and Warren had run as an entry for so long that it disconcerted him to think of Senator Winston; Winston up one rung on the ladder. He was irritated that Winston had made the first move and made it effortlessly. It had nothing to do with his own career, but suddenly he felt a shadow on the future. Winston had seized the day all right, and the fact of it depressed him. His friend was clever and self-assured in his movements; he took risks; he relished the public part of politics. Winston was expert at delivering memorable speeches on the floor of the House; they were evidence of passion. For Winston, there was no confusion between the private and the public; it was all one. LaRuth thought that he had broadened and deepened in twelve years in the House, a man of realism, but not really a part of the apparatus. Now Winston had stolen the march, he was a decisive step ahead.

LaRuth may have made a mistake. He liked and understood the legislative process, transactions that were only briefly political. That is, they were not public. If a man kept himself straight at home, he could do what he liked in the House. So LaRuth had become a fixture in his district, announcing election plans every two years from the front porch of his family's small farmhouse, where he was born, where his mother lived still. The house was filled with political memorabilia; the parlor walls resembled huge bulletin boards, with framed photographs, testimonials, parchments, diplomas. His mother was so proud. His life seemed to vindicate her own, his successes hers; she'd told him so. His position in the U.S. Congress was precious, and not lightly discarded. The cold age of the place had given him a distrust of anything spectacular or . . . capricious. The House: no place for lost causes.

Annette was looking at him, hands on hips, smiling sardonically. He'd taken off his coat and was now in shirt sleeves. She told him lightly that he shouldn't feel bad, that if *he* ran for the Senate he'd have to shave off his beard. Buy new clothes. Become prolix, and professionally optimistic. But, as a purchase on the future, his signature . . .

"Might. Might not," he said.

"Why not?"

"I've never done that here."

"Are you refusing to sign because you don't want to, or because you're piqued at Warren? I mean, Senator Winston."

He looked at her. "A little of both."

"Well, that's foolish. You ought to sort out your motives."

"That can come later. That's my business."

"No. Warren's going to want to know why you're not down the line with him. You're pretty good friends. He's going to want to know *why*."

"It's taken me twelve years to build what credit I've got in this place. I'm trusted. The Speaker trusts me. The chairman trusts me."

"Little children see you on the street. Gloryosky! There goes trustworthy Lou LaRuth—"

"Attractive, liberal," he said, laughing. "Well, it's true. This resolution, if it ever gets that far, is a ball buster. It could distract the House for a month and revive the whole issue. Because it's been quiet we've been able to get on with our work, I mean the serious business. Not to get pompous about it."

"War's pretty important," she said.

"Well, is it now? You tell me how important it is." He put his drink on the desk blotter and loomed over her. "Better yet, you tell me how this resolution will solve the problem. God forbid there should be any solutions, though. Moral commitments. Statements. Resolutions. They're the great things, aren't they? Fuck solutions." Thoroughly angry now, he turned away and filled the glasses. He put some ice and whiskey in hers and a premixed martini in his own.

"What harm would it do?"

"Divert a lot of energy. Big play to the galleries for a week or two. Until everyone got tired. The statement itself? No harm at all. Good statement, well done. No harm, unless you consider perpetuating an illusion some kind of harm."

"A lot of people live by illusions, *and what's wrong with getting this House on record?*"

"But it won't be gotten on record. That's the point. The thing will be killed. It'll just make everybody nervous and divide the place more than it's divided already."

"I'd think about it," she said.

"Yeah, I will. I'll tell you something. I'll probably end up signing the goddamned thing. It'll do Warren some good. Then I'll do what I can to see that it's buried, although God knows we won't lack for gravediggers. And then go back to my own work on the school bill."

"I think that's better." She smiled. "One call, by the way. The chairman. He wants you to call first thing in the morning."

"What did he say it's about?"

"The school bill, dear."

Oh shit, LaRuth thought.

"There's a snag," she said.

"Did he say what it was?"

"I don't think he wants to vote for it anymore."

Winston was after him, trying to force a commitment, but LaRuth was preoccupied with the school bill, which was becoming unstuck. It was one of the unpredictable things that happen;

there was no explanation for it. But the atmosphere had subtly changed, and support was evaporating. The members wavered, the chairman was suddenly morose and uncertain; he thought it might be better to delay. LaRuth convinced him that was an unwise course and set about repairing damage. This was plumbing, pure and simple: talking with members, speaking to their fears. LaRuth called it negative advocacy, but it often worked. Between conferences a few days later, LaRuth found time to see a high school history class, students from his alma mater. They were touring Washington and wanted to talk to him about Congress. The teacher, sloe-eyed, stringy-haired, twenty-five, wanted to talk about the war; the students were indifferent. They crowded into his outer office, thirty of them; the secretaries stood aside, amused, as the teacher opened the conversation with a long preface on the role of the House, most of it inaccurate. Then she asked LaRuth about the war. What was the congressional role in the war?

"Not enough," LaRuth replied, and went on in some detail, addressing the students.

"Why not a congressional resolution demanding an end to this terrible, immoral war?" the teacher demanded. "Congressman, why can't the House of Representatives take matters into its own hands?"

"Because"—LaRuth was icy, at once angry, tired, and bored— "because a majority of the members of this House do not want to lose Asia to the Communists. Irrelevant, perhaps. You may think it is a bad argument. I think it is a bad argument. But it is the way the members feel."

"But why can't that be *tested*?? In votes."

The students came reluctantly awake and were listening with little flickers of interest. The teacher was obviously a favorite, their mod pedagogue. LaRuth was watching a girl in the back of the room. She resembled the girls he'd known at home, short-haired, light summer dress, full-bodied; it was a body that would soon go heavy. He abruptly steered the conversation to his school bill, winding into it, giving them a stump speech, some flavor of home. He felt the students with him for a minute or two, then they drifted away. In five minutes they were somewhere else altogether. He said good-bye to them then and shook their hands on the way out. The short-haired girl lingered a minute; she was the last one to go.

"It would be good if you could do something about the war," she said.

"Well, I've explained."

"My brother was killed there."

LaRuth closed his eyes for a second and stood without speaking.

"Any gesture at all," she said.

"Gestures." He shook his head sadly. "They never do any good."

"Well," she said. "Thank you for your time." LaRuth thought her very grown-up, a well-spoken girl. She stood in the doorway, very pretty. The others had moved off down the hall; he could hear the teacher's high whine.

"How old was he?"

"Nineteen," she said. "Would've been twenty next birthday."

"Where?"

"They said it was an airplane."

"I'm so sorry."

"You wrote us a letter, don't you remember?"

"I don't know your name," LaRuth said gently.

"Ecker," she said. "My brother's name was Howard."

"I remember," he said. "It was . . . some time ago."

"Late last year," she said, looking at him.

"Yes, that would be just about it. I'm very sorry."

"So am I," she said, smiling brightly. Then she walked off to join the rest of her class. LaRuth stood in the doorway a moment, feeling the eyes of his secretary on his back. It had happened before; the South seemed to bear the brunt of the war. He'd written more than two hundred letters, to the families of poor boys, black and white. The deaths were disproportionate, poor to rich, black to white, South to North. Oh well, he thought. Oh hell. He walked back into his office and called Winston and told him he'd go along. In a limited way. For a limited period.

Later in the day, Winston dropped by. He wanted LaRuth to be completely informed and up to date.

"It's rolling," Winston said.

"Have you talked to Wein?"

"I've talked to Wein."

"And what did Wein say?"

"Wein agrees to the revisions."

"Complaining?"

"The contrary. Wein sees himself as the spearhead of a great national movement. He sees scientists moving into political positions, cockpits of influence. His conscience is as clear as rainwater. He is very damp."

LaRuth laughed; it was a private joke.

"Wein is damp in Cambridge, then."

"I think that is a fair statement, Uncle Lou."

"How wonderful for him."

"He was pleased that you are with us. He said he misjudged you. He offers apologies. He fears he was a speck . . . harsh."

"Bully for Wein."

"I told everyone that you would be on board. I knew that when the chips were down you would not fail. I knew that you would examine your conscience and your heart and determine where the truth lay. I knew you would not be cynical or pessimistic. I know you want to see your old friend in the Senate."

They were laughing together. Winston was in one of his dry, mordant moods. He was very salty. He rattled off a dozen names and cited the sources of each member's conscience: money and influence. "But to be fair—always be fair, Liberal Lou—there are a dozen more who are doing it because they want to do it. They think it's *alright*."

"*Faute de mieux*."

"I am not schooled in the French language, Louis. You are always flinging French at me."

"It means 'in the absence of anything better.'"

Winston grinned, then shrugged. LaRuth was depressed, the shadow lengthened, became darker.

"I've set up a press conference, a half-dozen of us. All moderate men. Men of science, men of government. I'll be out front, doing all the talking. OK?"

"Sure." LaRuth was thinking about his school bill.

"It's going to be jim-dandy."

"Swell. But I want to see the statement beforehand, music man."

Winston smiled broadly and spread his hands wide. Your friendly neighborhood legislator, concealing nothing; merely your average, open, honest fellow trying to do the right thing, trying to do his level best. "But of course," Winston said.

Some politicians have it; most don't. Winston has it, a fabulous sense of timing. Everything in politics is timing. For a fortnight, the resolution dominates congressional reportage. "An idea whose time has come," coinciding with a coup in Latin America and a surge of fighting in Indochina. The leadership is agitated, but forced to adopt a conciliatory line; the doves are in war paint. Winston appears regularly on the television evening news. There are hearings before the Foreign Affairs Committee, and these produce pictures and newsprint. Winston, a sober legislator, intones *feet to the fire*. There are flattering articles in the news magazines, and editorial support from the major newspapers, including the most influential paper in Winston's state. He and LaRuth are to appear on the cover of *Life*, but the cover is scrapped at the last minute. Amazing to LaRuth, the mail from his district runs about even. An old woman, a woman his mother has known for years, writes to tell him that he should run for President. Incredible, really: the Junior Chamber of Commerce composes a certificate of appreciation, commending his enterprise and spirit, "an example of the indestructible moral fiber of America." When the networks and the newspapers cannot find Winston, they fasten on LaRuth. He becomes something of a celebrity, and wary as a man entering darkness from daylight.

He tailors his remarks in such a way as to force questions about his school bill. He finds his words have effect, although this is measurable in no definite way. His older colleagues are amused; they needle him gently about his new blue shirts.

He projects well on television, his appearance is striking; his great height, the black suits, the beard. So low-voiced, modest, diffident; no hysteria or hyperbole. (An intuitive reporter would grasp that he has contempt for "the Winston Resolution," but intuition is in short supply.) When an interviewer mentions his reticent manner, LaRuth smiles and says that he is not modest or diffident, he is pessimistic. But his mother is ecstatic. His secretary looks on him with new respect. Annette thinks he is one in a million.

No harm done. The resolution is redrafted into harmless form and is permitted to languish. The language incomprehensible, at the end it becomes an umbrella under which anyone could huddle. Wein is disillusioned, the media look elsewhere for their news, and LaRuth returns to the House Education and Labor Committee. The work is backed up; the school bill has lost its momentum. One month of work lost, and now LaRuth is forced to redouble his energies. He speaks often of challenge and commitment. At length the bill is cleared from committee and forwarded to the floor of the House, where it is passed; many members vote aye as a favor, either to LaRuth or to the chairman. The chairman is quite good about it, burying his reservations, grumbling a little, but going along. The bill has been, in the climatic phrase of the newspapers, watered down. The three years are now five. The billion is reduced to five hundred million. Amendments are written, and they are mostly restrictive. But the bill is better than nothing. The President signs it in formal ceremony, LaRuth at his elbow. The thing is now law.

The congressman, contemplating all of it, is both angry and sad. He has been a legislator too long to draw obvious morals, even if they were there to be drawn. He thinks that everything in his life is meant to end in irony and contradiction. LaRuth, at forty, has no secret answers. Nor any illusions. The House of

Representatives is no simple place, neither innocent nor straight-forward. Appearances there are like appearances elsewhere: deceptive. One is entitled to remain fastidious as to detail, realistic in approach.

Congratulations followed. In his hour of maximum triumph, the author of a law, LaRuth resolved to stay inside the belly of the whale; to become neither distracted nor moved. Of the world outside, he was weary and finally unconvinced. He knew who he was. He'd stick with what he had and take comfort from a favorite line, a passage toward the end of *Madame Bovary*. It was a description of a minor character, and the line had stuck with him, lodged in the back of his head. Seductive and attractive, in a pessimistic way. *He grew thin, his figure became taller, his face took on a saddened look that made it nearly interesting.*

from *The Last of the Southern Girls*

WILLIE MORRIS (1934–1999)

> Journalist, essayist, novelist, and editor William Weaks Morris
> was born in Jackson, Mississippi, and grew up in nearby Yazoo
> City where he began his career as a journalist writing for his
> high school newspaper. Upon his return to the United States
> after studying as a Rhodes scholar at Oxford University, he
> took an editorial position at the *Texas Observer*, a liberal
> weekly newspaper focusing on political and social issues. He
> took an associate editorial position at *Harper's* magazine and,
> four years later, at the age of thirty-three, became the publica-
> tion's youngest editor-in-chief. Morris's inclusion of contro-
> versial material in the magazine, specifically Norman Mailer's
> "Steps of the Pentagon," fostered an ideological confrontation
> with the magazine's owners, resulting in his resignation and
> the subsequent mass exodus of his loyal staff. This opportu-
> nity allowed Morris to focus on his own writing. He returned
> to Mississippi in 1980 to take a position as writer-in-residence
> at the University of Mississippi at Oxford, before resettling in
> Jackson ten years later. His writing in a variety of forms,
> including *North Toward Home* (1967), *Yazoo: Integration in a
> Deep-Southern Town* (1971), *My Dog Skip* (1995), and *My
> Cat Spit McGee* (1999), won him both popular and critical
> praise. Following is an excerpt from *The Last of the Southern
> Girls* (1973).

Her friends and enemies had been wondering what would
become of her. She had lived in Washington for twelve years.
They asked themselves if she intended to remain its *enfant terrible* for the rest of her days. Most of the women disliked her
and were jealous of her, for good reason. Most of the men lusted
for her but were somewhat obsequious before her, for better reason still. Washington in the age when American omnipotence
had had its day was exceedingly contradictory, yet those who
were mystified by it, or perhaps frightened by it, seldom recog-

nized that its vast bureaucratic mazes and the tangled actualities of its institutional power disguised the most ingenuous simplicity. It had all the illusions of a large city, compounded by the sources and appurtenances of national authority which gave it its character. Yet strip off these layers and there, for any outsider to see, lay the quintessential American small town. It was one of the few capitals of the world that was not the most interesting place in its country, like Bern, perhaps, The Hague, Canberra, *Brasília!* There were many causes of this, the Southern founders for a beginning, and the very act of compromise which brought it into being, but at the heart of it, certainly, was its especial political nature and the dire transience of our politics. It was a large city but not a truly communitied one, being as it was and always had been a kind of national waystation, a least common denominator of a disparate society; it was the capital of a great modern power but the practitioners of that power, as they knew best of all, were impermanent residents, susceptible to the arcane predilections of our people. So that in the best echelons of its society the truly permanent citizens—the politicians who managed to stay on year after year, the journalists and the columnists and the television personalities, the lawyers and businessmen with the most fruitful connections, the most entrenched and powerful of the civil servants, the foreign service officers, three or four dozen key foreigners, the retired diplomats and statesmen and respectable hangers-on—were not a very large group at all. Practically everyone in this community knew everyone else. The outsider also usually forgot that, numerically, Washington was essentially a black city, with narrowing white enclaves scattered throughout. With the inexorable movement to the tranquillity of the outlands, so expressive of what America had become in her day, the old aspiring federal city outside these enclaves of modern high-rises and the more settled places was a maw of bureaucracies and tenements. So in describing a fixed white society in our most chameleon of American metropolises, one must keep in mind a small threatened island.

Its political character and small town ambience gave an unusual quality to the nature of its talk, exacerbated in the

1960's by an ill-tempered restiveness owing to the saddest of our many wars. Its people seemed not to take language seriously. In this regard the political melted into the social in ways that were childish and destructive. *They seemed not to understand the consequences of words.* They babbled away to anyone about anything, principally about each other. Words should have real weight for intelligent members of the species, who must perceive by now that they can evoke and titillate and inspire and damage and delude as effectively as actions, yet language in this locale seemed somehow off at the edges of perception. The most rapt confessionals between friends, the most desultory persiflage between confidants, entered the public domain swiftly, circling and gyrating and eventually returning home. One is not speaking here so much of conventional gossip but of the whole illusory, circuitous, and benighted trajectory of human talk when talk has little root or foundation. Not that Washington was not princely ground for the more mundane gossip, for indeed it was—unlike Manhattan Island in those years, which was too colossal and fragmented for gossip to have much more blood and ooze in it than the quip. But when words and their consequences meant nothing, and when everyone talked to everyone about everyone else, and when the dimensions of the permanent community within the larger metropolis remained relatively contained and homogeneous, one tended finally to become confused, perhaps, about truth and fantasy, about sympathy and malice, about friendship and enmity. And what, pray, must all of this have done to the nature of privacy? How could the privacy of the soul acquit itself against that most underestimated of human sins? For that sin, after all, was *calumny*.

This was the milieu in which Carol Hollywell, née Templeton, a Southern debutante from the Mississippi River town of De Soto Point, Arkansas, had grown from girlhood into maturity. They talked of her incessantly and she, being a child of this most unusual city, talked also of them. In a town, so Southern in character, where females were then such appendages to ambitious husbands and where the more independent seethed under this

inferiority, where society was ordered for males and the urges of
their politics—a place of powerful men, and women they married when they were young, Mrs. Holmes said axiomatically, of
hostile wives whose men had vanished long before into the toils
and sweats and circumlocutions of their calling—she was both
unattached, being a divorcée for two years, and outspoken.
When she first met people, she talked with them as if she had
been familiar with them and their kin for a very long time. Her
eyes in such moments moved constantly, and so did her lips; her
whole being, indeed, hummed with motion. She could be charming, fine-humored, and inexhaustibly garrulous, but still she was
a girl of immediate caprices: swift to act, often perhaps a little
too swift, and swifter yet to anger. There was a large strain of
design and crudeness in her; chaos, commotion, and even emotional calamity often followed in the wake of her tempestuous
pride, and her life unfolded from one crisis to the next, at first
with a deft, histrionic aplomb, as if she could only survive on
catharsis. But all this coexisted with a loveliness and grace, for
an aura of romance and beauty surrounded her, there was a rare
electricity to her movements, she seemed touched with gold, and
people would stare at her in the streets or in the restaurants, not
just because of this radiance, but something more: the good
juices and spirits of life which encompassed her, her elegance
and proud defiance. These strangers when touched by this magnetism might sense that she was fully observant of herself, and
that she viewed herself with an unusual regard. At an election
party one year, for instance, where she followed the men into a
paneled library on Foxhall Road for brandy, leaving the women
to dwell on her audacity, three United States Senators stood in a
corner watching the election results on television. She was con-
versing quietly with the Secretary of Commerce, on whose right
she had sat at the expensively catered dinner and who had been
so entranced with her candid observations that his wife had
watched him quizzically from across the room, when the three
Senators burst into exuberant shouts. "What on earth is it?" she
asked one of them. "*Claiborne's been re-elected!*" he replied, for

Senators, as it is known to some, are all but maternal in their protectiveness of colleagues. "Claiborne!" she said. "He's the only liberal I know whose victory is a defeat for liberalism," causing all the men in the room, including His Honor the Secretary, to stare wordlessly at her before returning glumly to their cigars. Sitting one evening in the Presidential box at the ballet with her escort, an influential but somewhat prosaic adviser on domestic affairs, she noticed the thousand pairs of eyes on them from below, then quite precipitously she leaned across and kissed the man on his nose. It was well known that she had suddenly declared at a glum buffet in Kenwood that she hoped her black brethren would soon achieve home rule because the city needed not only soul but *pizang* (a word she had added to her repertoire, curiously enough, in her first year at the University of Mississippi) almost as bad as that particular buffet needed it. In a place where the best men, in the words of Carol Hollywell's ebullient Washington friend Jennie Grand, "fucked beneath themselves," she had had affairs with a United States Senator, a Yale man in the State Department, a Presidential adviser, and three mighty men of the media—and in the bright new spirit of the day had proven superior to them all. In a society where young women were expected to sit quietly at the table, she teemed with anecdotes and observations fully worthy of her heroine Alice Roosevelt Longworth. Hence she was much in demand among the younger political set, and though she considered herself a solid moderate-to-liberal Democrat, she crossed partisan lines with little difficulty and, in fact, considerable pleasure. There was a warrant officer who followed within a few yards of the President of the United States wherever he went, even sitting just outside his bedroom, or his bathroom when he had to go there, carrying a black briefcase with the day's special code for the nuclear deterrent. People talked about the time she suddenly embraced this man, kissing him on the cheek, and asking, "Is it a lucky number today?" Little wonder that most Washington matrons considered her an unfeminine parvenu, a willful bitch, and that in moods of sad introspection before she turned thirty-three she told herself she was wasting her life, and indeed had become little more than the court jester. In a city where dinner parties broke up at 11 P.M., when even the randy young men went home to their memoranda at that drastic stroke of the clock, she was known to entertain for perambulating homosexuals, New York novelists, professional football players, women reformers from the Midwest, with more than a few of these entertainments raging perilously toward dawn. All of Georgetown knew she occasionally rode a motor-scooter in the shortest mini-skirt in Washington, and that she had once been serenaded from her front steps by four drunken Southern Congressmen wearing Scottish kilts.

All of Georgetown, for that matter, knew that she could give proper but gay dinners as well, for diplomats, civil servants, professors from the university, and foreigners spending their obligatory two days in the "capital of the world." They knew she was an exceptionally good cook in the American way who prepared her own food and served only the best wines, that she was an earthy but ingratiating hostess, and that her townhouse, which she had decorated by her own wits, was a dazzling place with its amusing bric-a-brac and its sharp joyous colors and its good comfortable old pieces of early American.

Just what did she want? they asked. With her trenchant tongue and her flamboyant Southern wit, they said, her hasty expressions and passionate imprecations, she could take over the leadership of the movement for the liberation of women just then sweeping the Grand Old Union. Quite obviously her mind was better than those curiously arch and emotionless girls who had become bywords in that revolution. Carol Hollywell did have flair, after all, and experience with conceiving and bearing and raising an actual human being. She was intrepid in her disdain of iron-maiden marriages, and indeed of all the formal circumscriptions; she believed in her inmost being that it was women who held American society together. But she had had her moments with the movement toward liberation and had found that the campfollow-ers and footsoldiers of it left an emptiness in her, as did all those Simón Bolívars of the clitoris against the forces of reaction behind the labia minora, majora, and the deeper but equally irrelevant

extras. "I mean, hell," she stunned a cadre of anti-chauvinist lib-
erationists one day by paraphrasing Mr. Mailer, "which is more
impressive, the anchovy or the cucumber?" Then why did she not
marry another wealthy man, a better breed of wealthy man this
time, and seek power more tactfully than before? Because, she
said, she had known wealth when she was merely twenty-six, and
had found it restricting. Or transport herself to Manhattan and
find a niche there in that citadel of trends and gestures? Because,
she replied, she did not like the steam that came out of the sewers
on its streets, and because Washington was her town and because
she was bound to it with all her longings and hopes.

What, indeed, did she want? She herself did not know.

The truth is that Carol Hollywell, being a Southern girl, was
American to the blood, and hence was both an irredeemable
romantic and a fitful pragmatist. She might suffer along the way,
as indeed she had, but she was going to do all right before it was
over. It might take a while, but she was prepared to wait her time.
Before her sudden fall from grace and power, hadn't the British
Ambassador once removed, an imperious London intellectual,
told her the night before he went home that she was the most
promising young woman in Washington? Hadn't Dean Acheson
kissed her on the cheek and said she had more vivacity than any
lady he had ever known? Hadn't Mr. Buchwald, master of the
droll and whimsical, deemed her the most jocose of raconteurs?
And hadn't Joseph Alsop himself pronounced her the most beautiful creature in Georgetown and said that only she had the imagination to amalgamate the executive, the legislative, and the judiciary
into a new form of governance, a little indigenous but largely
Anglophilic?

She was tall and slender, about five eight, with dark-brown
hair and wisping curlicues that tumbled into her eyes, enough of
it to set off a face with expressions so varied that she could seem
a different person altogether from the one she had been five minutes before: a healthy American face with sturdy bloodlines. It
could be an amusing face, and a mean and calculating one, and

then straightforwardly and wholesomely beautiful, and mock serious in a way that fooled everyone, and in rare moments there would be a look around her mouth, an expectant look, at once tender and vulnerable. Her bright green eyes were touched with mischief. There was structure in the bones, and beauty that would likely last: and small breasts, and long slender legs that kept a summer's tan. She had an agreeable Southern voice, medium-pitched, with enough of the Deep South in it yet, and loud enthusiastic laughter that curdled the women and often frightened the men away. There was about her a slight suggestion of the Southern tomboy. She had never thought of herself as beautiful, yet she had heard it told her so often since her debutante days along the river that she had taken full advantage of the proposition, and it had spoiled her, making her a little headstrong and high-strung. Her wit could be as self-serving as it could be self-deprecatory, but fortunately for her the latter won the day. "I've had two rivers in my life," she would say, "the Mississippi and the Potomac. I'm fast, murky, and polluted." A likable girl? That was too plain a word for her, but those very few who knew her well saw character there, and impulsiveness and generosity, and the most curious disguised naiveté and innocence: a woman of the world, true, but beneath that the child who grew up in a time when the quiet streets of a small Southern town were the limits of that world, and all the streets and houses and pathways were where she remembered they belonged. She was, in fact, born at almost the last moment in time when it was possible to get, firsthand, a feel of what the older Southern life had been. The South was the root of her strength, though she did not know it yet, the irascibility of the South, that and her innate sense of the absurd, the one naturally following the other. Those who dwelled with their feelings were the ones who were drawn to her, and people hated her and people loved her, for she defied prediction, and she was not to be effaced.

. . .

She had come up to the Hill to work on the staff of a Congressman from Arkansas, a remote acquaintance of her uncle. The Congressman's most recent campaign cards had pronounced him "Against Every Ism But Americanism," helping him to re-election for a fifth term over a female justice of the peace with one leg. She was twenty-one, recently out of Ole Miss with a degree in political science, and considerable applied knowledge of the insane Mississippi dances, three-day drinking sprees, and orgiastic roadtrips to Memphis and New Orleans which gave the University of Mississippi its unique distinction before the great American academy. She had also left a 230-pound Johnnie Rebel linebacker who had been elected Colonel Rebel the year before she was Miss Ole Miss and who, as a luminary in the Fellowship of Christian Athletes and president of Sigma Alpha Epsilon fraternity, had obtained a sturdy foothold in the Memphis real estate market, a chain of drive-in hardware stores, and a partnership with the Chrysler-Plymouth dealer. She had been the most "popular" girl on the campus, a little too irreverent perhaps for her own good but not excessively so, and she had read enough textbook politics to get her by in Washington City while she learned what might be wanted there of her. Washington City! That is what her grandmother, the eighth daughter of a Confederate brevet-colonel, had called it, and the name itself had been resonant and mysterious and slightly alien to her all during her childhood. She had ordered a guide to her nation's capital, and in her last days home she sat in one of her shaded childhood haunts on Anderson's Ridge overlooking the river and traced her way around the city with her fingers, absorbing there in Arkansas all of L'Enfant's nostalgia for Versailles.

On a fine June morning in 1957 she stepped off the Crescent Limited in Union Station. On arriving in the vast echoing hall, she followed a porter pushing the cartful of new, polished leather luggage acquired in Memphis, walking gingerly on her toes, smiling for no reason at all at inessential strangers—and then, safely in a taxicab, admired the marbled certitude of Columbus out front, fresh to the New World on a ship's prow. She radiated warmth and foolishness and good will; she smiled when she read the inscription in stone on Union Station: *He who would bring home the wealth of the Indies must carry the wealth of the Indies with him.* An onlooker on that day would have become aware of the rush and flow of the blood through her, the robustness of her body, a robustness which seemed so extraordinarily vital because it was not in the least merely voluptuous, a young woman who was entirely resolute about her beauty. Even then she recognized somewhere down in the heart of her the restless gnaw of ambition. Because she was intelligent if not bookish, and resourceful in the ways of society, and heiress to a good Southern name with a United States Senator in its genealogy, and recipient of 750 dollars a month for life from her grandfather's estate, she harbored scant fears of intimidation or inferiority. And like the splendid Scarlett, whom she adored and envied for having lived during a magnificent calamity so commensurate with her gifts and whom she had secretly emulated at scores of weddings and balls down on the river, she hoped all the men on the Hill would soon beseech her to be allowed to fetch her barbecue. And she was not far wrong.

Even before she took her position with the Congressman she rented a small apartment near Wisconsin Avenue in Georgetown, painting it herself in bright colors and furnishing it with the early American pieces she had bought at auctions in the countryside. How she loved the city! She loved to stand in high places on spring evenings and look down at the monuments and edifices and the broad boulevards bordered with their great shade trees to admire the vistas opening from one of L'Enfant's circles, to gaze across from the Lee House at Arlington in a hazy autumn light toward the nest of its bureaucracies, its parks and plazas, to walk the quiet backways of Georgetown and browse in the tiny shops, to tarry among the dogwoods and sweet covers of honeysuckle and wildcrab among the ravines and hillsides of Rock Creek Park, to hear the bells of Washington Cathedral on dark lonesome Sundays, to find out-of-the-way places in northern Virginia and to see the battlefields at Fredericksburg, Chancellorsville, Spotsylvania, Bull Run, and the Wilderness. She imagined Lincoln walking all over the city alone during the Civil War, and the levees at the old Willard, and Whitman on his rounds of the emergency hospitals, and Mrs. Madison's drawing-room, and the rhetoric thundering forth from the inaugurals in front of the Capitol. She adored the corridors of Old Treasury with its great eagles and pilasters, and the pigeons and starlings in the tree-shaded parks, and Rochambeau in bronze in Lafayette Square, and the surging crowds that emerged in late afternoons from the monumental gray buildings of the Triangle, and the wooded reaches of the Potomac leading down into the Chesapeake, and the passageways and enclaves of the Capitol: here, on Capitol Hill, down the Mall and Pennsylvania Avenue to the Treasury, was the clash and play of the intractable Continent. And she would be part of it!

Later, on the Hill, she would come to know many of the young people who were working as researchers and assistants. "The presence of power," one of the most promising of them said to her, a little mysteriously, "begets ambiguity," but she was immediately at home in those unrestrained environs, for unlike certain other parts of Washington it had a nimbus of her hometown to it, an easy buoyance, a shared sense verging on fellowship of being commonly at the mercy of thistly electorates hundreds of miles removed. She would grow then to love the final nights of sessions when the House of Representatives whiled away the last hours waiting on a conference committee, or making perfunctory insertions in the *Record*, or enjoying the antics of the sugar lobbyists, and when the liquor flowed freely and the old horny House members, usually perpetual Southerners from the reddest hills or the blackest deltas, came uncertainly in pursuit of her. On one of these first closing nights she sat above the Mall with two or three young Congressmen and their assistants, drinking Scotch from paper cups in the twilight, watching the lights of the city come on and the sun on the marble and limestone all about her, feeling in a girlish glow the promise and variety of this new place she had chosen for herself.

Her first assignment for her Congressman was to investigate the complexities which might be lurking in a bill he intended to introduce in the new session. The bill, which had inspired considerable enthusiasm in her employer and various members of his staff, would replace the forty-eight American flags which encircled the Washington Monument with the flags of the forty-eight states.

"How should I research it, sir?" she asked him.

"Just get out and talk to people! Find out what the sentiment is. I'm sure everybody's for it. Everybody and his brother! Just think of all the different colors flappin' there in the breeze."

"Yessir."

She did not perform any pertinent formal investigations, but she thought about the prospective legislation on the way home, and the next afternoon she arranged to see her Congressman in his office.

"Well, what did you find out, pretty girl?"

"Congressman, it looks very controversial."

"*Controversial!* Who the hell thinks?"

"Everyone I talked to on the Hill—lawyers, economists, A.A.'s. They say you'll be accused of being the man who . . ."

"Accused of what?"

". . . the man who took down the American flag from the Washington Monument."

His broad open face was suddenly washed with sadness. For a time he said nothing, looking silently at his great gnarled hands and the stacks of paper on his desk and the signed photographs of Orval E. Faubus.

"By god, honey, you're right! That could get us into real trouble back home."

"Yessir."

"Now go get me Tommy!" he shouted. "It was *his* idea."

Naturally she was disillusioned when her second task for the

Congressman was to read all of Winston Churchill's major speeches to prepare a memorandum for him on how he could best emulate Churchill's oratory in Arkansas. She was disappointed not because of Churchill, but because she did not wish this mission in any measure to juxtapose that marvelous old Tory with her Congressman. The Congressman saw himself as a descendant of the lordly Southern Bourbons, but in fact he was a small backcountry yeoman who had once raised cabbage and eggplants and soybeans: shrewd in the ways of the Hill but little more enlightened in her haughty opinion than the cows and livestock and country people who were his constituents, the first two generally outnumbering the last. "This man has no class," her uncle had told her. "Learn the Hill fast and then get something better."

"Well, little lady," the Congressman had said to her, "I think you've done a real good job on the Churchill memo."

"Thank you, Congressman."

"I even intend to take your advice on most of it, and I don't take advice from many men."

"I'm flattered."

"Yes ma'am, pretty girl, I intend to give that version you did of his Iron Curtain speech in Marked Tree next month, and I'm using a little of the speech he gave to the House of Commons in September 1941, in Paragould in August. Just the high points."

"Yessir, Congressman."

"Little lady, you're goin' a far way."

Not too far as it turned out, but just up the street to the Senate Office Building. She worked four months for the Congressman. Then quite unexpectedly one night she found an entrée into Georgetown society, and this event would rearrange her whole existence.

"The Peacock Room"

ROBERT HAYDEN (1913–1980)

Robert Hayden was born and raised in the Paradise Valley ghetto of Detroit. Despite extreme myopia that worsened throughout his life, he became an early and avid reader. While acting in a Langston Hughes play in his college years, Hayden showed Hughes his first attempts at poetry, only to be told by the elder poet that they were derivative. After work in the late 1930s researching local black folklore and history for the Federal Writer's Project in Detroit and his marriage in 1940, Hayden enrolled in the English master's program at the University of Michigan. After taking his M.A., he was offered a position as assistant professor of English at Fisk University in Nashville, Tennessee, in 1946. In 1949, Hughes and Arna Bontemps published the anthology *The Poetry of the Negro*, and several of Hayden's poems of black history were included, the best known of which is "Middle Passage." The 1950s were largely unproductive for Hayden, but the changing aesthetics and politics of the 1960s were a boost to his creativity. Hayden left Fisk in 1969 to teach at his alma mater, the University of Michigan. He was elected to the American Academy of Poets in 1975 and in 1976 was the first African American to be appointed consultant in poetry to the Library of Congress. The following poem appeared in Hayden's 1975 collection, *Angle of Ascent*.

---

in memory of Betsy Graves Reyneau

Ars Longa   Which is crueller
Vita Brevis   life or art?
      Thoughts in the Peacock Room,
where briefly I shelter. As in the glow
(remembered or imagined?)
      of the lamp shaped like a rose

my mother would light
for me some nights to keep
    Raw-Head-And-Bloody-Bones away.

Exotic, fin de siècle, unreal
and beautiful the Peacock Room.
    Triste metaphor
Hiroshima Watts My Lai.
Thus history scorns
    the vision chambered in gold
and Spanish leather, lyric space;
rebukes, yet cannot give the lie
    to what is havened here.

Environment as ornament.
Whistler with arrogant art designed
    it, mocking a connoisseur
with satiric arabesque of gold
peacocks on a wall peacock blue
    in fury trampling coins of gold.
Such vengeful harmonies drove
a rival mad. As in a dream
    I see the crazed young man.

He shudders in a corner, shields
his face in terror of
    the perfect malice of those claws.
She too is here—ghost
of the happy child she was that day.
    When I turned twelve,
they gave me for a birthday gift
a party in the Peacock Room.
    With shadow cries

the peacocks flutter down,
their spread tails concealing her,
      then folding, drooping to reveal
her eyeless, old—Med School
cadaver, flesh-object
      pickled in formaldehyde,
who was artist, compassionate,
clear-eyed. Who was beloved friend.
      No more. No more.

The birds resume their splendored pose.
And Whistler's portrait of
      a tycoon's daughter gleams
like imagined flowers. What is art?
What is life?
What the Peacock Room?
Rose-leaves and ashes drift
its portals, gently spinning toward
      a bronze Bodhisattva's ancient smile.

"D.C."

RITA DOVE (1952–   )

Rita Dove made her mark at an early age writing stories and plays for her classmates to perform. In 1970, she was named a Presidential Scholar, enabling her to visit the White House with the other top 100 high school seniors in the country. She attended Miami University in Ohio, where she graduated summa cum laude as a National Achievement Scholar, and later studied at West Germany's Tubingen University on a Fulbright scholarship. Dove received her M.F.A. in 1977 from the University of Iowa's Writer's Workshop. She went on to write several books of poetry, a prose work, and a full-length play, earning recognition through both minimizing the distance between the written and spoken word and her treatment of racial issues in the context of daily life. In 1987 Dove became the second African American to receive the Pulitzer Prize for poetry for her collection *Thomas and Beulah*. She was named Poet Laureate in 1993, becoming the first African American writer and the second woman to receive this honor. She also served as special consultant in poetry for the Library of Congress. She is Commonwealth Professor of English at the University of Virginia in Charlottesville, where she resides with her husband and daughter. Among her poetry collections are *On the Bus with Rosa Parks* (1999) and *The Darker Face of the Earth* (1996), and her prose includes *Through the Ivory Gates: A Novel* (1993) and *Fifth Sunday: Stories* (1985). The following poem appeared in *The Yellow House on the Corner* (1980).

1
Roosters corn wooden dentures
pins & thimbles embroidery hoops
greenbacks & silver snuff & silver

brontosaurus bones couched on Smithsonian velvet

2

A bloodless finger pointing to heaven, you say,
is surely no more impossible than this city:
A no man's land, a capital askew,
a postcard framed by imported blossoms—
and now this outrageous cue stick
lying, reflected, on a black table.

3

Leaving his chair under the giant knee-cap,
he prowls the edge of the prune-black water.
Down the lane of clipped trees, a ghost trio
plays Dixie. His slaves have outlived him
in this life, too. Harmonicas breathe in,
the gray palms clap: "De broomstick's jumped, the world's
not wide."

from *Cadillac Jack*

LARRY MCMURTRY (1 9 3 6 –   )

Larry McMurtry was born in Wichita Falls, Texas. He received a B.A. from North Texas State University in 1958 and an M.A. from Rice University in 1964. His first novel, *Horseman, Pass By*, was published in 1961. This initial publication brought support for McMurtry's work, including a Guggenheim fellowship in 1964. In 1969, McMurtry moved to northern Virginia where he lived until moving into an apartment over the bookstore he opened in Georgetown. McMurtry has owned several rare and used bookstores, including one in Archer City, Texas. During his time in Washington, he continued to write. His subject, which began as an investigation of rural life and place, shifted to explore the movement from country to urban life. His 1982 novel *Cadillac Jack*, from which the following selection is taken, tells the story of a man leaving rural life for Washington, D.C. McMurtry has written numerous screenplays and novels, including his Pulitzer Prize–winning *Lonesome Dove* (1985) and *Terms of Endearment* (1975), both made into motion pictures. His nonfiction includes *Crazy Horse* and *Walter Benjamin at the Dairy Queen: Reflections at Sixty and Beyond*, both published in 1999.

It feels silly to kiss a smile. At best you just sort of bump teeth. With Boss even that might be sexy, but as things stood, or as we stood, it seemed even sillier than it might have in another context.

I quickly lost belief in the notion that she had meant to kiss me. I felt embarrassed, but Boss seemed not the least bit embarrassed. She had a lot of confidence in her powers, it seemed.

"These people aren't hungry," she said. "These people are just bored."

She kept hold of my wrist and concentrated on edging ever closer to the velvet ropes.

She was a good edger, too. The trick seemed to be to move

sideways, using one's lead elbow like a plow. As I watched, Boss plowed right between two short glassy-eyed Indonesians, her bosom passing just over their heads. A couple of tall, gloomy-looking Scandinavians had been blocking our view all along, but Boss somehow sidled right between them.

In three minutes we were standing next to the velvet ropes, directly in front of the tureen of caviar. Boss's eyes were shining and she was not even particularly sweaty, although there was a bead or two on her upper lip.

"You better get ready," she said.

Despite my constant immersion in the passions of auctions, I could not get over the avidity of this crowd. Even those who were glassy-eyed from the heat and the crush were trembling with eagerness.

Ten seconds later the ropes were removed. It was as if the roof had opened, dropping about five hundred people directly onto a feast.

I had no sensation of moving at all, but in an instant Boss and I were at the caviar bowl. I stood directly behind her, functioning like a rear bumper. People bumped into me, rather than her. A thicket of hands reached past me, trying to reach the bowl and slop a little caviar on some toast. There were little brown Indonesian hands, on arms long enough to reach around both Boss and myself. There were fat hands, mottled hands, be-ringed hands, skinny hands, and hands with sweaty palms. Having them waving all around me, like a sea of reeds, was creepy. I didn't even feel like I was among people. I felt like I was surrounded by a lot of wet plants.

While people were trying to reach around us, Boss and her peers were eating caviar. One of her peers was Sir Cripps Crisp, who must have been as good at edging as Boss was. He appeared out of nowhere and began methodically popping little caviar-heaped wedges of toast into his mouth.

Boss did the same, from time to time passing me a wedge. Once in a while she looked around at me and grinned, a fish egg or two momentarily stuck to her lips.

"Beastly," Sir Cripps said, while heaping himself another wedge. He was obviously a practiced man. In a second he could erect a neat pyramid of fish eggs on his wedge of toast. While his mouth worked on one pyramid his hand would be erecting the next.

His complaint was not lost on Boss.

"What's the matter with you, Jimmy?" she asked.

I was startled to hear Sir Cripps spoken to so familiarly, but he himself was not in the least offended. He actually raised his eyebrows when Boss spoke to him. They went up so slowly that it seemed they were probably powered by a little motor in his head, as if they were stage curtains. His eyes were an attractive and rather twinkly blue. It may have been the sight of Boss with fish eggs on her lips that caused them to twinkle.

"Beastly there's no vodka," he said. "Very irregular."

Boss opened a mother-of-pearl cocktail purse and took out a tiny silver flask. She opened it, took a swig, and handed the flask to Sir Cripps, who took a swig and handed it to me. They both looked at me impatiently, so I took a swig, too.

"You know Jimmy, don't you?" Boss asked, in much the way she had asked if I knew Spud Breyfogle.

I nodded, and Sir Cripps continued to erect pyramids of caviar.

"Jimmy writes the best cables in town," Boss said, giving him a little pat. "He used to bring 'em over and read 'em to me. Then we'd get drunk and he'd write a few in Latin. I think one of the ones in Latin nearly started a war, didn't it, Jimmy?"

Sir Cripps shrugged. "Only in Maseratu," he said. "Not difficult to start a war in Maseratu. Very excitable people."

Between the two of them they put away an amazing amount of caviar.

Being tall I was able to scan the crowd. Cindy was at the shrimp table, between Boog and Spud Breyfogle. Boog was gobbling shrimp, and Spud was dispensing a good deal of tightly wound charm for Cindy's benefit.

Meanwhile, Sir Cripps, whom I had considered to all intents and purposes a dead man, had come alive and was twinkling at Boss in a manner that suggested he might even still be capable of romance. He looked quite animated, perhaps because Boss was allowing him a snort of vodka after every wedge of caviar and toast.

Then I happened to notice the hapless Eviste Labouchere, a few steps away at the couscous bowl. Hapless is a word that might have been coined especially for him. In a room containing five hundred gluttons he still managed to stand out, thanks to the rate at which he was stuffing down the couscous. He ate like he was starving. Of course, he might have been starving. For all I knew he hadn't eaten since the Penrose dinner. Certainly he looked awful. He had clearly been living in his tux for several days, and at some point had come into contact with a dog, or at least with a place where a dog had spent time. His dinner jacket was covered with dog hairs. He had a wild, almost demented look in his eye as he scooped couscous out of the giant bowl.

Lilah Landry, his one-time date, was standing between the couscous and the caviar, watching Eviste go at it. She looked faintly sickened. Perhaps the sight of him gobbling couscous had brought home to her the fact that he wasn't really a star.

I think I must have looked at her at the precise moment when their romance ended. Eviste didn't notice it ending, but I did. Boss and Sir Cripps were having a tête-à-tête, and had forgotten me, so I had nothing to do but look. Also I was faintly worried about what sort of lubricity Spud might be whispering in Cindy's ear.

While I was pondering the general inconclusiveness of life, Lilah arrived at my side, tall, beautiful, and dizzy.

"How you?" she said, startling me.

"I'm fine," I said, trying to appear composed and at ease.

"How's Eviste?" I asked, in an attempt to make conversation.

Lilah just continued to smile her famous smile. The minute some women get through with a man their brains simply erase them, as tape recorders erase tape. Coffee had never bothered to erase me, but she had erased any number of Roberts and Richards. I had the feeling that at the very moment the equivalent of an empty tape was whirling through Lilah's brain—a tape that had once contained memories of Eviste Labouchere.

To make up for my unnoticeable opening note, I offered her some caviar. This was possible because Boss and Sir Cripps had quietly vanished, leaving me undisputed access to the bowl.

Instead of taking the wedge of toast and caviar I offered her and feeding it to herself, Lilah leaned over and nipped off half the wedge, in the process exposing much of the creamy bosom that had so recently harbored a pug.

Then she straightened up and chewed lazily for a moment.

"Well, I vow and declare," she said. "Look who's here."

Before I could look she caught my wrist, leaned over, and ate the rest of the wedge.

As a bosom-tilter, Lilah Landry was world class. By tilting adroitly she managed to make her bosom seem more interesting than anyone who could possibly have arrived in our vicinity, and even while I was enjoying the exhibition, I had the definite sense that someone was emitting heat waves of displeasure.

When I finally looked around I saw that the arrivee was the small redhead in the khaki safari suit.

"It wouldn't be a Washington party without you eating out of some man's hand, would it, Lilah?" she said.

The redhead had a face that put me in mind of a drill, and a voice that suggested sandpaper.

Lilah didn't seem in the least disturbed by the remark. She just gave me a blithe look and moved off toward the seafood table. Before I knew it I was alone with the redhead.

"Hello, Jack," she said, shaking hands. "Don't you think we ought to talk?"

I would have been more inclined to think so if I had had some inkling of what she did. All I knew was that she put me in mind of drills. She had an intense, button-eyed manner, and she didn't let go of my hand.

"Do you want some caviar?" I asked.

The question stumped her momentarily. For a second or two her face lost its drill-like aspects and just looked like the face of a small hungry woman.

"George would kill me if I ate some," she said a little wist-fully. "He doesn't approve of this regime. I don't think he'd tol-erate it if I ate their caviar."

"It's difficult living with a moralist," she added. "George is not flexible. His moral vision is twenty-twenty. If I eat one bite of this caviar he'll throw a fit."

Instead of talking, we began to walk through the thinning crowd. While we were walking I saw a reporter's notebook sticking out of her handbag, which explained what she did, at least. She was a reporter, not a Cabinet member.

Most of the people in the thinning crowd looked sleepy. They had stuffed, now they wanted to sleep. In fact, some of the older diplomats had started sleeping already; they were being guided toward the exits by their well-trained wives.

Suddenly the spectral figure of Eviste Labouchere wobbled up. He spotted Khaki and rushed to embrace her as a colleague.

"Ah Khakee, Khakee!!" he exclaimed.

"Get lost, you little turd," Khaki said, in unsentimental tones.

Eviste looked a little hurt by Khaki's remark, which was more or less the rhetorical equivalent of a splash of acid.

"But Khakee," he said woefully. "I am going your way. I will give you a ride on Anouk."

"Like shit you will," Khaki said.

"George will probably strangle you when he hears about this," she added, in her sandiest tones. Once again she was burn-ing with displeasure—her heat had a Saharan quality.

If Khaki was the pitiless desert, Eviste was the lost Legionnaire, the one who is never going to make it back to the fort. He stood looking woeful for a moment and then turned and stumbled away.

"Who's Anouk?" I asked, thinking Eviste might have a giant girl friend hidden away somewhere. After all, he had just offered Khaki a ride on her.

"That's what he calls his motor scooter," Khaki said, looking disgusted. "He named it after Anouk Aimée."

"At Home in Washington, D.C."

GORE VIDAL (1 9 2 5 –   )

> Gore Vidal was born at the United States Military Academy in
> West Point, New York, but considers Washington his "native
> city." Vidal's father, Eugene Vidal, was the director of air com-
> merce under President Franklin Roosevelt; his maternal grandfa-
> ther, Thomas P. Gore, was a senator from Oklahoma. Grandfather
> Gore was a great influence and instilled in Vidal a great passion for
> politics, a value that led Vidal to twice run for the U.S. Congress.
> Vidal has had many careers: member of the President's Advisory
> Committee on the Arts (1961–63), host for the *Hot Line* television
> program (1964), cofounder of the New Party (1968–71), and co-
> chair of the People's Party (1970–72), among them. He has writ-
> ten over twenty-five novels, numerous teleplays, screenplays, stage
> plays, short stories, and essays. Among his works are many related
> to Washington, including his novel *Season of Comfort* (1949), sev-
> eral of his American Chronicles (notably *Washington, D.C.*
> [1967], *Lincoln* [1984], and *The Smithsonian Institution* [1998]),
> and his memoir *Palimpsest* (1995). The following essay first
> appeared in the *New York Review of Books* in 1982.

Like so many blind people my grandfather was a passionate
sightseer, not to mention a compulsive guide. One of my first
memories is driving with him to a slum in southeast Washington.
"All this," he said, pointing at the dilapidated red brick buildings, "was once our land." Since I saw only shabby buildings and
could not imagine the land beneath, I was not impressed.

Years later I saw a map of how the District of Columbia had
looked before the district's invention. Georgetown was a small
community on the Potomac. The rest was farmland, owned by
nineteen families. I seem to remember that the Gore land was next
to that of the Notleys—a name that remains with me since my
great-grandfather was called Thomas Notley Gore. (A kind reader

tells me that the land-owning Notleys were located elsewhere in Maryland.) Most of these families were what we continue to call—mistakenly—Scots-Irish. Actually, the Gores were Anglo-Irish from Donegal. They arrived in North America at the end of the seventeenth century and they tended to intermarry with other Anglo-Irish families—particularly in Virginia and Maryland.

George Washington not only presided over the war of separation from Great Britain (*revolution* is much too strong a word for that confused and confusing operation) but he also invented the federal republic whose original constitution reflected his powerful will to create the sort of government which would see to it that the rights of property will be forever revered. He was then congenial, if not controlling, party to the deal that moved the capital of the new republic from the city of Philadelphia to the wilderness not far from his own Virginia estate.

When a grateful nation saw fit to call the capital-to-be Washington City, the great man made no strenuous demur. Had he not already established his modesty and republican virtue by refusing the crown of the new Atlantic nation on the ground that to replace George III with George I did not sound entirely right? Also, and perhaps more to the point, Washington had no children. There would be no Prince of Virginia, ready to ascend the rustic throne at Washington City when the founder of the dynasty was translated to a higher sphere.

Although Washington himself did not have to sell or give up any of his own land, he did buy a couple of lots as speculation. Then he died a year before the city was occupied by its first president-in-residence, John Adams. The families that had been dispossessed to make way for the capital city did not do too badly. The Gores who remained sold lots, built houses and hotels, and became rich. The Gores who went away—my grandfather's branch—moved to the far west, in those days, Mississippi. It was not until my grandfather was elected to the Senate in 1907 that he was able to come home again—never to leave until his death in 1949.

Although foreign diplomats enjoy maintaining that Washington is—or was—a hardship post, the British minister in 1809, one

Francis James Jackson, had the good sense to observe: "I have procured two very good saddle horses, and Elizabeth and I have been riding in all directions round the place whenever the weather has been cool enough. The country has a beautifully picturesque appearance, and I have nowhere seen finer scenery than is composed by the Potomac and the woods and hills about it; yet it has a wild and desolated air from being so scantily and rudely cultivated, and from the want of population. . . . So you see we are not fallen into a wilderness,—so far from it that I am surprised no one should before have mentioned the great beauty of the neighborhood. The natives trouble themselves but little about it; their thoughts are chiefly of tobacco, flour, shingles, and the news of the day." *Plus ça change.*

Twenty years ago, that well-known wit and man-about-town, John F. Kennedy, said, "Washington perfectly combines southern efficiency with northern charm." I think that this was certainly true of the era when he and his knights of the Round Table were establishing Camelot amongst the local chiggers. By then too many glass buildings were going up. Too many old houses were being torn down or allowed to crumble. Too many slums were metastasizing around Capitol Hill. Also, the prewar decision to make an imperial Roman—literally, Roman—capital out of what had been originally a pleasant Frenchified southern city was, in retrospect, a mistake.

I can remember that when such Roman palaces as the Commerce Department were being built, we used to wonder, rather innocently, how these huge buildings could ever be filled up with people. But a city is an organism like any other and an organism knows its own encodement. Long before the American empire was a reality, the city was turning itself into New Rome. While the basilicas and porticoes were going up, one often had the sense that one was living not in a city that was being built but in a set of ruins. It is curious that even in those pre-nuclear days many of us could imagine the city devastated. Was this, perhaps, some memory of the War of 1812 when the British burned Capitol and White House? Or of the Civil War when southern troops invaded the city, coming down Seventh Street Road?

"At least they will make wonderful ruins," said my grandfather, turning his blind eyes on the Archives Building; he was never a man to spend public money on anything if he could help it. But those Piranesi blocks of marble eventually became real buildings that soon filled up with real bureaucrats, and by the end of the Second World War Washington had a real world empire to go with all those (to my eyes, at least) bogus-Roman sets.

Empires are dangerous possessions, as Pericles was among the first to point out. Since I recall pre-imperial Washington, I am a bit of an old Republican in the Ciceronian mode, given to decrying the corruption of the simpler, saner city of my youth. In the twenties and thirties, Washington was a small town where everyone knew everyone else. When school was out in June, boys took off their shoes and did not put them on again—at least outside the house—until September. The summer heat was—and is—Egyptian. In June, before Congress adjourned, I used to be sent with car and driver to pick up my grandfather at the Capitol and bring him home. In those casual days, there were few guards at the Capitol—and, again, everyone knew everyone else. I would wander on to the floor of the Senate, sit on my grandfather's desk if he wasn't ready to go, experiment with the snuff that was ritually allotted each senator; then I would lead him off the floor. On one occasion, I came down the aisle of the Senate wearing nothing but a bathing suit. This caused a good deal of amusement, to the blind man's bewilderment. Finally, the vice president, Mr. Garner—teeth like tiny black pearls and a breath that was all whisky—came down from the chair and said, "Senator, this boy is nekkid." Afterward I always wore a shirt on the Senate floor—but never shoes.

I date the end of the old republic and the birth of the empire to the invention, in the late thirties, of air conditioning. Before air conditioning, Washington was deserted from mid-June to September. The president—always Franklin Roosevelt—headed up the Hudson and all of Congress went home. The gentry withdrew to the northern resorts. Middle-income people flocked to Rehobeth Beach, Delaware or Virginia Beach, which was slightly more racy. But since air conditioning and the Second World War arrived, more or less at the same time, Congress sits and sits while the presidents and their staffs never stop making mischief at the White House or in "Mr. Mullett's masterpiece," the splendid old State, War and Navy building, now totally absorbed by the minions of President Augustus. The Pentagon—a building everyone hated when it was being built—still gives us no great cause to love either its crude appearance or its function, so like that of a wasp's nest aswarm.

Now our Roman buildings are beginning to darken with time and pigeon droppings while the brutal glass towers of the late twentieth century tend to mask and dwarf them. But here and there in the city one still comes across shaded streets and houses; so many relics of lost time—when men wore white straw hats and suits in summer while huge hats decorated the ladies (hats always got larger just before a war) and one dined at Harvey's Restaurant, where the slow-turning ceiling-fans and tessellated floors made the hottest summer day seem cool even though the air of the street outside was ovenlike and smelled of jasmine and hot tar, while nearby Lafayette Park was a lush tropical jungle where one could see that Civil War hero, Mr. Justice Oliver Wendell Holmes, Jr., stroll, his white moustaches unfurled like fierce battle pennants. At the park's edge our entirely own and perfectly unique Henry Adams held court for decades in a house opposite to that Executive Mansion where grandfather and great-grandfather had reigned over a capital that was little more than a village down whose muddy main street ran a shallow creek that was known to some even then as—what else?—the Tiber.

from *Migrations of the Heart*

MARITA GOLDEN (1 9 5 0 –   )

> A native Washingtonian, Marita Golden grew up observing the
> lives of the residents of her mother's boardinghouses unfold
> "like a thrilling, irresistible narrative." After earning a bache-
> lor's degree in English and American Studies from American
> University in 1972, Golden worked at a newspaper in Baltimore
> and earned a master's degree in journalism from Columbia
> University. She left her job as a producer at a public broadcast-
> ing affiliate in 1975 to marry an architecture student she had
> met at Columbia and move with him to his native Nigeria.
> Golden's first book, *Migrations of the Heart* (1983), from
> which the following selection is taken, draws from Golden's
> own experience as an American wife in Lagos. Other publica-
> tions include *A Woman's Place* (1985), *Long Distance Life*
> (1989), *And Do Remember Me* (1992), and *The Edge of
> Heaven* (1998). She has edited *Wild Women Don't Wear No
> Blues: Black Women Writers on Love, Men, and Sex* (1993)
> and, with Susan Richards Shreve, *Skin Deep: Black Women
> and White Women Write About Race* (1995). Golden was the
> recipient of the Washington, D.C., Commission on the Arts'
> Mayor's Arts Award for Excellence in 1992. She teaches in the
> creative writing program at Fairfield University. She was a
> founder of the African American Writers' Guild.

I

My father was the first man I ever loved. He was as assured as a
panther. His ebony skin was soft as the surface of coal. The vig-
orous scent of El Producto cigars was a perfume that clung to
him. The worn leather seat of his taxi, a stubborn aroma, had
seeped into his pores, and like a baptism, the smells rubbed onto
me from the palms of his hands.

In school he went as far as the sixth grade, then learned the rest on his own. Part of the rest he bequeathed to me—gold nuggets of fact, myth, legend dropped in the lap of my mind, shiny new pennies meant to be saved. By his own definition he was "a black man and proud of it." Arming me with a measure of this conviction, he unfolded a richly colored tapestry, savored its silken texture and warned me never to forget its worth.

Africa: "It wasn't dark until the white man got there."

Cleopatra: "I don't care WHAT they tell you in school, she was a black woman."

Hannibal: "He crossed the Alps with an army of five hundred elephants."

The Sphinx (pointing with a tobacco-stained index finger to a page in the encyclopedia): "Look at the nose, see how broad it is? That's your nose. That's my nose too."

Bitter, frightening tales of slavery dredged by his great-grand parents from memories that refused to be mute. Passed to him. Passed to me. And when he recounted the exploits of Toussaint L'Ouverture, pausing to remind me that L'Ouverture meant "The Opener," inside his eyes I saw fire and smoke float over the hills of Haiti, and his voice stalked the room amid the clanging of swords, the stomp of heavy boots.

Our most comfortable stage was his taxicab. On frigid winter Saturday afternoons and warm summer evenings, I rode in the front seat with him. Always, it was an adventure. As much as anything else in his life, my father cherished the look of surprise and unease that invaded the faces of white passengers as he regaled them with quotes from Jefferson, Tolstoy, or Frederick Douglass. Pouncing on them unawares with the sharpness of his intellect, he brought their blanched faces from behind the *Wall Street Journal* or the *New York Times*. Their baffled respect, blooming in the form of a generous tip or an awed, "Mister, you're pretty smart," sealed his victory.

Together we visited the homes of women, who plied me with Kool-Aid and cookies and spoke to him in a language of double meanings and invisible but obvious desire. Women adored my father. He took them seriously enough to strip his fantasies before them. He listened as intensely as he spoke, and his reactions confirmed the legitimacy of their dreams. All of his women were like my mother, women who had turned daydream desire into tangible reality through houses, cars, money. All theirs. And, like my mother, these women, who had flexed their muscles in the face of fate and circumstance, looked at him with eyes that said, "I will give this all to you." My father never refused anything. He accepted their allegiance or a loan of money with equal ease as his due. He was a hard, nearly impossible man to love when love meant exclusive rights to his soul. Yet he relied on their steadfastness to enhance the improvisational nature of his life. Hearing their screen doors slam behind us as we walked to my father's cab, I trembled as though implicated in a crime. For, returning home, I met my mother's worried interrogation and watched her large hands tie themselves in knots after I helplessly nodded in assent when she asked if we'd visited Dorothy or Mamie that day.

My father's friends were men with names like Lucky and Sweets, men whose eyes rendered other verdicts on their lives. I watched them develop potbellies and saw gray sprout at their hairlines as they stood, year after year, before the fire-engine-red Coke machine in Sam's Sunoco gas station, waiting for the number to come out. In a shifting, eternal circle, they parried and joked, voices edgy, cloaked in gruff humor as they stood wondering if 301 or 513 would come out that day and "make them a man." Because of his luck with women and money, they called my father Goldie.

They were not his real friends—they feared him too much. Shuddered in the wake of his determination, which cast consideration aside. And they trembled, windswept and lost, in the face of his poorly hidden belief that he was and always would be better than the rest. Much like the characters who peopled the Africa he created for me, and for whom he felt an unbridled affinity, my father viewed his life as a stage. Those around him were an audience from whom he demanded total loyalty but to whom he gave mere lightning flashes of his soul. And I loved him with blind faith. Could never imagine having to forgive him anything. So when I had to, I could not.

My father grabbed life by the arm and wrestled it into squealing submission. My mother cleared the same terrain with a faith and self-possession that both fueled and ruined some of her dreams.

Greensboro, North Carolina, must have fit her like a coat too small, buttons missing, hem unraveling and torn. The town, steeped and cured in humility and patience, could never have imagined her hopes. So at nineteen she fled. One summer night, while her parents and younger brothers slept, she crept out of bed. Crouching on the floor, she retrieved a cardboard suitcase wrapped in string that had been hidden beneath her bed for three days. After pinning a note to her pillow, she walked out into the full-moon night. Standing on the porch, she felt her heart hacking a path out of her chest. Placing the suitcase on the porch, she rubbed her sweating palms on the side of her dress. Crickets echoed in the night air and fireflies illuminated the web of knee-high front-yard grass. And, as on every evening of what had been her life up to then, the pure, heartfelt country silence reached out for her. Struggling out of its grasp, she picked up the suitcase. Licked her lips for courage. And, imagining her mother's face the next morning discovering the empty bed and her wizened hands reaching for the letter, she scurried down the steps. It was 1928 and she was headed north.

Washington, D.C., was as far north as she got. There she settled with a cousin who'd arrived the year before. Her first job was cleaning government office buildings. But soon she discovered more gratifying outlets for her industry. Driven by caution, she scrupulously saved her earnings yet daringly, shrewdly bet small amounts on the numbers. She hit them regularly and plowed the winnings into property. Soon she owned four boarding houses and leased two others, a material affluence which at that time equaled a virtual empire for a black woman. Indeed, my mother was blessed, for she had her own. Each month, when she wrote her parents, she slipped a money order between the pages of the folded letter. And seven years after her arrival in the city dotted with historical monuments and scarred by Jim Crow laws, my mother drove, prosperous and proud, back to Greensboro in her own 1935 Ford.

Her mother sat on the porch in a rocking chair, stringing beans that afternoon. Her feet touched the splintered boards and she set the bowl of beans on the table beside her, stood up and clutched the banister. "Be-A-trice, whose car that you drivin?" she called out with only modest interest.

"It's mine, mama," her daughter called back, parking the car before the house with considerable skill.

"Yours?"

"Yes, mama, mine."

My mother was now walking dramatically up the steps to the porch. She wore a dark-purple suit and a hat that resembled a box was perched on her head. Her hands held white gloves and a small brown leather clutch bag.

"You want to go for a ride?" she asked, delighted to be offering such a treat.

Her mother, who had witnessed greater miracles than this every Sunday in church, merely folded her arms and shook her head in disgruntled amazement. "Be-A-trice, can't you write your own folks no more? It's been three months since we last heard from you."

If she'd had her way, my mother would have been an actress. Like the best of them, her presence was irresistible. My father used words to control and keep others at bay. For my mother language was a way to reassure and reward. My father demanded loyalty. My mother inspired it in the host of friends whom she cared for and melded into her life. She was a large, buxom woman, with caramel-colored skin and a serene face that gave little indication of the passion with which she imbued every wish, every commitment. Her hands were large, long-fingered. Serious hands that rendered punishment swiftly and breathlessly, folded sheets and dusted tables in a succession of white folks' homes long after she was mistress of several of her own. Hands that offered unconditional shelter and love. In every picture of her there is freeze-framed a look of sadness rippling across her glance, as though there is still just one more thing she wants to own, to do, to know. She wore perfume, fox fur throws casually slung over her shoulders and lamb coats, as though born to wear nothing less. My father confided to me offhandedly once, "When I met your mother I thought she was the most beautiful woman I'd ever seen."

She had been married once before. That husband had loved her with a precision and concern my father could never imagine. But after ten years she divorced him, his spirit routed, mauled by years of drinking into a shape she could barely recognize.

My father was her Armageddon. The thirteen years of their marriage, a music box wound too tight, played an off-key song of separation and reunion. The arguments and fights were nearly always murderous. Sculpted like hot wax around the dry bones of their unyielding wills was a love that joined and informed them of each other in ways that were unbearable and soothing. They fought over my father's women. But mostly, with a special viciousness, over power, symbolized by my mother's property. Her will shimmered with so much eloquence and strength that my father felt duty bound to try to break it. He almost did.

Year after year he insisted the houses be put in his name. Some were, and my father lost them with obscene swiftness, bartering them to pay his own gambling debts. My mother, now more reckless than wise and entrapped and enshrined by her love for my father, lost the rest. She gambled the way she had lived her life—with everything she had. Soon the modest empire dwindled to one house. Like pearls falling to the floor, the houses scattered, rolling across my mother's hopes into unseen cracks and crevices. Finally, irretrievable.

In the wake of a fight, my father, a wounded lion, would storm out of the house. A chaste calm settled over us all then. A peace so unfamiliar, so welcome that my mother was rarely comfortable with it. Perhaps within it she heard the mocking voice of a solitude she could neither accept nor respect. Maybe she missed the purpose, the scratching, blood-pumping tension my father provided. I think she was afraid. But my father always returned, swaggering, triumphant, forgiven. Pounced on at the front door by me with kisses, arms, legs enfolding. Greeted by my mother with a faint, resigned smile that resembled relief.

Still, my mother suffered inside the silence of that marriage. A silence that was loudest during the fight, the argument, the shout. During the last, most bitter years of their union she frequently sought renewal through pilgrimages to the home of her former husband. Some evenings I went with her to his small basement apartment. We ate dinner around a card table in the center of the disheveled but clean room. As a centerpiece, a plastic flower sat in an empty coffee jar. As my mother talked, Mr. Robinson listened gratefully, his gray eyes shining in the dim half-light. The room was stuffed with tightly packed cardboard boxes that sat beneath year-old funeral home calendars tacked to the wall. Sometimes I napped on an iron folding cot in a corner.

Drifting between sleep and wakefulness, I heard their voices waltz overhead, hushed but not hiding. My father's women handed him the tools with which to conquer them. Mr. Robinson gave my mother a way to stay alive.

But it was the houses that really mattered. And years after the fact, my mother was never able to understand or forgive herself for losing them. Sunday afternoons she used to pack me, one of her girlfriends, and the woman's daughter into her 1958 Pontiac and drive around Washington looking at houses. She sat behind the steering wheel and discussed them with Miss Johnnie Mae as though she was choosing a dress for a special occasion.

In the houses we lived in she paid homage to the home she'd known in Greensboro. For she crowded the mantelpieces and shelves with the same abundance of tiny ceramic knickknacks, doilies, and plants, cherished only for Sunday china, that her mother had used to bring grace to the tiny house on McConnell Road. And, as at my grandmother's house, all the houses had large back yards and screened-in back porches. She would put cast-off sofas there in the summer and gossip with the people next door while stirring a pitcher of iced tea. The houses were solid, unequivocal. Proper Victorian houses that demanded a certain majesty of their owners. On Saturday mornings we attacked the house in a frenzy of cleaning. While my mother polished the hardwood floors, I swept down three flights of stairs and hallways that never ended. Dusted the dark-brown massive bureaus in her bedroom, the upright piano, and vacuumed the oriental rug claiming the living room floor.

In the summer I took up residence in the attic. In its cool, spacious recesses I pasted pictures from *Life* and *Look* on the walls. Under a loose floorboard I hid reams of poetry and my diary, which charted my anguished journey into adolescence. Most of all I read books for comfort and salvation.

Leaning against the walls in that secret womb, I read *Ivanhoe, Vanity Fair, Tom Jones, Oliver Twist*. For two weeks my heart bled over the fate of Emma Bovary. One summer I lay stretched out on blankets there and read all of Jane Austen and Charlotte Brontë. Books simply saved me. Between their pages I transcended the horrors of my parents' marriage and the stark loneliness that regularly ambushed me.

My half-sister, ten years my senior, was as gregarious as I was shy, and sallied like a storm cloud over my life. While I was a studious bookworm, she was a sparkling sunburst. Alienated from each other by parentage and age, we paid over and over for the sins of the father, the love of the mother. Surely I symbolized to my sister the end of the possibility of love between our mother and Mr. Robinson. This was my crime. Never could I prove my innocence.

And I came to this halting, uncertain sisterhood weighed down, nearly crushed by a self-doubt planted and confirmed by everything I ever saw. The idea that I could be beautiful was eclipsed by the specter of my sister's light skin and long hair. Whatever hope I nurtured of being loved for my looks was sabotaged by the straightedged shadow she cast. Never could I imagine her lonely. Never could I envision her afraid.

She was lithe and petite, while I remained chubby into my late teens. Doted on, adored because of her looks and effervescent personality, this acceptance from others reinforced her natural openness and won her not just friends but loyal fans. But I was not pretty. My skin was brown. My hair short. I was not loved by strangers, for, unlike my sister, I was afraid to take them at face value. The poems and daydreams that steadily erupted in my mind encased me in a world that belonged to me, that few could enter. This world was barrier and refuge. So I became a flower, wilting and gasping as I spiritually clung to walls and corners, terrified that my voice would be rejected or, even worse, merely ignored. Only as women were we able to fill the chasm that separated and bound us. But at seven, at ten, at thirteen I ran from her shadow.

The houses gave my mother her identity. They taught me carefully, unknowingly, about life. The second and third floors belonged to the roomers, and I spent disgraceful amounts of time rummaging through the whispers and shouts swirling behind those doors. Crouched on the floor outside Mr. and Mrs. Benton's room, I held my breath and heard her thin, whining voice rise in weak defense against a charge of stupidity or indolence spat out by her husband. She was a slender, birdlike woman, brimming with self-apology. Once a week she received a beating from her husband, who on Friday evenings at six o'clock shed the forced, jovial mood that carried him through the week as quickly as he removed his coat.

Outside Marlene Jasper's door, I was tutored in the essence of love and desire. Hiding in the darkened stairwell, I watched her boyfriend, a muscular, jovial construction worker, enter her room as Marlene murmured a surprised, soft hello.

A waitress in a nearby black-owned restaurant, she rushed noisily down the steps every morning at 7:15, hair uncombed, her gaze still wrapped in sleep. She was a hurricane streaking through the dining room, spilling coffee on her chest, moaning over unpolished shoes.

We were friends. She told me wry, funny stories about her family and her lovers as she cooked minute steaks and fried yams in butter, always enough for two, forcing me to eat dinner with her. Taking a fierce drag on a cigarette, much the way I imagined she would kiss a man, she gazed at her empty plate and wiggled her white-stockinged toes stretched out before her. There were days, she said, when something hurled her without warning into a world of bloody dreams and sleepless nights. "Sometimes I want to be somebody else," she told me, folding her hands to steady her voice. "My life is too small. Some days I feel its fingers wrapped around my neck." Then she folded her hands around mine. "But I'm scared to make myself up all over again. What if I find out God didn't give me enough to work with?" In hot pursuit of her life, it remained a phantom nonetheless, leaving her more puzzled than afraid. Even at twelve I could see why men loved her. Could not resist her husky laugh and the tender fragility of her face. And because I looked on that face more steadily than most, I saw and measured the pain embedded between the laugh lines creasing the sides of her mouth. So, outside her door I listened to bedsprings creak and mellow laughter and her voice, plaintive and bruised after all, ask about tomorrow and the day after that.

These were the people who moved with us to new homes when a house was relinquished to pay the debts my parents incurred. A caravan of people and furniture streamed out of the house like ants on those Saturday mornings. The moving vans resembled dinosaurs patiently waiting to be fed. Mr. Carter, who smoked a pipe and never came out of his room except to go to work and the bathroom, pounced on my mother with bitter complaints about a radio one of the movers had dropped. My father stood imperially amid the movement, surveying the activity with the eminence of a sheik watching his army follow him across the desert. And I, anxious and excited, carrying my goldfish bowl in one hand, my scrapbooks in the other, navigated the cluttered steps, wondering what this new house would teach me.

Finally my parents separated. On a spring afternoon so ripe it seemed incapable of betrayal, my mother packed two suitcases with our clothes and left the last house she owned. After an argument earlier that day, my father warned her to be gone by the time he returned in the evening. That night, standing on the porch of the house to which we fled, he explained to an old family friend, chagrin and forced laughter rumbling through his voice, "She knows I didn't mean it. I've said the same thing before and she never left. What happened today?" My father was as embarrassed as my mother was liberated by her act. That she had conspired in the destruction of her financial autonomy frightened her more than any threat he could make. She left my father not because of his warning but to find a phoenixlike second chance tucked away between the folds of her prayers.

Six months later we moved into a low-income housing project near George Washington University. The small, neat cluster of four buildings was surrounded by a phalanx of high-rise apartments that included the Watergate. My mother was fifty-five years old, vanquished but not defeated. Once a week my father came to our apartment to give me an allowance. Still in good form after years of practice, she coaxed her share as well. Battleworn, randomly scarred, my parents sat in the tiny kitchen savoring cups of coffee, appraising one another with the charity of grateful survivors of an emotional war. Sheer endurance had carved wisdom into the blood.

2

The April evening was muggy, our apartment listless beneath the darkness. *The Wild Wild West* filled the television screen as my mother sat on the sofa beside me, her arthritic knee propped on the coffee table. I watched the television set indifferently, my mind rummaging through a forest of more immediate concerns— the money for my senior class ring due next week, ordering a copy of the yearbook, where I should buy my prom dress. The heat was a blanket tucked under my chin. My skin was prickly with sweat. Kicking off my sandals, I started unbuttoning my blouse when the voice of an announcer interrupted the program to say that Martin Luther King had been shot in Memphis, Tennessee. My mother struggled upright and grabbed my arm, the wedding band she still wore cutting into my flesh. The flutter of her heart echoed in the palm of her hand and beat in spasms against my skin. Then fear crawled into the room with us. As she huddled me to her breast, I heard her small, whimpering cry. It sounded like hymns and eulogies dripping from the air inside a tiny, parched black church. In mourning already, she released me and wept softly, dabbing her eyes with a handkerchief.

The screen once again filled with scenes of the Old West. Listening to my mother's sobs, my body was set on edge by a raw, hard-edged anger that nothing in my life up to then had prepared me for. In that flashing, endless moment that had come on like a seizure, the blood of my belief in America seeped through my flesh and formed a puddle at my feet.

Dazed, disbelieving, I reached for the phone and began calling friends. They had all heard the news. Grief, sudden and deep, stripped us of speech. We clung mutely to the phone as though it were a life raft bobbing in a sea of cold, lapping madness. If we could just hear another's voice, even stilled and hurt like our own, then life might go on.

But Washington's ghetto, long voiceless and ignored, scrawled an angry cry along its streets, using bricks, bottles and torches for its song of sorrow. We knew no one man had killed the prophet. Rather, the combined weight of racism and an absence of moral courage had crushed him. A constitution ignored, laws denied, these were the weapons. America pulled the trigger. For three days and nights a fury of looting and burning cleansed and destroyed the inner core of the city. National Guard troops cordoned off the affected areas. President Johnson appealed on television for an end to the violence, a convulsion spreading across the country. Pacing the apartment, unable to go out because of the curfew, I sympathized with the rioters. A sense of impotence hounded me. I was still numb, catharsis beyond my grasp. I envied their freedom, rooted in the fact that nobody cared about their will or collective rage unless it spilled over the bounds of the ghetto. So the rage continued, taking shape in a death wish-like spiral that devoured only the ghetto, until it was spent and whimpers of regret replaced the shouts.

I walked the streets demolished by the riots a few days after the troops had left and the fires had died. Block after block was filled with only huge store frames turned black from the flames, a damp smell of ashes hanging over each one. Pictures of Robert Kennedy still hung precariously in many store windows. Mountains of rubbish filled the streets. The "Soul Brother" signs that had been pasted on the store windows too late lay burned around the edges among piles of trash. The streets were choked with cars from the Maryland and Virginia suburbs, whites popping their heads out of car windows, snapping pictures.

The days after King's death saw an invisible barricade of tensions rise between the white and black students at Western High School. The black students did not know then that in a few months many of us would repudiate our white friends, no longer finding them "relevant." Finding instead their mere presence inconsistent with a "commitment to the struggle," which is what our lives became overnight. We did not know it, but some of us sensed it, caught tortured, shadowy glimpses of it in the changes festering like mines in the open, dangerous field we would enter upon graduating in June.

Andrea McKinley, small-boned as a deer, with a finely honed sharp wisdom, declared while we were leaving a civics class together that perhaps King's death was a blessing. Shrugging her thin shoulders, removing her glasses and rubbing her eyes, still red from tears, she said, "Let's face it. The movement has changed. He was from another era. He couldn't deal with the ghetto and I think he knew it."

"But how can you say that?" I screamed. "That's the most callous thing I ever heard." We stood in a corner of the crowded hallway, each hugging books to her chest as for support.

"Do you think that's an easy conclusion for me to come to?" Andrea asked, her look unmasked and pained. "What I'm talking about is a struggle with different rules. Rules that talk about what's really important—power, community control and identity. How can you talk about love to people who aren't even listening?" I had never imagined Andrea, so cool and intellectual, capable of such unflinching anger. At eighteen she had the demeanor of the Rhodes scholar she would later become. But at that moment her words sprang from the same place within her where my belief in America had snapped. Her tirade frightened me because she so precisely articulated my own doubts. It also inspired me because in the midst of a vacuum it offered hope.

"I'm going to spend the summer with my sister working with SNCC before I go to Oberlin," she said.

"That means you'll be going south?"

"Yes. Probably Mississippi."

"It's a battleground down there," I whispered, ashamed of the fear evident in my trembling voice.

"Marita, the front lines are everywhere."

"I feel like the world's turned upside down. I felt safe before. Now I don't know," I moaned.

"You don't feel safe because now you see the truth. You see how they lied. Integration. Civil Rights." She spat out the words harshly, her voice a train rushing out of control.

"Just yesterday we cloaked our anger in folk songs and fingers pointed at society," I said.

"Yesterday we had faith," she countered. "Yesterday we were willing to wait. I've got a class and I'm already late," she said hurriedly, glancing at her watch.

"We'll talk some more. We *have* to." Unexpectedly, she squeezed my shoulder, as awkwardly as I'd imagined it would be, and strode quickly down the hall.

In the deserted hallway the silence struck me like a gong. I stood there feeling very old. Unwise. And afraid to look over my shoulder. I wanted to cut the rest of the day, walk through Georgetown and look in the opulently decorated store windows, which were like wrapped packages of silver and gold waiting to be opened. I wished desperately to be frozen in time at that moment, with only this image in my brain. So I ran down the stairs and out the main entrance into a sun so radiant it stabbed my eyes. But even a sun that pure did not destroy the emotional turbulence that whispered in my ear the rest of that day.

"The New Washington: An Inside Story"

GARRISON KEILLOR (1951–   )

Garrison Keillor was born in Anoka, Minnesota. His big break came during his freshman year at the University of Minnesota when he interviewed for a job in radio. This interest sparked a career that by itself is storied and recognized. Keillor's radio program, *A Prairie Home Companion,* aired on National Public Radio from 1974 to 1987 and from 1993 to the present, and won a George Foster Peabody Broadcasting Award. Keillor would go on to win a Grammy in 1987 for the audio version of his novel *Lake Wobegon Days*; the novel itself was nominated for the Los Angeles Times Book Award in 1986. Keillor has also won two Cable Ace Awards and was inducted into the Museum of Broadcast Communications and Radio Hall of Fame in 1994. The author of twelve books or collections—including two children's books—and the producer of numerous recordings, Keillor is a frequent contributor to the *New Yorker, Harper's,* and the *Atlantic Monthly.* The following selection, "The New Washington: An Inside Story," first appeared in the *New Yorker* in 1983.

Mr. Wick said he thought that economically pinched Americans of today enjoyed viewing the luxurious Washington way of life of the Reagan Administration members, much as Americans who suffered in the Depression enjoyed watching Hollywood stars in the movies. "During the Depression," said Mr. Wick, "when people were selling apples and factories were still and guys were jumping out windows because they lost everything, people would go to the movies. They loved those glamour pictures showing people driving beautiful cars and women in beautiful gowns, showing that people were living the glamorous good life."

—The Times, *quoting Charles Z. Wick,*
a member of Mr. Reagan's Kitchen Cabinet

An autumn afternoon in Washington—mysterious, delirious Washington!—and all along glittering, office-lined Pennsylvania Avenue a fleet of gleaming stainless-steel buses was loading up tourists for the two-hour guided excursion of Governmentville, Image City, Tax Town, or, as it's often referred to by its residents, Our Nation's Capital. Sturdy, sweaty, plainly dressed, and somewhat pinched, the visitors from Iowa, Alabama, Vermont, Kansas, Idaho put their money down and climbed aboard—the dumpy, dull-faced folks Norma Desmond once called "those wonderful people out there in the dark." They sat down wearily and waited for a brief glimpse of the glamorous good life, a glimpse that would make their own defeated and despair-filled lives a little bit more bearable.

"See the Homes of Department Heads," the signs beside the waiting buses read. "See the Homes of Alexander Haig, Donald Regan, James Watt, William French Smith & Many Many More. See Exclusive Restaurants, Stores, Hotels, Apartment Complexes! Visit Sites of Gala Affairs. See Malt Shop Where Sandra O'Connor Was Discovered."

"Yesterday I seen William French Smith come out of a candy store," a large woman in pink stretch-pants and a "Wahoo for Washington!" T-shirt confided to a gaunt, sad-eyed woman sitting next to her on the first bus. "Wally says to me later, he says, 'Myrt, it musta been someone else,' but I knowed it was him. He was as close to me as that little gimpy guy in the cardigan up there. He give me a big smile and I about fell over. Then he got into the biggest limo you ever seen, and away he went. I'll remember that as long as I live. You know what they call him? They call him 'the Attorney General of the United States.' Ain't that beautiful?"

"You got the binocs, Myrt?" a skinny old man in the seat behind her piped up.

"In my purse," she snapped. "You can't see nothing anyway. Blind as a bat," she added, muttering to herself.

Her seatmate pulled the lever on the armrest of the reclining seat and leaned back and closed her eyes. "Me and Carl scrimped and saved for two years to come here," she said wearily. "I wait-ressed at the Elks Lodge on weekends, he worked nights at the worm ranch, now here we are—I can't believe it. Last night I dreamed I saw a striped tent on the White House lawn and an orchestra playing and beautiful cars parked in the driveway and women in beautiful gowns walking across the grass. I walked up to the front gate and the Secret Service said, 'Oh, hi, Mary Frances!' and I looked down and I had on a yellow chiffon gown, with rubies and emeralds and diamonds all over, and I walk in and the first person I see is David Stockman. He looks at me and I look at him and I start to run and he runs after me and in the Rose Garden he grabs me and takes me in his arms and he is gasping for breath and his big eyes are looking into mine and he says, 'Don't ignore what you feel this moment! Don't pretend that you don't feel exactly what I feel! I *need* you, Mary Frances. I've wanted this all my life—your intensity, your passion, your hunger for life!' Then I woke up in the Travelodge and Carl was asleep and the TV was on. It was *him* on the TV, talking about budget cuts, just like Carl does, but it was different—it was a certain way he looked at me, a way he smiled. I don't say this to Carl, but I have strong feelings I will not be going back to Des Moines."

"Tickets, ladies?" A young man in a blue blazer was standing in the aisle next to them, with the faint trace of a smirk etched across his tanned, handsome face. He had heard some of what Mary Frances had said, and as he punched the last tickets and jumped off the bus he could hardly keep from laughing out loud.

"What's so funny, Chuck?" his friend and fellow-worker Jim asked him quizzically.

"Couple doozies in that load," Chuck snorted. "Buncha nuts. One of 'em thinks Stockman is trying to seduce her on *Meet the Press*."

Jim turned, a faraway look in his eyes. In the distance he saw the Washington Monument beyond the White House and the Treasury. Maybe I'm crazy, too, he thought to himself.

A former campus radical, Jim had first felt drawn to Nancy Reagan in September 1980. On television, smiling and clapping for her husband, she sometimes turned and looked directly into the camera and seemed to ask Jim to come to Washington to help her and her family in an important mission that would be revealed to him later. "America is the land of promise," she seemed to say. "I want you to be very happy."

Now he and Chuck shared a studio apartment in Potomac Beach, where Jim often heard his friend, a neoliberal, attack Washington as a city of sham, a maker of myths, a vender of illusions, and ridicule the tourists as rubes and suckers. Jim also had his doubts about the tourists—the hordes of dreary men and women with their souvenir tax-cut pens and their souvenir hats shaped like the Capitol dome, who bought issues of *Federal Romance* and *U.S. Government Confidential*, and trudged the city streets looking for the rooming house where Stockman lived when he was only a congressman, the booth at Le Bistro Louis XIV where columnist George Will holds court, the parking lot where George Bush lived (for two months in 1978) in the back seat of a 1965 Buick, when his name was Waldo Pflueger and all he had was a dream of success and a box of Ritz Crackers. There was something forlorn about it all, Jim knew, and yet whenever he walked down the Mall at night and looked across the Potomac to Arlington and saw there on the hill behind the old Lee mansion the illuminated fifty-foot letters that spelled WASHINGTON, he felt the pull of the dream that supported his life and kept him going—the dream of becoming an Assistant Secretary of the Interior.

Interior—the very word breathed mystery, hinted at intimate secrets to be discovered, suggested the glamorous life of the Administration insider. Jim had recently borrowed two hundred dollars from his mother, back in Topeka, to enroll in the Academy of Administration, a night school on the second floor of a dingy stucco building around the corner from Dupont Circle. Max Hugel had gone there. So had Drew Lewis, James Baker, and Edwin Meese. Every Tuesday and Thursday night, Jim attended Spokesman class, and every Wednesday night he worked with a small improvisational press-conference group in the basement of a church. On Friday nights, he took dancing lessons. One evening there, his speaking instructor took him aside. "Listen, kid," he said, putting a sympathetic arm around the young man's shoulders, "I know you think it could happen tomorrow—the call from the Interior that will make all of this worth it, but, believe me, I've seen this town eat people up and spit them out. You're a nice guy. Go home, marry the girl, raise a family. Someday you'll thank me."

"I am aware that I do not speak well," Jim wrote his sweetheart that night. "But did you know that they have speechwriters here in Washington who make these big guys sound a lot smarter than they really are? Judy, I still believe that with one lucky break I can become an Assistant Secretary, right alongside James Watt, and I hope that you still believe. Someday I will send for you and we will live in a $750,000 house in Georgetown and be invited to fabulous parties. Please don't give up on me, darling, for it is your faith that gives me faith in myself."

As the tour bus rolled past the Pentagon ("The fourth-floor corner window where you see the blue satin drapes is the office of Casper Weinberger," the bus loudspeaker blared out. "In his office Mr. Weinberger keeps more than seventy-five suits, some valued at more than one thousand dollars each, and three hundred pairs of shoes, many of them custom-made in Europe and flown to this country"), across the Potomac ("On these historic waters, members of the Cabinet frequently spend long weekends aboard their luxury yachts, some of which are up to one hundred feet in length. The President's yacht is two hundred feet in length and can remain completely submerged for up to three weeks"), and past the Lincoln Memorial ("Here, a few short weeks ago, Mr. Reagan celebrated the passage of his tax bill with a dinner party for three thousand. Marine parachutists entertained the guests with precision jumps into the Reflecting Pool, as freshman members of Congress served cold tenderloin of beef and candied carrots. The fruit salad alone came to more than six thousand dollars"), Wally and Carl stared straight ahead, stunned by the thought of the bundle this trip was costing them. Myrt and Mary Frances were planning on a night on the town next, with cocktails at Nero's and dinner at the Top Hat—a blowout from which they were unlikely to escape for less than a hundred bucks per couple. Both men had hoped to return home the next morning, but now their wives were talking about renting a cab to revisit some of the high points of the bus tour. Myrt was sure she had seen Pat Buchanan peering out from the garage beside his palatial McLean, Virginia, residence, and Mary Frances had spotted a semi parked in front of the Charles Percy mansion, with "Venice Catering" emblazoned on the trailer. A man in a formal white suit was unloading crates of demitasse cups from it, using a silver forklift. Mary Frances was sure the Percys were preparing for a party, and she had a strong hunch that David Stockman would be there. "Don't laugh, Myrt, but I feel that if I could only touch him it might clear up my arthritis," she whispered.

Minutes before, riding past the vice-presidential mansion at the Naval Observatory ("Il Gazebo della Marina"), she and Myrt had pressed their faces against the window, hoping for a glimpse of George Bush. They had read his biography, *The Rest of Him: The George Bush Story,* and loved it—the saga of an unemployed tile-setter who, while on his way to the welfare office one day, had spotted a scrap of newspaper stuffed in the coin-return of a pay telephone, unfolded it, and read that Mr. Reagan was conducting a national talent search for a vice-president—but there was no sign of Mr. Bush in the yard now, although they did see two black Alfa-Romeos with gold trim, a large steel cage containing three ocelots, and several servants busily hanging flaming torches from the trees.

What they didn't know was that George Bush was sitting alone in the seat directly behind Wally and Carl. How could they? He was wearing dark glasses, a red wig, and a false face that had taken him three hours to apply. And yet, for George Bush, it was worth all the trouble.

He had never learned to accept the luxurious way of life of the Reagan Administration. In his heart, he was only himself, a mere tile-setter, and after all these months he still felt uneasy in his mansion, with its Moorish-style ballroom paneled in walnut and red brocade, its gold-leaf ceilings and marble floors, its terra-cotta figurines of mermaids and serpents and Egyptian deities, its grand staircase ascending to the gymnasium-sized master bedroom with the canopied bed done up to resemble a Chinese pagoda, its immense moat surrounding the mansion, its ornate Mayan lawn statuary, its giant swimming pool in the shape of the White House. No, he escaped from his new home whenever he could and mingled unnoticed among the common people. It gave him perspective, he thought, to see Washington from the outside. For a few hours now and then, he could be himself and not a glamorous figure admired by millions. "My dream is to buy a few acres in some little town where the *New York Times* isn't delivered, where the *CBS Evening News* doesn't go, where you and I can keep a few chickens, raise vegetables, and be real people together," he had said to his wife one night on the South Portico of the White House, to which they had slipped away for a few minutes from a lavish party attended by hundreds of persons whom he had privately described as "phonies."

The bus rolled to a stop in front of Lafayette Square, and as the disguised man made his way down the aisle he was tempted momentarily to reveal himself to the two women and to take them into the White House and show them the plain truth about Washington. But no, he suddenly decided; it was far better to let them keep their dreams. Without their illusions, he thought sadly to himself, they would be utterly destroyed.

"Excuse me," Myrt said, tapping him on the arm. "Can you tell me which way is the Justice Department?"

"Sorry," he mumbled, avoiding her eyes. "I'm a stranger here myself."

There are millions of stories in Washington. These have been some of them.

Carl, Wally, and *Myrt* returned to Des Moines the next evening, where they continued to follow the activities of the Reagan Administration on television and in the newspapers. *Myrt* keeps a scrapbook on William French Smith.

Mary Frances remained in Washington, hoping to get a job chopping vegetables in the White House commissary. Several weeks later, she was hired as a waitress in the Senate Dining Room, where Jesse Helms, Howard Baker, and David Durenberger regularly sit in her assigned area. Through Senator Baker, she obtained a one-night waitress appointment for a gala dinner at the Reagans' ranch and was flown out to California and back. She had a color photograph taken of herself with the First Family. "The Reagans are good eaters," she wrote to *Myrt*, "but David Stockman is awful finicky. He sent his lobster back to the kitchen three times. I coulda killed him."

Chuck was discovered one day by *George Bush*, who overheard him ridicule the Republican elite and promptly hired him as a personal aide. The two often drive around the city in an old car and do ordinary things. *Mr. Bush* has been seen recently walking along the C. & O. Canal, looking at exhibits in the Smithsonian, or eating a hot dog on the south side of L Street, between Nineteenth and Twentieth.

Jim was happy for *Chuck,* and yet his friend's good fortune also depressed him, pointing up as it did his own slim prospects. One night, after writing long letters to his parents and to Judy, he took a bus to Arlington and walked up the hill through the cemetery to the base of the illuminated WASHINGTON. He climbed the "W" and stood there for a long moment, admiring the dazzling lights of the city. Then he threw himself over the edge. His fall was broken by a safety net installed there many years before, but as he landed his head hit his knee—a sharp blow, causing complete amnesia. Three days later, he was found in a pitiable condition by a wealthy Administration couple, who prefer to remain anonymous. They took him into their home, and have surrounded him with every imaginable luxury. This does not seem to have restored his faculties.

"Writing About, Living in Washington"

SUSAN RICHARDS SHREVE (1939–   )

Ohio native Susan Richards Shreve was educated at the University of Pennsylvania and the University of Virginia. She is the author of twelve novels, including *The Visiting Physician* (1996) and *Plum and Dagger* (2000), as well as numerous books for children and young adults. She has won awards from the Guggenheim Foundation and the National Endowment for the Arts and has taught at Bennington College, Columbia University, and Princeton University. Shreve has been a frequent contributor of short stories and essays to periodicals and of documentary essays to the *PBS NewsHour*. She has taught at George Mason University since 1976 and was the founder of its M.F.A. program in creative writing. The following essay was first presented at a conference on Washington and Washington writing at the Center for Washington Area Studies at George Washington University in 1986.

My parents were married on New Year's Day in 1937 in the parlor of my grandmother's house. No one, so I have been told, approved.

First off, my father was from the wrong side of the tracks. In small midwestern towns, there are, even today, two sides. He was a man of unpredictable genes. No midwestern farmer. And then for years, my mother had been engaged to marry a splendid young athlete whose pictures in basketball shorts doing jump shots and lay-ups are in my attic. She agreed to leave the basketball player several weeks before the wedding, but my father, committed as he was to emergencies, found Donna, a tall voluptuous blond, late thirties Harlow, in mid-December, and on Christmas Day a week before the wedding, he maintained in earnest that he was undecided about marriage.

I think he made it up. My father saw my mother when she was

twelve years old sitting on the veranda of her house with the quiet and contented air of the well-born on the bottom side of the century, just after the first war. He decided about marriage then. He crossed the tracks on Valentine's Day to bring her chocolates which he gave to her father because my mother wouldn't come to the door.

"He was too small," my mother said, "and skinny as a pole. Anyway," she insisted, "my friends would have laughed. He was younger than I was and didn't play sports. Instead," she said, "he wrote stories."

I expect my father found Donna just in time to protect himself with understudies in the wing, to seal my mother's commitment to this persistent dark horse.

Besides, as I have said, he liked emergencies. A simple wedding in the company of outraged relations was not enough.

"I suppose," my mother said on Christmas Day after the news about Donna, "that if you come on New Year's Eve, I'll know the wedding is on."

"I'll try my very best to let you know before then," my father said.

Twenty-one years later, my parents were announcing my engagement to a man not unlike the basketball player who lost out in his list of accomplishments—a young man of his time whose talents unlike my father's were perfectly suited to the moment. My parents had planned a large party with friends and relations from out of town, but the day before the party, the man I was to marry broke his leg playing football and could not attend the celebration. Immediately, my father sent out telegrams to everyone invited. "ENGAGEMENT OFF," he said. He was a writer, known for absolute clarity.

For weeks I received small notes on blue Crane's stationery, on sheets with violet borders from well-meaning aunts. How sorry they were to hear about the trouble, advising me to get busy and put the man out of my mind, to look for someone else more loyal.

"Jeez," I said to my father. "What did you tell Aunt Lindsay and grandmother and Mrs. Henry?"

"That the party was off," my father said. "That's all."

"You said the engagement was off," my mother said with surprising sharpness. She had after all dedicated that year to the careful arrangement of her daughter's future and did not want slip-ups. "You forgot the word party," she said.

"By accident," my father said sheepishly.

It may have been because the man I married was tall and blond, unreasonably successful for a boy. Or that he reminded my father of the ex-basketball player or his own impossible dreams for himself. Or that I was his daughter.

All of these and more that I don't know yet or don't understand. What I do know is that we inherit from the lives of our parents a complex of patterns which can give a sense of order to our lives. When I write, I am looking for these patterns.

My mother didn't know my father well before she married him although they had grown up in the same Ohio town. He was a crime reporter for the *Post* in Cincinnati, and she was teaching school in Urbana, waiting for the basketball player to get a job and marry her. Her own father said she had to wait. He also said she must teach school. Not go to New York to be an artist or a model or a dancer in that order, as she wished to be. In New York, she would be, he promised her darkly, open to false advances, low-life companions. She must have a serious profession teaching school.

When I got my first job teaching school, my mother told me fiercely that I was throwing my life away. And with all my opportunities. I could be an actress or television writer. I could produce plays. Something worthwhile. I mention this so you will understand why a careful and old fashioned woman, as I describe my mother, could be carried off by a crime reporter, a Welshman from the wrong side of the tracks.

On their way to Cincinnati, driving at night, after the wedding ceremony and the disappointed relations, my father spotted a brown paper bag in the middle of the highway and stopped.

There was, he claimed in dead earnest, a baby in the paper bag.

"A baby?" my mother asked incredulously. "How do you know?"

"Look for heaven's sake," he said to her, as though her sense of sight had failed her in an instant. "Can't you tell?"

She looked. There were lights on the highway and headlights on their car so she could see the paper bag perfectly It appeared to be a brown paper bag which gave no evidence of concealing a baby. But it did move, she noticed, as my father rushed to rescue it from the middle of the road.

Filled with a sudden and unfamiliar excitement, she began to believe that he was right and would return with a small baby which he'd dump from the paper hag onto her lap. She straightened her skirt in anticipation.

"Well?" she asked as he opened the door by the driver's seat. "What is it?"

My father got in, tossed the paper bag in the back seat, and turned on the engine.

"Nothing," he said and drove off into the night with his new bride, headed for Cincinnati.

"Why," my mother dared to ask sometime later, "did you think there was a baby in the paper bag?"

"There could have been a baby," my father said simply.

Anything, of course, is possible and so my reasonable mother agreed that "yes," there could have been a baby.

"Besides," my father said later. "I couldn't imagine that it was simply an empty paper bag."

Our house was full of stories. Every night when my father came home from work, I wanted to be there, not to miss my role in whatever high drama might be played out in our kitchen. It was not so much that he told us stories, although he did that too, but he made our lives into stories. I grew up believing that there could be a baby in an empty paper bag.

My parents moved from Toledo, Ohio, to Washington in 1943. I was three years old. We came because my father who had wanted to go to Europe as a correspondent joined radio censorship for the wartime office which cleared the news before it reached the American people. He moved my mother and me into the only place we could find, which in the winter of 1943 was occasionally heated and always full of soldiers passing through Washington on their way to Europe. I had rheumatic fever shortly after we arrived and so my early life was attended by a certain amount of drama of which I was the center. It was not a bad time, and I was not bored. There were plenty of soldiers, and my mother was good company. I listened to soap opera on the console radio and played out melodrama of my own design with paper dolls on my bed. I expected, as children do, that my life was ordinary. I expected as well that it was easy to die. A child must be armed for it, ready for combat. I remember only one angry winter, fed up with staying in bed, that I undressed my doll, Ann Shirley, named for the healthy dimpled child idol of the time, and asked my mother to put the naked doll out in the snow so she would die. My wonderful mother did just that, walked around the house to my window so I could see her and put Ann Shirley in the snow where, I had determined, she would catch pneumonia and die.

For several years after I got well, I went through a ritual with my mother before I went to sleep. "Promise me that I won't be poisoned," I asked. "That I won't be kidnaped in the middle of the night or bitten by the poisonous snake under my bed. Promise me that I won't die."

My mother was an honest and literal woman and would not make promises she could not keep. But after nights up with me, she compromised and promised me faithfully that I would make it through the night.

I see dark shadows everywhere, even now. Roach poison mysteriously in the orange juice, kidnappers lurking in the basement thinking our house belongs to the wealthy senator from Colorado, viruses transmitted by pigeons which flood Washington every fall. Living, I instinctively believe, requires energy, a readiness to fight.

I have been careful with my children. They are not growing up with my father's stories from his crime reporter days or my precarious childhood. They do not need to believe, as I seem to, that we live in a state of emergency. But of course, however careful we are as parents, these legacies outdo us.

Recently when I was in New York, I spoke long distance with

my eldest son who told me about the fine day he had in school, about lacrosse and his girlfriend with long yellow hair, a conversation punctuated by black reminders of the dangers of New York. Was my door locked? Did I go out at night alone? Did I remember the woman from Washington struck by a taxi as she waited for the bus? Was I traveling by subway ever?

When I was a child, I made up events as if I were in the midst of them, turned them into stories in my mind, casting myself in the heroic role. Once waiting at Garfinckel's for my mother to try on suits, I spotted a child hiding under the dress racks. I imagined the kidnapper of the Lindberg baby in the dressing rooms, waiting for the child's mother to move out of sight so that he could whisk the little girl away. In the nick of time, I warned the mother and pulled the child, chewing Juicy Fruit, from under the dress rack.

"That didn't happen," my mother told me in distress as we drove home from Garfinckel's.

"Yes, it did," I said. "I was there. You were in the dressing room."

"You made it up," my mother went on.

"I think it happened," I said. "Anyway I did find the little girl in the nick of time."

"She tells lies," my mother told my father at dinner time, her sadness absolute.

"She exaggerates," my father said.

"Whatever," my mother said, exasperated. "She doesn't tell the truth."

Even now my mother will telephone about a book of mine she's reading.

"Look at page 96," she'll say. "Aunt Lucy doesn't drink too much. She's going to be furious."

"The woman on page 96 isn't Aunt Lucy," I say. "I made her up."

"She has lavender hair," she'll insist. "What other woman do you know with lavender hair?"

I was rigorous about honesty when I was growing up. I never cheated in school, or stole Lifesavers from G. C. Murphy's, or lied regarding my whereabouts when I skipped classes, or blamed another child in the class for my own not infrequent misbehavior. I knew hypocrisy in myself and others as though it were painted turquoise. But even when I was small, invention seemed to me as true as the facts of things, sometimes truer because it showed the facts for what they were.

I went to a Quaker school in Washington, D.C., and in my last years there, post-McCarthy and the 1954 Supreme Court decision on integration, amidst the liberal whisperings of the next era, the senior class spent hours in small, earnest groups discussing issues.

"My uncle came over last night," one boy said in the senior shack, "and we discussed the crisis in the Middle East."

"We have on-going debates every night after dinner," another girl said, "about the conflict between science and religion. It can be incredibly tense."

Another claimed to spend hours talking with his father about civil rights and the nature of God and the influence of Puritan morality on the twentieth-century state of mind.

I was at a loss. Dinner was not a serious occasion at our house. It was important to have good food and tell good stories. It was important to laugh a lot and accept with grace stories told by others at your expense. There were often unimpressive guests. A painter who left a life-sized nude and life-sized Lincoln in our attic, who changed his name from time to time if he found a new one in the obituaries. An exquisite woman, a former actress, with her great dane, who drank herself to death after my father died. A black man given to the occasional shooting of his relations, for whom my father created jobs at our house whenever he was fired from a proper job my father had found him downtown. These were regulars, but there were others in and out who stayed for dinner and sometimes didn't leave for days. My father had a deep affection for decent people down on their luck—not the usual hand licking variety who wander woefully from one free meal to the next, but odd people and good ones who simply did not get on well in the world as it is arranged.

It was not, however, a group for intellectual discussions in the parlor after supper.

"Other people in our class have real conversations at dinner," I told my father one night. "They learn something."

"What would you like to learn about?" my father asked.

"For example today at lunch we were talking about civil rights and were there intrinsic differences between blacks and whites?"

"You're worried because we're not a thinking family," he said without appropriate concern.

The painter was there that night and the woman with the great dane called Zelda. My brother sat at the table carefully collecting his supper in a linen napkin and Jimmy was there on parole, having recently made the front page of the *Post* after major difficulties with his wife.

I knew the story my father told that night because it was true and I had been there when it happened.

At the end of the war, my parents bought a farm in Vienna, Virginia, then rural and Southern. The farm included three tenant farmers with piles of children, crops and animals tended by the black families who had lived there under owner protection, barely paid for generations, a not uncommon post-slavery arrangement.

My father was a Northerner, a midwesterner from that vast central expanse between the oceans, peopled by ordinary Protestant farmers of moderate disposition who grew up in small towns knowing a handful of Jews, some Catholics and one or two black families; a score of Polish jokes. They believed in democracy the way fundamental Christians believe in Genesis. He left home at seventeen, but you don't leave everything behind.

My father set about treating those tenant farmer decently, to show the other white southerners in farms around what democracy was all about. He paid the farmers equal wages, had them to supper, to sit at the table with us, and even I knew they weren't comfortable taking meals in our dining room. He went down to their places and played poker, had their children up to play with me. Nobody in the village said much, but one woman warned my mother at the market that trouble was afoot, she'd heard from Mrs. Able at Bailey's Crossroads.

"The neighbors are hoping for trouble," my father said.

On the Fourth of July, my father butchered a pig who had grown so fat he had to be cut out of his pen. From the back porch of the house I watched him shoot the pig and cried for the sweet pig and for my father who had to shoot him.

When my father came back to the house, he told my mother it had taken all the ammunition that he had to kill that pig.

That night after supper we heard shots, same as the ones I'd heard when the pig was shot, and shortly afterwards the women and children from the houses on the farm streamed into our kitchen, full of bruises, spilling blood on the floor.

"They're going to kill us," they said. "They've beaten us," "They're crazy with drink," and my little friend, Janie, wrapped her arms around my mother's white skirt, striping it like candy cane.

My father bolted the door, turned out the lights, and sat on a chair with the empty, pigshooting rifle across his knee. The men came soon.

"Let them go," they shouted at my father.

"Not on your life," my father shouted back.

"We'll kill you if you don't."

"I'll shoot the first one who walks through this door," my father said.

They must have known he had an empty gun. They had been with him when he shot the pig. In fact the gun belonged to one of them.

My mother called the police. They said they wouldn't come.

"That's not our job," they said.

"Not even when there are guns?"

"Let the women and children go," the officer said.

"They'll be killed," my mother said.

"They won't be killed, but you ought to know it's not your business anyway," he said.

"Let them go," my mother said to my father when she put down the phone.

"Those men are drunk," my father said. "They could kill someone."

"It's not our business," my mother said, and she unbolted and opened the back door, motioned to the women who filed out of the dark kitchen into the silver light of evening and their men.

No one was killed. Contrite, my father sat in the chair at his bedroom window all night watching the houses where the farmers lived which were quiet until dawn.

"Some civil rights discussion," I said later to my brother, but he was not sympathetic.

When I grew up in Washington, it was a small, sleepy Southern town, populated largely by people whose allegiances were elsewhere. There was an "old Washington" whose children attended Episcopalian schools and dancing classes, who went to law school and practiced in respectable firms, but their lineage was political as well—defeated or retired senators who could not leave the town and stayed after their terms were up. The rest of us came to Washington because our fathers were elected or got someone else elected or were good as well as noted at what they did.

I wanted to be famous. It was not a pipe dream. It seemed that everyone I knew was famous or had been famous once.

It was a segregated city in the years I was in school. White families, even Northerners like ours, had 'live-ins' at little cost, and Lula lived with us for years; often her children lived with us as well. She was a college-educated black woman who could not get a federal job in post-war Washington. I spent weekends with her as the only white child at a black movie theatre or birthday party or chicken supper at the Baptist Church.

I went to a school noted for its liberal education, its respect for individual rights, its tolerance of alien points of view. Nixon's children went there. So did the children of one of the most reactionary senators from the South. The school turned down the children of Ralph Bunche because they were black. As a young girl, I was aware of paradox, and so were most of those with whom I grew up. I didn't have unquestioned faith in anything except my family. Nothing was absolute. A man like Senator

Joseph McCarthy rose and fell like an erupted volcano in a few short years of my adolescence.

Children of Power is a story which takes place in seven days in 1954 about a group of children who persecute the daughter of a Chairman of the F.C.C. for his protection of a defeated Senator McCarthy.

I wanted to write a book about Washington which was not political, but had to do with power as the basis of exchange. I had left Washington when I was seventeen, post-McCarthy, had lived all over this country and Europe and returned with my children to live in Washington, post-Watergate. I had a feeling coming home that I hadn't realized the expectations of my childhood, that I hadn't done much and wasn't ready to return to the town of superlatives where everyone wants to be the "brightest" and the "best."

One of the things, however, that characterizes Washington and the country as well is mediocrity, a paring down, a filing away of distinctions, the melting pot.

McCarthy interested me because he did terrible things and was well-liked by people who knew him. We let him get away with what he did. We have a tendency in this country, perhaps because of our great size and wealth, to make giants of our villains and heroes. Nothing short of Paul Bunyan will do.

I am struck by the violence here, the odd juxtapositioning of violence and freedom in a land, as Gatsby saw it, nearly equal to a man's capacity to dream. I grew up with cowboy movies, first voted in the election that began the decade of assassination. My mother told me when she was sixty that I had lost more friends than she had by double at least—first to automobiles and then suicide. One of my classmates killed a black woman at a debutante party. Another killed his wife.

When I was in high school I went to a party at Karla Hennings' house in Georgetown, and someone had hung a dead cat on the front door of Senator Hennings' house in the posture of crucifixion. When I started *Children of Power*, I thought of that cat and what its being there on the senator's front door suggested about our growing up. All of our growing up. Not just the children of Washington.

When Karla Hennings grew up, she married John Dean. I saw them once at a visit to the obstetrician. Probably in part, I wrote this book because Karla Hennings and I were together at the doctor's office, young wives with a short history, round-bellied with our first sons.

My father wanted to be a fiction writer.

"He was a fine non-fiction writer," my mother has told me, "but not much good at fiction." And that may be true. It is also true that he was a fatherless boy who came of age at the end of the Depression, and he would have been crazy to be a fiction writer. He wanted to make money and eat well and ride in taxicabs. I did all that while I was growing up.

I didn't write fiction while my father was alive. Perhaps it is true that I was only free to write after my father died. It is also true that in the manner of families, my parents set me up in this business; I have inherited my father's shop, passed from father to child with the responsibility for maintaining its essential character in changing times.

"How I Started to Write"

CARLOS FUENTES (1928–)

Before Panamanian-born Carlos Fuentes's distinguished career as a novelist, playwright, and critic, he served in several important positions in Mexican government and higher education. A lifetime of fiction, including the novels *Terra Nostra* (1976) and *Diana, the Goddess Who Hunts Alone* (1995), have earned him some of the most distinguished awards in world literature, and his criticism and nonfiction, including writings on human rights and Latin American politics, have been recognized by honorary degrees from Cambridge University, Georgetown University, and Dartmouth College, among others. Fuentes currently teaches at Brown University. The following essay is from his *Myself and Others* (1988).

As a young Mexican growing up in the U.S., I had a primary impression of a nation of boundless energy, imagination, and the will to confront and solve the great social issues of the times without blinking or looking for scapegoats. It was the impression of a country identified with its own highest principles: political democracy, economic well-being, and faith in its human resources especially in that most precious of all capital, the renewable wealth of education and research.

Franklin Roosevelt, then, restored America's self-respect in this essential way, not by macho posturing. I saw the United States in the thirties lift itself by its bootstraps from the dead dust of Oklahoma and the gray lines of the unemployed in Detroit, and this image of health was reflected in my daily life, in my reading of Mark Twain, in the images of movies and newspapers, in the North American capacity for mixing fluffy illusion and hard-bitten truth, self-celebration and self-criticism: the madcap heiresses played by Carol Lombard coexisted with the Walker Evans photographs of hungry, old-at-thirty migrant mothers, and the nimble tread of the feet of Fred Astaire did not silence the heavy stomp of the boots of Tom Joad.

My school—a public school, nonconfessional and coeducational—reflected these realities and their basically egalitarian thrust. I believed in the democratic simplicity of my teachers and chums, and above all I believed I was, naturally, in a totally unselfconscious way, a part of that world. It is important, at all ages and in all occupations, to be "popular" in the United States; I have known no other society where the values of "regularity" are so highly prized. I was popular, I was "regular." Until a day in March—March 18, 1938. On that day, a man from another world, the imaginary country of my childhood, the President of Mexico, Lázaro Cárdenas, nationalized the holdings of foreign oil companies. The headlines in the North American press denounced the "communist" government of Mexico and its "red" president; they demanded the invasion of Mexico in the sacred name of private property, and Mexicans, under international boycott, were invited to drink their oil.

Instantly, surprisingly, I became a pariah in my school. Cold shoulders, aggressive stares, epithets, and sometimes blows. Children know how to be cruel, and the cruelty of their elders is the surest residue of the malaise the young feel toward things strange, things other, things that reveal our own ignorance or insufficiency. This was not reserved for me or for Mexico: at about the same time, an extremely brilliant boy of eleven arrived from Germany. He was a Jew and his family had fled from the Nazis. I shall always remember his face, dark and trembling, his aquiline nose and deep-set, bright eyes with their great sadness; the sensitivity of his hands and the strangeness of it all to his American companions. This young man, Hans Berliner, had a brilliant mathematical mind and he walked and saluted like a Central European; he wore short pants and high woven stockings, Tyrolean jackets and an air of displaced courtesy that infuriated the popular, regular, feisty, knickered, provincial, Depression-era little sons of bitches at Henry Cooke Public School on Thirteenth Street N.W.

The shock of alienation and the shock of recognition are sometimes one and the same. What was different made others afraid, legation parquet, even if the Angel Gabriel had announced me as a future Mexican writer of some, albeit debatable, merit.

So if I could not be born in a fictitious, extraterritorial Mexico, neither would I be born in that even more fictitious extension of the United States of America, the Canal Zone, where, naturally, the best hospitals were. So, between two territorial fictions—the Mexican legation, the Canal Zone—and a mercifully silent close-up of John Gilbert, I arrived in the nick of time at the Gorgas Hospital in Panama City at eleven that evening.

The problem of my baptism then arose. As if the wasters of the two neighboring oceans touching each other with the iron fingertips of the canal were not enough, I had to undergo a double ceremony: my religious baptism took place in Panama, because my mother, a devout Roman Catholic, demanded it with as much urgency as Tristram Shandy's parents, although through less original means. My national baptism took place a few months later in Mexico City, where my father, an incorrigible Jacobin and priest-eater to the end, insisted that I be registered in the civil rolls established by Benito Juárez. Thus, I appear as a native of Mexico City for all legal purposes, and this anomaly further illustrates a central fact of my life and my writing: I am Mexican by will and by imagination.

All this came to a head in the 1930s. By then, my father was counselor of the Mexican Embassy in Washington, D.C., and I grew up in the vibrant world of the American thirties, more or less between the inauguration of Citizen Roosevelt and the interdiction of Citizen Kane. When I arrived here, Dick Tracy had just met Tess Truehart. As I left, Clark Kent was meeting Lois Lane. You are what you eat. You are also the comics you peruse as a child.

At home, my father made me read Mexican history, study Mexican geography, and understand the names, the dreams and defeats of Mexico: a nonexistent country, I then thought, invented by my father to nourish my infant imagination with yet another marvelous fiction: a land of Oz with a green cactus road, a land-scape and a soul so different from those of the United States that they seemed a fantasy.

A cruel fantasy: the history of Mexico was a history of crushing defeats, whereas I lived in a world, that of my D.C. public school, which celebrated victories, one victory after another, from Yorktown to New Orleans to Chapultepec to Appomattox to San Juan Hill to Belleau Wood: had this nation never known defeat? Sometimes the names of United States victories were the same as the names of Mexico's defeats and humiliations: Monterrey. Veracruz. Chapultepec. Indeed: from the Halls of Montezuma to the shores of Tripoli. In the map of my imagination, as the United States expanded westward, Mexico contracted southward. Miguel Hidalgo, the father of Mexican independence, ended up with his head on exhibit on a lance at the city gates of Chihuahua. Imagine George and Martha beheaded at Mount Vernon.

To the south, sad songs, sweet nostalgia, impossible desires. To the north, self-confidence, faith in progress, boundless optimism. Mexico, the imaginary country, dreamed of a painful past; the United States, the real country, dreamed of a happy future.

The French equate intelligence with rational discourse, the Russians with intense soul-searching. For a Mexican, intelligence is inseparable from maliciousness—in this, as in many other things, we are quite Italian: *fuberia,* roguish slyness, and the cult of appearances, *la bella figura,* are Italianate traits present every-where in Latin America; Rome, more than Madrid, is our spiri-tual capital in this sense.

For me, as a child, the United States seemed a world where intelligence was equated with energy, zest, enthusiasm. The North American world blinds us with its energy; we cannot see our-selves, we must see *you.* The United States is a world full of cheer-leaders, prize-giving, singin' in the rain: the baton twirler, the Oscar awards, the musical comedies cannot be repeated else-where; in Mexico, the Hollywood statuette would come dipped in poisoned paint; in France, Gene Kelly would constantly stop in his steps to reflect: *Je danse, donc je suis.*

Many things impressed themselves on me during those years. The United States—would you believe it?—was a country where things worked, where nothing ever broke down: trains, plumbing, roads, punctuality, personal security seemed to function perfectly, at least at the eye level of a young Mexican diplomat's son living in a residential hotel on Washington's Sixteenth Street, facing Meridian Hill Park, where nobody was then mugged and where our superb furnished seven-room apartment cost us 110 pre-inflation dollars a month. Yes, in spite of all the problems, the livin' seemed easy during those long Tidewater summers when I became less of what was different than of themselves, of their own incapacity to recognize themselves in the alien.

I discovered that my father's country was real. And that I belonged to it. Mexico was my identity yet I lacked an identity; Hans Berliner suffered more than I—headlines from Mexico are soon forgotten; another great issue becomes all-important for a wonderful ten days' media feast—yet he had an identity as a Central European Jew. I do not know what became of him. Over the years, I have always expected to see him receive a Nobel Prize in one of the sciences. Surely, if he lived, he integrated himself into North American society. I had to look at the photographs of President Cárdenas: he was a man of another lineage; he did not appear in the repertory of glossy, seductive images of the salable North American world. He was a mestizo, Spanish and Indian, with a faraway, green, and liquid look in his eyes, as if he were trying to remember a mute and ancient past.

Was that past mine as well? Could I dream the dreams of the country suddenly revealed in a political act as something more than a demarcation of frontiers, on a map or a hillock of statistics in a yearbook? I believe I then had the intuition that I would not rest until I came to grips myself with that common destiny which depended upon still another community: the community of time. The United States had made me believe that we live only for the future; Mexico, Cárdenas, the events of 1938, made me understand that only in an act of the present can we make present the past as well as the future: to be a Mexican was to identify a hunger for being, a desire for dignity rooted in many forgotten centuries and in many centuries yet to come, but rooted here, now, in the instant, in the vigilant time of Mexico I later learned to understand in the stone serpents of Teotihuacán and in the polychrome angels of Oaxaca.

Of course, as happens in childhood, all these deep musings had no proof of existence outside an act that was, more than a prank, a kind of affirmation. In 1939, my father took me to see a film at the old RKO-Keith in Washington. It was called *Man of Conquest* and it starred Richard Dix as Sam Houston. When Dix/Huston proclaimed the secession of the Republic of Texas from Mexico, I jumped on the theater seat and proclaimed on my own and from the full height of my nationalist ten years, "Viva México! Death to the gringos!" My embarrassed father hauled me out of the theater, but his pride in me could not resist leaking my first rebellious act to the *Washington Star*. So I appeared for the first time in a newspaper and became a child celebrity for the acknowledged ten-day span. I read Andy Warhol *avant l'air-brush:* Everyone shall be famous for at least five minutes.

"The Myth of Blackbirds"

JOY HARJO (1951–   )

> Joy Harjo was born in Tulsa, Oklahoma, and was educated at
> the University of New Mexico and the University of Iowa. Her
> publications include *In Mad Love and War* (1990) and *The
> Woman Who Fell from the Sky: Poems* (1996). Among her hon-
> ors are the Williams Carlos Williams Award, the Delmore
> Schwartz Poetry Award from New York University, the New
> Mexico Governor's Award for Excellence in the Arts, and the
> Lifetime Achievement Award from the Native Writers Circle of
> the Americas. Harjo is a founding board member of the Native
> Arts and Cultures Foundation. She lives in Albuquerque, N.M.
> The poem below first appeared in the *Kenyon Review* in 1991.

The hours we counted precious were blackbirds in the density of Washington.
Taxis toured the labyrinth with passengers of mist as the myth of ancient
love took the shape of two figures carrying the dawn tenderly on their
shoulders to the shores of the Potomac.

We fled the drama of lit marble in the capitol for a refuge held up by sweet,
everlasting earth. The man from Ghana who wheeled our bags was lonesome
for his homeland, but commerce made it necessary to carry someone else's
burdens. The stars told me how to find us in this disorder of systems.

Washington did not ever sleep that night in the sequence of eternal nights.
There were whirring calculators, computers stealing names, while spirits
of the disappeared drank coffee at an all-night café in this city of disturbed
relativity.

Justice is a story by heart in the beloved country where imagination weeps.
The sacred mountains only appear to be asleep. When we finally found the
room in the hall of mirrors and shut the door I could no longer bear the
beauty of scarlet licked with yellow on the wings of blackbirds.

This is the world in which we undressed together. Within it white deer intersect with the wisdom of the hunter of grace. Horses wheel toward the morning star. Memory was always more than paper and cannot be broken by violent history or stolen by thieves of childhood. We cannot be separated in the loop of mystery between blackbirds and the memory of blackbirds.

And in the predawn when we had slept for centuries in a drenching sweet rain you touched me and the springs of clear water beneath my skin were new knowledge. And I loved you in this city of death.

Through the darkness in the sheer rise of clipped green grass and asphalt our ancestors appear together at the shoreline of the Potomac in their moccasins and pressed suits of discreet armor. They go to the water from the cars of smoky trains, or dismount from horses dusty with fatigue.

See the children who became our grandparents, the old women whose bones fertilized the corn. They form us in our sleep of exhaustion as we make our way through this world of skewed justice, of songs without singers.

I embrace these spirits of relatives who always return to the place of power, whatever the outcome in the spiral of beauty. And I particularly admire the tender construction of your spine which in the gentle dawning is a ladder between the deep in which stars are perfectly stars, and the heavens where we converse with eagles.

I guide your hip home to me with my hand which is more than a hand, rather a river of effervescent water. And I am thankful to the brutal city for the space which outlines your limber beauty. To the man from Ghana who loves the poetry of the stars. To the ancestors who do not forget us in the concrete and paper illusion. To the blackbirds who are more than blackbirds. And to you, sweetheart, as we make our incredible journey.

from *Thereafter Johnnie*

CAROLIVIA HERRON (1947–   )

> Washington-born Carolivia Herron graduated from Coolidge
> High School in D.C. and then attended Eastern College (for-
> merly Eastern Baptist College), where she received a B.A. in
> English. She earned an M.A. in English at Villanova University.
> Herron went on to complete an M.A. in creative writing and a
> Ph.D. in comparative English and literary theory from the
> University of Pennsylvania. As a Fulbright Scholar, Herron had
> the opportunity to study in such places as Mexico and Congo.
> She wrote the children's book *Nappy Hair* (1997) based on an
> old family story, and in 1991 she edited the selected works of
> Angelina Weld Grinke for the Schomburg Library of Nineteenth-
> Century Black Woman Writers. The following chapter from
> Herron's *Thereafter Johnnie* (1991) is titled "Faerie Tale." She
> lives in Washington, D.C.

---

*Once upon a time my mother loved my father but my father left
my mother one early morning in February. He left her gifts of
money and jewels but he left. So my mother took the gifts of
money and jewels wrapped them and kept them, wrapped me in
a blanket. My mother put on her hat her coat her gloves she held
me in her arms she came down from the penthouse of the
Washington Hilton. Her heart was broken.*

She finds she rents a room in a house in River Terrace with a
porch that looks toward the Eastern Branch of the Anacostia
River and from there we hear the nearby intersections of roads,
waters, electricity, telephones, bridges of Minnesota Avenue and
Benning Road. She withstands late winter. Snow comes hard late
to Washington City this winter. Her days are one continuous day
within which she steps an ice skater between the walls. Cracking.

Losing balance. Collapsing. Falling upon the frozen floor. She tries to sleep. The blackness beyond the icicles keeps her awake. She lies on her stomach, her elbows bent. Both slightly cupped hands against the mattress. Terror and the soft pillow at her side. My mother, Patricia. A murderer comes, breaking through the lock and shattering the sliding glass door he stalks to her bed and slits her throat. I watch. She raises herself up trying to focus upon him. Nothing. She pulls the comforter around her head. Icicles pierce the air beyond the glass, hung tears. Only it is too cold for tears unless a freezing thing should cry as it died, unless a toss of warm Atlantic seawater should arrive suddenly at Arctica, dropping so late so fast upon Washington City this winter. Icicles gather light into stagnant flame, glance through sparkling glass and white white curtains, icicles clear cold like my own eyes, my white blue eyes in my coal black face looking at my mother my eyes, elongated, distorted, multiplied along the rims of the eaves of the porch imprisoning stalactites of cold vision my eyes, empty, crystal, terrifying eyes, out of blackness. Crystal, as crystal as the polished Venetian glass bird the one my mother loved and broke in her anger once, a frozen crystal river encroaching upon the sea, the sea.

"Daddy, Daddy." As if there is hope. As if he presses his cheek in the warmth between her neck and shoulder. She is delivered up to the altar of sheer absence, given to the white walls who answer her whimpering calls with that exact despair from which her soul cannot recover. "Daddy, Daddy," brown velvet eyes "Daddy, Daddy," I see those brown eyes open on the room, she seeks him upon the wall dust, casts her yearning upon innocent walls, "Daddy!" It can happen, yes, it can happen. Those lovers never to be seen again have returned. They have stomped at last through the doors of the forsaken. There have been knocks on doors. It can happen, "Daddy! Daddy!" and anguish leaps as a stone leaps against the seawall in Cinquetera south of Puerto Escondido on the Pacific of Mexico leaps to her throat, breaks her head, cracks her face, rips through to the sheet, tears holes in the mattress, shredding, unleashing—she leaps from the bed, crashes hard against the wall, her head hard, the wall, the wall, out. Then through the glass porch door groping, groveling the drifted snow on the brown wooden floor of the porch beneath the icicles screams, screams once—brushes off the snow calmly and the dirt, smooths back her hair comes calmly back into the room. She washes her hands, she smooths her hair, she returns to her bed. Some innocent, it is probably some innocent who has been murdered. How much it must hurt to be killed. My mother hears the young, high-pitched wavering cry of a child who casts such a long cry upon the air, it must be that it has been murdered. There have been murderers there have been betrayers who murdered little children burned them up thoroughly drenched them in oil and set fire to them or left them naked on hills to freeze and starve or cracked their unknit skulls upon stone cement or stabbed them or raped them or fed them to wolves. Fed them to the wolves. I have seen the wolves. The wolves come quietly over the frozen Anacostia River. They come at sunrise and eat the children.

River Terrace Apartments. Water. The Potomac River the Eastern Branch the Anacostia River. There are shelves of ice sculpted from frozen mud. The sun is bright mist filling cold air. When the air is so bright it is hard to see. My mother cannot see. Sunmist. The absolute directed act of light upon matter. Sunmist of vision, my mother, the unveiling of objects. There are blank holes in the sidewalk upon which she walks. Her eye focuses on a small white stone. Her eye imagines it on velvet under glass at Dumbarton Oaks Museum. A small white stone the emblem of her enchantment, it means nothing and yet she cannot move another step she cannot move she cannot see. A small white stone singled out as the milestone of the indistinguishable moment beyond which her mind cannot go, no, no further, her mind, no further. This, this is the moment she has been waiting for, my mother. Monomaniacal. Thoroughly insane. Beyond return my mother. She sees a white stone in Dumbarton Oaks Museum under glass and sticky fingered children peering over railings at it. A white stone washed up or down the water courses, deserted remnant of lost oceans, small featureless skull. A white stone on the sidewalk at River Terrace beside the Eastern Branch of the Anacostia River before which my mother falters.

The beauty of torture, the delight of slavery, the joy of being tied up bound down whipped beaten drawn quartered stretched broken into the ground is this—the mind is free. Is this, this, there is no way out, giving up is simplified. With warm flesh in shreds, limbs broken torn, guts lashed slashed hung hooked, body held down trussed up bent over, skin fingernails toenails stripped off, breasts cheeks ears eyes stuck stung pierced, feet palms knees elbows shaved and shaved again to the bone, limbs pinned open spread askew separated detached, genitals mauled, split, sliced, eliminated it's easy, so easy, so finally and absolutely easy. It must be endured. In such extremity the impulse toward life, living, is uncomplicated, smooth with minimal variation. It simply must be endured. That is all. It must be endured. There is no escape. There is nothing that can be done. The mind can rest. After so much perturbation, so much weighing of possibility, so much consideration of choice, opportunity, alteration, adjustment, coercion, influence, reversal, reconsideration—nothing. Nothing can be done. The mind is free, free, free indeed. Free at last. Released from complications of survival, from the necessity to devise its own release, caught then forever, in flame, tarred and feathered, castrated, raped the mind discovers infinite stillness—there are no decisions to make. It's just like love.

My mother stands on a sidewalk in River Terrace, I am in her arms, she looks down upon an arbitrary white stone. The afternoon light is hard. She wants to go back to her family on Sixteenth Street. She wants to leave Anacostia and return uptown. She wants to see Janie, at the convent. They have all turned from you, my mother. What will you do to save your soul from the terror that slices through sunlight scattering the air the wind the sound of the traffic frightening everything away my mother what will you do what shall we do my mother my mother while the light cuts down so cold against us my mother this terror that will not stand forth clearly in this terrifying light but scatters shatters in the eyes breaking into fragments of glistening ice slivers of light, my mother, lost, holding the scream within your body against me I feel it what shall we do?

Frantic. You cannot stand here looking down at this white stone forever. You must move at last, and when you move what will you do? You do not know how to save your soul. You will die with this unbearable grief around your heart battering at me through your body. I feel it. You are utterly alone except for me, a baby in your arms. You cannot go home. If you could only receive enough sun inside your chest my mother, you could be a princess, you could dance in a golden skirt and your heart would not be broken. Your heart is broken.

And maybe after a while you could learn to do other things, my mother. You could learn to play tennis or swim or drive a car. And what if you really do belong in the world after all and the prophecy is wrong that says you must lose your soul? Why should you lose your soul? Why does so much horror lie upon you? Why don't you give up and live? like my Aunt Sister Cynthia Jane and my Aunt Eva? Why should you be daemonic with dreams and prophecies? You don't want to die, you want to go home.

Janie, Janie with the other nuns doesn't think of Joseph. She has Mary and Jesus, she doesn't need Joseph. He was a lonely boy to grow up and marry God's wife and daughter, Joseph, the visionary sinner, king of adulterers, avenger. Incest. He thought he was chosen, he was a child pariah, brooding, skulking against the walls of the temple when they spoke of the hope of Israel. He thought he was the one. He thought the sunlight was on him.

Later, nauseated, in his trade, wondering, wood shavings sifting through his fingers with thoughts, he saw the virgins passing his door, Mary. What of Joseph? Patricia, my mother hates the world and does not want to be in it. Hated. Did not want to be in it. And I am tired. I have been telling and telling to you this story from Washington City and I don't know where I am. Where is Washington City? What has happened? Why can I not see? Is it a flood that has washed away the city and am I caught behind a flood that has washed away and dried? I? Am I speaking from the depth of the sea, or has the sea receded and do I speak from a dark box cast up upon drying sand? Is there sand where everything was? Where is the place where my mother and I walked before I came to this dark marble box? I will not see them again, my people, Washington. So solitary, that was once full of people.

I am telling a story the story of my mother's look and her loveliness and me. When she woke up to me for my mother it was like falling asleep.

Once upon a time
Once upon a time my mother loved my father but my father left my mother one early morning in February. He left her gifts of money and jewels but he left. So my mother took the gifts of money and jewels wrapped them and kept them, wrapped me in a blanket. My mother put on her hat her coat her gloves she held me in her arms she came down from the penthouse of the Washington Hilton. Her heart was broken. She found she rented a room in a house in River Terrace while winter ended. She took a cab to Diotima in Eastland Gardens. Diotima once at the Benning Heights Community Center once when I was held within my mother's body Diotima had been kind. My mother found her again after I left my mother's body they drank tea while Diotima fell in love with my mother and my mother did not fall in love with Diotima.

Diotima looks from her window in Eastland Gardens. We are coming. What is it? A branch budding quietly? We are coming. The cab bringing us moves as a glittering sliver between slices of light, thin, substanceless as a curve of dust in the slant of a venetian blind, or protruding light through a tear in a curtain, or sheer light. We are coming. My mother stands with the sun in her face, holding me, stricken, Pietà reversed, the stricken mother over the grieving child who is me.

Diotima enters the room bringing tea a steaming teapot two cups a bronze tray. Diotima steps upon the floor mats, they flatten beneath her steps and lift back. Diotima sits across the table from my mother. My mother leans against a large pillow, white with small orange flowers.

A flickering speck at the edge of vision. A branch budding quietly. It is spring.

A tea leaf floats a slow circle in my mother's cup. My mother moves her hand almost plucks out the speck, a torn tea leaf does not pluck it out, lifts the cup instead. The screens between the rooms are beige with gold leaves. The leaves are raised as in brocade. The light in the room is sharp, the light leaves my mother and me in shadow. The crystal table takes fire from the light, Diotima floats in brightness and shade. She is not beautiful as my mother is beautiful. Mottled light waves on the screen behind Diotima, and where the screen has been left open the shadows, tree shadows, limbs, dance on the woven mats.

A flickering speck at the edge of vision. What is it? A branch budding quietly?

Diotima turns her eyes between mother and child. Touch, Diotima, touch the rich color of my skin, caress, only a flicker of fingers on hand my mother's hand, your fingers caress, but touch the rich color of my skin black dark black coal black night black ebony black polished black anthracite black pearl black midnight black tar black macadam black onyx black touch, but caress my mother the desert color, sand beige dry, and with the circled fluff of hair gentle, gently touch her, my chill, freezing, not burning but frozen desert mother.

"I thought I would return to my family by now. I thought this would not be long. Now I know they will not take me back. My father has given me money and ordered me to leave Washington, to leave the United States in fact. He feels that as long as I am anywhere near him I will hurt his career as a doctor. He says I destroy his skill by needing him too much. I shall never leave. I've been studying where to hide here in Washington, I've decided on Georgetown. Help me, Diotima, please help, I can buy a house in your name. He won't find me. I cannot leave Washington."

"Buy a house in Georgetown? But what about black folks? In Georgetown the black people are almost all gone. We would be alone and what if your father or one of your father's patients should see you there anyway? To hide from him you won't be able to go out. They would recognize you. You would never be able to go out at all. You would be so sad. And you would get sadder."

"Yes, I know, yes, I've looked at it, I want it. I need rest, I need to rest for a while. In Georgetown there is space with no one in it, there is no one I know nobody I recognize and no real D.C. black people, in Georgetown the Potomac River is calm, I can rest with Johnnie, and with you Diotima if you help me. We can buy a house I could stay there with a window with the Potomac River a soft chair gold velvet and rest my sadness in peace."

"But Georgetown! Georgetown. I've never wanted to live away from a black community. I never have, ever since I left Mexico and came here and had to live around gringos, in Mexico we blacks were just Mexicans like everybody else, my father couldn't take it here and went back. White people up here don't want us in Georgetown and why should we want them? Why can't you live here? There's Anacostia, Kenilworth, Eastland Gardens, Deanwood, Parkside, Mayfair, Capitol Heights, River Terrace, Langston, Benning Heights, there are so many neighborhoods for us here."

"I can't stay here, Diotima, I'm going to leave Anacostia I hate Anacostia, I hate Kenilworth, I hate Eastland Gardens and Deanwood and Parkside and Mayfair, how I hate Capitol Heights and River Terrace and Langston and Benning Heights, I hate Anacostia. My mother grew up in Kenilworth everybody who has ever known me walks through Kenilworth all the time, my family is known too much around here and I can't stay here.

"I'll live in Georgetown Diotima where nobody ever hurt me I was never hurt in Georgetown I want a place in Georgetown as far as I can get west in Washington as Anacostia is east. I want a tall house on the Potomac my father has given me money I could be there you and me and Johnnie all three of us. I've thought and thought. We can do it. Let's get away from here. Let's get away from the Eastern Branch. Let's get ourselves together and go hid-

den above the river and send out for everything. Every afternoon
Johnnie and I will walk by evening by night by fog by the water
by the Potomac. In the winter you and me and Johnnie will
gather ourselves in from the cold. We will have a fireplace. I'll
have a place to rest my sadness." She stands. My mother stands
up with me clutched in her arms.

"He has made me swear I shall leave the country he doesn't
want me here I shall not leave the country or the city the money
is contingent upon my departure you could help me with your
family in Mexico you could divert the money he won't know
where I am. Help me, Diotima, help me, help me. We must find
things to fill our house, we must find furniture and dishes and
rugs and the chair, the golden velvet chair I want so much, I
want to sit in it Diotima, I want to sit in it right now and when
I look out of the window I don't want to look at Anacostia, no,
never, I hate it here, let me get free let me go let me out of here
and everybody who's not here is up on Sixteenth Street or North
Portal Estates I've got to get out of here Diotima help me, help
me Diotima we have to move we have to move fast get the house
ready fast it's April I have to be there fast, fast the house must be
bought and prepared and filled before autumn Diotima I'm telling you you've got to help me please help me Diotima. Diotima.
Help me Diotima." Her language halts, the flow cuts off, then
softly, "I can do it, we can do it, believe me, help me."

My mother pauses. Pauses again. Diotima is afraid. What is it?
What has happened? Diotima looks at my mother's entranced
suffering body. I am forgotten, cramped in one arm, the left arm,
while she lifts her right hand in a gesture rising in repudiation, a
gesture with which to cast off all relationship, a blue satin cloth
in that hand, presumably for me but not mine, not mine, blue
satin sky and her right hand rising in a gesture that is her signature, higher against that sky, no, no I won't have it I don't want
it I shall not take it if you force me to live I will tear it down, that
gesture of utter repudiation what does it portend my mother? "I
do not want it, Diotima. I want no part of this world. I shall
have no part of this place. This Anacostia. Let me get to a place

another place where this place this Anacostia this Kenilworth this Mayfair this Eastland Gardens becomes the other place, that place, another place where I am not, where I never come. I shall not be a part of this ground. I will not live as it lives. I repudiate it and I ask you to come with me away Diotima," her lovely hand her beige brown arm lifted upon the pale blue sky of the cloth held high casting away the clouds of heaven my mother my beautiful mother in horror as she holds me against her beige marble breast, a sculptor's breast, smooth, perfect, classic, the curve of her legs beneath swirled lavenders and blues for spring, spring swirling within the eyes of Diotima, my mother's exhausted arm uplifted, held, my mother, Diotima, their eyes meet and Diotima stands up. In that silence. "What has happened? What is so wrong? What has made you so unhappy?"

"Yes, you see, I'm probably insane. But I must hide somewhere . . . he has almost killed me. I don't have a home. My head hurts I've been raving all the way let me have my house."

Once upon a time my mother loved my father but my father left my mother one early morning in February. He left her gifts of money and jewels but he left. So my mother took the gifts of money and jewels wrapped them and kept them, wrapped me in a blanket.

My mother put on her hat her coat her gloves she held me in her arms she came down from the penthouse of the Washington Hilton. Her heart was broken. She found she rented a room in a house in River Terrace while winter ended. She took a cab to Diotima in Eastland Gardens. Diotima once at the Benning Heights Community Center once when I was held within my mother's body Diotima had been kind. My mother found her again after I left my mother's body they drank tea while Diotima fell in love with my mother and my mother did not fall in love with Diotima. Then we all moved to Georgetown and after a while they deserted me and escaped into death and homecoming, and I, I alone, lived unhappily forever after within the struck diamond of Washington City.

"Marie"

EDWARD P. JONES (1951–   )

Edward P. Jones grew up in Washington, D.C., and was educated at the College of the Holy Cross and the University of
Virginia. *Lost in the City* was nominated for the National Book
Award in 1992, and his novel *The Known World* received the
2004 Pulitzer Prize for Fiction and the International IMPAC
Dublin Literary Award. His novel *All Aunt Hagar's Children*
was published in 2006. Jones is a professor of creative writing
at George Washington University. The following story first
appeared in the *Paris Review* in 1992.

The next appointment was two weeks later, 8:30, a good hour,
and the day before a letter signed by John Smith arrived to remind
her. She expected to be out at least by twelve. Three times before
eleven o'clock Marie asked Vernelle Wise if the man, Mr. Green,
who was handling her case, was in that day, and each time the
woman assured her that he was. At twelve, Marie ate one of the
two oranges and three of the five slices of cheese she had brought.
At one, she asked again if Mr. Green was indeed in that day and
politely reminded Vernelle Wise that she had been waiting since
about eight that morning. Vernelle was just as polite and told her
the wait would soon be over.

At 1:15, Marie began to watch the clock hands creep around
the dial. She had not paid much attention to the people about
her, but more and more it seemed that others were being waited
on who had arrived long after she had gotten there. After asking
about Mr. Green at one, she had taken a seat near the front and,
as more time went by, she found herself forced to listen to the
conversation that Vernelle was having with the other receptionist next to her.

"I told him . . . I told him . . . I said just get your things and
leave," said the other receptionist, who didn't have a nameplate.

"Did he leave?" Vernelle wanted to know.

"Oh, no," the other woman said. "Not at first. But I picked up some of his stuff, that Christian Dior jacket he worships. I picked up my cigarette lighter and that jacket, just like I was gonna do something bad to it, and he started movin' then."

Vernelle began laughing. "I wish I was there to see that." She was filing her fingernails. Now and again she would look at her fingernails to inspect her work, and if it was satisfactory, she would blow on the nails and on the file. "He back?" Vernelle asked.

The other receptionist eyed her. "What you think?" and they both laughed.

Along about two o'clock Marie became hungry again, but she did not want to eat the rest of her food because she did not know how much longer she would be there. There was a soda machine in the corner, but all sodas gave her gas.

"You-know-who gonna call you again?" the other receptionist was asking Vernelle.

"I hope so," Vernelle said. "He pretty fly. Seemed decent too. It kinda put me off when he said he was a car mechanic. I kinda like kept tryin' to take a peek at his fingernails and everything the whole evenin'. See if they was dirty or what."

"Well, that mechanic stuff might be good when you get your car back. My cousin's boyfriend used to do that kinda work and he made good money, girl. I mean real good money."

"Hmmmm," Vernelle said. "Anyway, the kids like him, and you know how peculiar they can be."

"Tell me 'bout it. They do the job your mother and father used to do, huh? Only on another level."

"You can say that again," Vernelle said.

Marie went to her and told her how long she had been waiting.

"Listen," Vernelle said, pointing her fingernail file at Marie. "I told you you'll be waited on as soon as possible. This is a busy day. So I think you should just go back to your seat until we call your name." The other receptionist began to giggle.

Marie reached across the desk and slapped Vernelle Wise with all her might. Vernelle dropped the file, which made a cheap, tinny sound when it hit the plastic board her chair was on. But no one heard the file because she had begun to cry right away. She looked at Marie as if, in the moment of her greatest need, Marie had denied her. "Oh, oh," Vernelle Wise said through the tears. "Oh, my dear God . . ."

The other receptionist, in her chair on casters, rolled over to Vernelle and put her arm around her. "Security!" the other receptionist hollered. "We need security here!"

The guard at the front door came quickly around the corner, one hand on his holstered gun and the other pointing accusingly at the people seated in the waiting area. Marie had sat down and was looking at the two women almost sympathetically, as if a stranger had come in, hit Vernelle Wise, and fled.

"She slapped Vernelle!" said the other receptionist.

"Who did it?" the guard said, reaching for the man sitting beside Marie. But when the other receptionist said it was the old lady in the blue coat, the guard held back for the longest time, as if to grab her would be like arresting his own grandmother. He stood blinking and he would have gone on blinking had Marie not stood up.

She was too flustered to wait for the bus and so took a cab home. With both chains, she locked herself in the apartment, refusing to answer the door or the telephone the rest of the day and most of the next. But she knew that if her family or friends received no answer at the door or on the telephone, they would think something had happened to her. So the next afternoon, she began answering the phone and spoke with the chain on, telling Wilamena and others that she had a toothache.

For days and days after the incident she ate very little and asked God to forgive her. She was haunted by the way Vernelle's cheek had felt, by what it was like to invade and actually touch the flesh of another person. And when she thought too hard, she imagined that she was slicing through the woman's cheek, the way she had sliced through the young man's hand. But as time went on she began to remember the man's curses and the purplish color of Vernelle's fingernails, and all remorse would momentarily take flight. Finally, one morning nearly two weeks after she slapped the woman, she woke with a phrase she had not used or heard since her children were small: You whatn't raised that way.

It was the next morning that the thin young man in the suit knocked and asked through the door chains if he could speak with her. She thought that he was a Social Security man come to tear up her card and papers and tell her that they would send her no more checks. Even when he pulled out an identification card showing that he was a Howard University student, she did not believe.

In the end, she told him she didn't want to buy anything, not magazines, not candy, not anything.

"No, no," he said. "I just want to talk to you for a bit about your life and everything. It's for a project for my folklore course. I'm talking to everyone in the building who'll let me. Please. . . I won't be a bother. Just a little bit of your time."

"I don't have anything worth talkin' about," she said. "And I don't keep well these days."

"Oh, ma'am, I'm sorry. But we all got something to say. I promise I won't be a bother."

After fifteen minutes of his pleas, she opened the door to him because of his suit and his tie and his tie clip with a bird in flight, and because his long, dark brown fingers reminded her of delicate twigs. But had he turned out to be death with a gun or a knife or fingers to crush her neck, she would not have been surprised. "My name's George. George Carter. Like the president." He had the kind of voice that old people in her young days would have called womanish. "But I was born right here in D.C. Born, bred and buttered, my mother used to say."

He stayed the rest of the day and she fixed him dinner. It scared her to be able to talk so freely with him, and at first she thought that at long last, as she had always feared, senility had taken hold of her. A few hours after he left, she looked his name up in the telephone book, and when a man who sounded like him answered, she hung up immediately. And the next day she did the same thing. He came back at least twice a week for many weeks and would set his cassette recorder on her coffee table. "He's takin' down my whole life," she told Wilamena, almost the way a woman might speak in awe of a new boyfriend.

One day he played back for the first time some of what she told the recorder:

> . . . My father would be sittin' there readin' the paper. He'd say whenever they put in a new president, "Look like he got the chair for four years." And it got so that's what I saw—this poor man sittin' in that chair for four long years while the rest of the world went on about its business. I don't know if I thought he ever did anything, the president. I just knew that he had to sit in that chair for four years. Maybe I thought that by his sittin' in that chair and doin' nothin' else for four years he made the country what it was and that without him sittin' there the country wouldn't be what it was. Maybe thas what I got from listenin' to father readin' and to my mother askin' him questions 'bout what he was readin'. They was like that, you see. . . .

George stopped the tape and was about to put the other side in when she touched his hand.

"No more, George," she said. "I can't listen to no more. Please . . . please, no more." She had never in her whole life heard her own voice. Nothing had been so stunning in a long, long while, and for a few moments before she found herself, her world turned upside down. There, rising from a machine no bigger than her Bible, was a voice frighteningly familiar and yet unfamiliar, talking about a man whom she knew as well as her husbands and her sons, a man dead and buried sixty years. She reached across to George and he handed her the tape. She turned it over and over, as if the mystery of everything could be discerned if she turned it enough times. She began to cry, and with her other hand she lightly touched the buttons of the machine.

Between the time Marie slapped the woman in the Social Security office and the day she heard her voice for the first time,

Calhoun Lambeth, Wilamena's boyfriend, had been in and out of the hospital three times. Most evenings when Calhoun's son stayed the night with him, Wilamena would come up to Marie's and spend most of the evening sitting on the couch that was catty-corner to the easy chair facing the big window. She said very little, which was unlike her, a woman with more friends than hairs on her head and who, at sixty-eight, loved a good party. The most attractive woman Marie knew would only curl her legs up under herself and sip whatever Marie put in her hand. She looked out at the city until she took herself to her apartment or went back down to Calhoun's place. In the beginning, after he returned from the hospital the first time, there was the desire in Marie to remind her friend that she wasn't married to Calhoun, that she should just get up and walk away, something Marie had seen her do with other men she had grown tired of.

Late one night, Wilamena called and asked her to come down to the man's apartment, for the man's son had had to work that night and she was there alone with him and she did not want to be alone with him. "Sit with me a spell, " Wilamena said. Marie did not protest, even though she had not said more than ten words to the man in all the time she knew him. She threw on her bathrobe, picked up her keys and serrated knife and went down to the second floor.

He was propped up on the bed, surprisingly alert, and spoke to Marie with an unforced friendliness. She had seen this in other dying people—a kindness and gentleness came over them that was often embarrassing for those around them. Wilamena sat on the side of the bed. Calhoun asked Marie to sit in a chair beside the bed and then he took her hand and held it for the rest of the night. He talked on throughout the night, not always understandable. Wilamena, exhausted, eventually lay across the foot of the bed. Almost everything the man had to say was about a time when he was young and was married for a year or so to a woman in Nicodemus, Kansas, a town where there were only black people. Whether the woman had died or whether he had

left her, Marie could not make out. She only knew that the
woman and Nicodemus seemed to have marked him for life.

"You should go to Nicodemus," he said at one point, as if the
town was only around the corner. "I stumbled into the place by
accident. But you should go on purpose. There ain't much to see,
but you should go there and spend some time there."

Toward four o'clock that morning, he stopped talking and
moments later he went home to his God. Marie continued holding the dead man's hand and she said the Lord's Prayer over and
over until it no longer made sense to her. She did not wake
Wilamena. Eventually the sun came through the man's Venetian
blinds, and she heard the croaking of the pigeons congregating
on the window ledge. When she finally placed his hand on his
chest, the dead man expelled a burst of air that sounded to
Marie like a sigh. It occurred to her that she, a complete stranger,
was the last thing he had known in the world and that now he
was no longer in the world. All she knew of him was that
Nicodemus place and a lovesick woman asleep at the foot of his
bed. She thought that she was hungry and thirsty, but the more
she looked at the dead man and the sleeping woman, the more
she realized that what she felt was a sense of loss.

Two days later, the Social Security people sent her a letter,
again signed by John Smith, telling her to come to them one
week hence. There was nothing in the letter about the slap, no
threat to cut off her SSI payments because of what she had done.
Indeed, it was the same sort of letter John Smith usually sent.
She called the number at the top of the letter, and the woman
who handled her case told her that Mr. White would be expect-
ing her on the day and time stated in the letter. Still, she suspected the Social Security people were planning something for
her, something at the very least that would be humiliating. And,
right up until the day before the appointment, she continued
calling to confirm that it was okay to come in. Often, the person
she spoke to after the switchboard woman and before the

woman handling her case was Vernelle. "Social Security Administration. This is Vernelle Wise. May I help you?' And each time Marie heard the receptionist identify herself she wanted to apologize. "I whatn't raised that way," she wanted to tell the woman.

George Carter came the day she got the letter to present her with a cassette machine and copies of the tapes they had made about her life. It took quite some time for him to teach her how to use the machine, and after he was gone, she was certain it took so long because she really did not want to know how to use it. That evening, after her dinner, she steeled herself and put a tape marked "Parents/Early Childhood" in the machine.

. . . My mother had this idea that everything could be done in Washington, that a human bein' could take all they troubles to Washington and things would be set right. I think that was all wrapped up with her notion of the gov'ment, the Supreme Court and the president and the like. "Up there," she would say, "things can be made right." "Up there," was her only words for Washington. All them other cities had names, but Washington didn't need a name. It was just called "up there." I was real small and didn't know any better, so somehow I got to thinkin' since things were on the prefect side in Washington, that maybe God lived there. God and his people. . . . When I went back home to visit that first time and told my mother all about my livin' in Washington, she fell into such a cry, like maybe I had managed to make it to heaven without dyin'. Thas how people was back in those days. . . .

The next morning she looked for Vernelle Wise's name in the telephone book. And for several evenings she would call the number and hang up before the phone had rung three times. Finally, on a Sunday, two days before the appointment, she let it ring and what may have been a little boy answered. She could tell he was very young because he said hello in a too loud voice, as if he was not used to talking on the telephone.

"Hello," he said. "Hello, who this? Granddaddy, that you? Hello. Hello. I can see you."

Marie heard Vernelle tell him to put down the telephone, then another child, perhaps a girl somewhat older than the boy, came on the line. "Hello. Hello. Who is this?" she said with authority. The boy began to cry, apparently because he did not want the girl to talk if he couldn't. "Don't touch it," the girl said. "Leave it alone." The boy cried louder and only stopped when Vernelle came to the telephone.

"Yes?" Vernelle said. "Yes." Then she went off the line to calm the boy who had begun to cry again. "Loretta," she said, "go get his bottle . . . Well, look for it. What you got eyes for?"

There seemed to be a second boy, because Vernelle told him to help Loretta look for the bottle. "He always losin' things," Marie heard the second boy say. "You should tie everything to his arms." "Don't tell me what to do," Vernelle said. "Just look for that damn bottle."

"I don't lose noffin'. I don't," the first boy said. "You got snot in your nose."

"Don't say that," Vernelle said before she came back on the line. "I'm sorry," she said to Marie. "Who is this? . . . Don't you dare touch it if you know what's good for you!" she said. "I wanna talk to granddaddy," the first boy said. "Loretta, get me that bottle!"

Marie hung up. She washed her dinner dishes. She called Wilamena because she had not seen her all day, and Wilamena told her that she would be up later. The cassette tapes were on the coffee table beside the machine, and she began picking them up, one by one. She read the labels: Husband No. 1, Working, Husband No. 2, Children, Race Relations, Early D.C. Experiences, Husband No. 3. She had not played another tape since the one about her mother's idea of what Washington was like, but she could still hear the voice, her voice. Without reading its label, she put a tape in the machine.

. . . I never planned to live in Washington, had no idea I would ever even step one foot in this city. This white family my mother worked for, they had a son married and gone to live in Baltimore. He wanted a maid, somebody to take care of his children. So he wrote to his mother and she asked my mother and my mother asked me about goin' to live in Baltimore. Well, I was young. I guess I wanted to see the world, and Baltimore was as good a place to start as anywhere. This man sent me a train ticket and I went off to Baltimore. Hadn't ever been kissed, hadn't ever been anything, but here I was goin' farther from home than my mother and father put together. . . . Well, sir, the train stopped in Washington, and I thought I heard the conductor say we would be stoppin' a bit there, so I got off. I knew I probably wouldn't see no more than that Union Station, but I wanted to be able to say I'd done that, that I step foot in the capital of the United States. I walked down to the end of the platform and looked around then I peeked into the station. Then I went in. And when I got back, the train and my suitcase was gone. Everything I had in the world on the way to Baltimore. . . .

. . . I couldn't calm myself down enough to listen to when the red-cap said another train would be leavin' for Baltimore, I was just that upset. I had a buncha addresses of people we knew all the way from home up to Boston, and I used one precious nickel to call a woman I hadn't seen in years, cause I didn't have the white people in Baltimore number. This woman come and got me, took me to her place. I 'member like it was yesterday that we got on this streetcar marked 13TH and D NE. The more I rode, the more brighter things got. You ain't lived till you been on a streetcar. The further we went on that streetcar—dead down in the middle of the street—the more I knowed I could never go live in Baltimore. I knowed I could never live in a place that didn't have that streetcar and them clackety clack tracks. . . .

She wrapped the tapes in two plastic bags and put them in the dresser drawer that contained all that was valuable to her: birth and death certificates, silver dollars, life insurance policies, pictures of her husbands and the children they had given each other and the grandchildren those children had given her and the great-grands whose names she had trouble remembering. She set the tapes in a back corner of the drawer, away from the things she needed to get her hands on regularly. She knew that however long she lived, she would not ever again listen to them, for in the end, despite all that was on the tapes, she could not stand the sound of her own voice.

from *Sisters and Lovers*

CONNIE BRISCOE (1952–)

Washington, D.C.–born Connie Briscoe attended Hampton University and received a master's degree in urban studies from American University in 1978. Briscoe has worked as a research analyst for a computer company and as associate editor for the Joint Center for Political and Economic Studies in Washington. In 1990, she became the first African American, and the first deaf, managing editor of the *American Annals of the Deaf,* a journal for educators of the hearing impaired. Her first book, *Sisters and Lovers,* was published to popular success in 1994. Her following novels, which include *Big Girls Don't Cry* (1996), *A Long Way From Home* (1999), and *Money Can't Buy Love* (2011) assess the experiences and struggles of middle-class black women in America.

Evelyn DuMont turned the silver Mercedes-Benz sedan onto Windmill Lane. She loved the way her new car handled. It felt so luxurious compared to her old Volvo. Not that the Volvo had been a bad car. It had served her well for more than a hundred and fifty thousand miles. But the Benz had so many more luxury features, like leather seats and cruise control. Her job as a psychologist in D.C. was almost an hour's drive from her home in the Maryland suburbs. The Benz made that long commute much more pleasant.

As she approached her house at the end of the block, her eyes fastened on two bicycles sprawled in the driveway behind her husband's Saab. How many times did she have to tell those children not to leave their bikes in the driveway? To put them back in the shed where they belonged when they'd finished riding them. At eight and thirteen years old, they could at least do that much without constantly having to be reminded.

She eased the Benz partway onto the front lawn and shut off the engine. Evelyn lived in one of the hundreds of Maryland subdivisions that consisted of driveways with cars, usually two or more per family, front lawns, usually green and manicured, and big, modern houses rising stately in the background. If Norman Rockwell were painting the typical American suburban scene of the latter decades of this century, this is what would fill his canvas.

She stepped out of the car with her briefcase and walked quickly up the driveway, scanning the block as she always did to see what her neighbors were up to. The Weldons next door had raked their leaves since that morning. She would have to remind Kevin or Andre to be sure to rake theirs this weekend.

She reached the top of the driveway and looked at the house three doors down. Two nights ago it had gone up in flames. Now it stood there, a mass of charred brick and scorched aluminum. She noticed that all the broken glass and other debris had been removed, probably by the insurance company repairing the house. Fortunately, the retired couple who lived there wasn't hurt seriously, although Elvin Johnson had given them all a good scare. His wife managed to escape before the fire trucks arrived, but there was too much smoke to go back for him. Regina stood on the front lawn, her nightgown and bathrobe blowing in the night breeze as she screamed and screamed, calling out to him. The neighbors gathered around and tried to calm her, and it took three of them to keep her from running back into the smoke-filled house to try to save him. The trucks finally came and rescued him and then rushed them off to the hospital. They were released later that night.

From what Louise Levinson across the street had told Evelyn and some of the others last night, Elvin was the cause of the fire. He'd dozed off on the sofa in the family room while smoking a cigarette. Evelyn had no doubt he was still drinking, even though Regina was going around telling everyone he'd quit. That would explain why he'd dozed off with a lighted cigarette in his hand and why he had been so slow to respond. It was exactly the kind of thing that happened when you were careless. The insurance company would pay to have the house rebuilt and for new furniture, but no one would be able to replace all their personal mementos—the family photo albums, the heirlooms, the souvenirs from their travels.

Then there was the problem of appearances. The Johnsons were the only other blacks in the subdivision, and his drinking embarrassed Evelyn to say the least. None of the neighbors said anything about skin color when they gossiped about Elvin Johnson's drinking habits, but Evelyn couldn't help feeling they somehow lumped her family with the Johnsons. Her husband always told her that it was a waste of time to worry about things like that. If anyone was narrow-minded enough to think that way, there wasn't a thing she could do about it. He was right, of course, but that didn't stop her from thinking about it. Well, maybe after this the man would get some help with his drinking problem.

She entered her house from the side door and stepped into the L-shaped country kitchen. One side of it was filled with shiny modern appliances—stove with built-in microwave, refrigerator with ice maker, double sink, dishwasher. The pantry and eating area sat in the other end, beneath a gleaming brass chandelier.

Evelyn was dying to kick off her heels and stretch her tired toes right there on the linoleum floor. Friday was always a long day for her, since she supervised a late therapy session with a group of women. But she would have to keep the shoes on until she got the children to remove their bikes from the driveway so she could park her car. She heard them arguing over the sound of the television in the family room, so she leaned over the stairs until she could just see Andre and Rebecca sitting on the leather couch watching a game show on the fifty-two-inch television screen. They stopped fussing with each other when they heard her at the top of the stairs. "Hi, you two," she said.

"Yo," Andre said, never taking his eyes off the television screen. He had his sneaker-clad feet propped up on the chrome and glass coffee table and was wearing the black leather bomber jacket he'd gotten a month earlier for his thirteenth birthday.

"Mama," Rebecca said, jumping off the couch. She walked around the table to the bottom of the stairs and looked up at her mother. "Andre's hogging the remote control. And he keeps changing the channel." She tossed her older brother a spiteful look. "How are we supposed to watch anything with you flipping the channel every two seconds?"

Andre folded his arms across his chest and sank defiantly into the sofa.

"Right now," Evelyn said, "I don't want to hear about any TV shows from either of you. I'm too tired. Just go put those bikes in the shed where they belong so I can park my car." She turned back toward the kitchen, thinking the matter was settled, but Andre's voice pulled her back to the top of the stairs.

"I'll get to it soon as I finish watching this," he said.

"You'll do it now. And get those feet off my good table. What's the matter with you?"

"Can't we finish watching this first, Mama?" Rebecca asked.

"I thought you didn't even like this show, Rebecca. But nevermind, you know the rules. Bikes in the shed when you finish with them." She clapped her hands at them to show she meant business. "Move. And I mean now."

Rebecca ran all the way up the stairs in less time than it took Andre to remove his high-tops from the table and stand up.

"What are you?" Evelyn teased as he poked along up the stairs. "An old man?"

He shoved his hands into his jacket pockets, and she followed the two of them as they walked into the kitchen. She noticed that the room was spotless, not a dirty dish in sight. That was a sure sign that no cooking had yet been done that evening.

"Have you eaten yet?" she asked.

"Daddy came home early and took us to McDonald's," Rebecca said.

"Oh, no, not that place. Did you start on your homework?"

"I finished mine," Rebecca answered, slipping into her jacket.

Andre reached the screen door and pushed it open. His pace had suddenly picked up a beat, as if he were a cat that had just discovered a dog was on its tail.

"Andre," she called after him. "Did you hear me just ask you a question?"

He paused, holding the screen door halfway open. "I heard you."

"And?"

"I haven't gotten around to it just yet."

"Then after you move your bike and finish watching this one show, go do your homework. You know the rules."

"Aw, Ma. It's Friday. There's this other show I wanted to watch at eight."

Evelyn shook her head. "You have to at least start your homework before TV on Fridays. And that's that."

"Aw, chill out, Ma. It's only on a half hour. The homework's not going anywhere before Monday."

"No, smartmouth. You think your father and I make rules just to have something to do?"

He kicked the door open and was out before Evelyn could say anything more, so she let his cheeky attitude slide. She just shook her head and followed with Rebecca at her side.

After pulling her car into the driveway, she came in and headed up the stairs to the bedroom. It felt good slipping out of her suit and heels and into a pair of jeans and one of her husband's sweatshirts. It drooped over her tall, slender frame, but she loved wearing it around the house because it was so roomy.

She went into the master bath and stood over one of the two sinks to wash the makeup off her face. Not that she wore much, with well-sculpted cheeks and thick eyelashes handed down from her father. Her sisters had them, too. Charmaine's were the prettiest, though, because she also had big almond-shaped eyes like their father. It seemed to Evelyn that Charmaine had gotten the best of about all the physical features, their father's eyes and their mother's shapely figure. Beverly had the best hair, though, thick and wavy like their father's.

She'd inherited the smarts. This hadn't seemed like much of a bargain until she got to graduate school and saw how far brains could carry her. Not that Beverly and Charmaine weren't smart, too. Evelyn just didn't think they used their intelligence as well as they could, especially Charmaine when it came to picking men.

She jumped when she heard a sound from behind her, and a bottle of bath oil toppled over on the marble vanity top. She looked up at her husband's dark brown reflection in the mirror as he stepped up behind her. The thing that had attracted her to Kevin besides his intelligence was his athletic six-foot three-inch frame. In fact, after graduating from Morehouse College in Atlanta, he was recruited by the New York Jets to play wide receiver but never made the team. He wound up taking a job in D.C. and they met shortly after that. She was almost six feet tall, and he was one of the few men she'd dated who was tall enough so that she could wear her heels and still have to look up. He placed his hands on her upper arms and squeezed gently.

"Still as beautiful as ever," he said.

She smiled and set the bottle upright. "You startled me," she said, holding up her cheek for his kiss. "Where were you?"

He planted a warm kiss on her face. "Downstairs in the den, going over some papers."

"Mmm. How was work today?"

He shrugged his shoulders and turned back into the bedroom. "Do you need to ask?" He sat on the edge of the bed and rolled a pencil he was holding across the handmade quilt.

She turned to face him, standing in the bathroom doorway. "I guess I keep hoping your feelings will change again. Just a few months ago you were all excited about that new case you've been assigned to."

"I have my ups and downs."

She walked to the side of the bed and slipped her feet into her bedroom slippers. "The leaves need raking."

"I'll get to it."

"It'll be dark soon. Why didn't you get Andre to do it earlier?"

He shrugged his shoulders. "He had homework to do."

"He wasn't doing any homework, he was watching TV."

"I definitely told them to go do their homework after we ate."

"They're always pulling the wool over your eyes, Kevin, especially Andre. You can't just tell them something and let it go. You have to keep checking on them."

"I know that, but like I said, I got wrapped up in these papers."

"You know as well as I do that if they think they can get out of something, they'll try, especially Andre. I don't know what's going on with him lately. He walks around the house wearing that leather jacket all day and it's like pulling teeth to get him to do his homework. His whole attitude is terrible."

"His grades haven't dropped, have they?"

"No, but he's. . . . You're not going to give me that boys will be boys stuff are you?"

Kevin waved his hand in the air. "The boy's fine. He's going through a phase, that's all."

"Then I hope it's a brief one. I had two sisters, so maybe I just don't know. Did you go through that?"

"Don't remember. Probably."

"Mmm. A lot of help you are." She smacked him playfully on the top of his head and headed for the door. "I'm going downstairs to eat. Is there anything besides that McDonald's food?"

"Some leftover lamb from yesterday, I think."

"Provided Andre didn't beat me to it."

"You got that right." He stood up. "Listen, uh, we need to talk."

She paused in the doorway and turned to face him. "I know."

He looked surprised at first, then he nodded. "I know you don't want to talk about this again but . . ."

"Then don't bring it up."

He smiled reluctantly. "I'm not letting you off that easy."

"That much I figured. Let's go downstairs and talk then. I'm starving."

She looked in the refrigerator for the lamb roast and whatever else she could find. Kevin sat at the table and rested his arms on top, twirling the pencil back and forth between his hands.

"The more I think about this, the better it seems," he said. "We could refinance the house to get our share of the money. But we wouldn't need to use all our equity, just part of it."

"You're not serious? That would be a big extra payment every month, Kevin. And with you not working . . ."

"Working part-time," he said. "I would still work at the firm at least twenty hours a week until we start bringing in clients. Of course, it will take us a while to get to that point. We have to raise the money, find office space, support staff."

"I don't know about this, Kevin." She removed the plate holding the roast and a bowl of salad from the refrigerator and set them on the countertop. "Doesn't look like enough here to make a meal."

"Why don't you eat the fish sandwich and fries from McDonald's?"

"You know I hate that stuff. I'll have to make do with this." She removed a knife from the drawer and turned the plate around, trying to find some meat. "I honestly don't know how one family of four can devour a whole lamb roast in twenty-four hours."

Kevin sat back and folded his arms across his chest. "Can we get back to the subject at hand, please?"

Evelyn took a deep breath. "I still don't get it. I know you've explained it to me, but for the life of me, I just don't understand why you want to leave one of the top law offices in the city to do something as risky as starting your own firm. You just made partner a year ago. They've been good to you."

Kevin twisted his mouth up in disgust. "I wouldn't call their treatment good by a long shot. They've been fair, but they've been a lot fairer to some of those white boys. You know that."

"At least you're a partner. Now you want to give it up, after all that work."

"Nothing compares to having your own firm, Evelyn. I'll be the senior partner."

Evelyn frowned. "Yes, but the senior partner of what? I read an article in *Black Enterprise* just the other day about the top black law firms in the country. There are only a few dozen, and they're all much smaller and bring in a lot less money than the firm you work for. That tells you something right there."

"I saw that. Yes, they're small by comparison. But those firms are doing well enough. A few have thirty to forty partners and associates, with revenues in the millions."

"But your firm has almost two hundred lawyers. Will they even let partners work part-time?"

"I can negotiate something, I'm sure. It'll be less money, of course."

"That's what I know. I don't see how we can pay all our bills and a new loan with you working part-time. The only real money we have saved is Andre and Rebecca's college savings plan. You aren't thinking of using that, are you? Because we can't touch that."

He shook his head. "Of course not. You think I would risk that?"

"You're willing to risk the house."

He dropped the pencil on the table and inhaled deeply, then released the air slowly. "I keep telling you, it's not a risk. I've gone over everything on paper a thousand times the past few weeks. You make enough to cover the bills, with me working part-time. We'll just have to cut back on the extras, like big summer vacations and new things for the house. I wish we had held off on that new car. The Volvo was running fine."

"Now you're ready to take my Mercedes."

"Nobody's talking about selling your car."

"We would have to if we couldn't make ends meet, Kevin. And we wouldn't be able to add to the college fund."

"You keep bringing that up. Andre's thirteen, Rebecca's only eight. We have plenty of time to save for their college educations."

"College costs a fortune these days. And I wasn't going to bring this up, but what about our plans to start saving to buy a bigger house, maybe in Potomac, in a few years?"

"We would still be able to do that. Eventually."

"That's what I mean. It would take forever if we go through with this."

"So what? This house is fine. You thought it was a dream come true when we moved here seven years ago."

Evelyn shrugged her shoulders. "It was then. You had just finished law school and started working at the firm. But it's nothing compared to living in Potomac or Bethesda or some of those places. And now that you've made partner we can afford them."

"You make it sound like we'll be living in poverty for the rest of our lives. It's not like things will be tight forever."

She placed her plate on the table and sat down across from him. "And how long do you think they'll be tight?"

"It's hard to say."

"That's what I know. That's part of the problem."

"A year. Two at the most."

Evelyn shook her head. "It'll be longer than that, Kevin. It takes a very long time to get a law firm going. And that's if it's successful. What if it fails?"

"It won't. Trust me, Evelyn. I'm not going into this blindly. Jeremy and I have looked at everything carefully. We've talked to a couple of others about coming in with us. I know we can make it work."

"And who's this Jeremy?"

"I told you, Jeremy Malone. Another attorney at the firm. Started in June. He was with a firm in Chicago before he moved here. You met him at the office picnic this summer. You don't remember?"

Evelyn frowned.

"He can't be all that hard to remember," Kevin said. "He's the only other black partner in the firm."

Evelyn nodded. "I remember now. How much is he supposed to be putting up?"

"The same as everybody else."

"Well, how much is that? You haven't told me much of anything."

"Only because you haven't seemed interested. Whenever I try to bring it up, you've got a million other things to do."

"Well, I'm listening now."

"If we get four people on board to start, about twenty-five thousand a piece."

"That's an awful lot of money. Is anyone else thinking of getting a second mortgage on their house?"

"Jeremy made some money when he sold his house back in Chicago. He's using that."

"And he's not buying a new one here? How does his wife feel about that?"

"He's divorced. She got her half from the sale of the house."

"Mmm. I just don't understand why you want to do this. Maybe if we were younger and just starting out, but we're not. I don't want to risk everything at this point on some—"

"I told you, it's not a risk."

"You keep saying that, but that's not the way I see it."

"I keep hoping you'll come around. It means a lot to me."

"I know. That's why it's hard for me to just come out and say no."

"Is that your answer—no?"

She looked down at her plate and picked at a slice of tomato with her fork.

He stood up. "Fine." He walked to the back door.

"Where are you going?"

"Out to rake the leaves."

"But it's almost dark now."

"So I'll rake them in the dark." He opened the door and a draft blew across her shoulders.

"You need a sweater," she said.

He didn't say anything, just quietly closed the door behind him. She looked down at the plate of cold lamb and wondered why she wasn't hungry anymore.

"The *Other* Invisible Man"

ESSEX HEMPHILL (1957–1995)

> Chicago-born Essex Hemphill grew up in southeast Washington, D.C. His poetry was published widely in journals, and his essays appeared in the *Advocate* and *Essence* magazines, among others. He received grants from the National Endowment for the Arts and the District of Columbia Commission for the Arts. His poetry appeared in the anthologies *The Poet Upstairs: A Washington Anthology* (1979), *In the Life* (1986), *New Men, New Minds* (1987), *Gay and Lesbian Poetry in Our Time* (1988), *Art Against Apartheid* (1990), and *Men and Intimacy* (1990), and was featured in Isaac Julien's film *Looking for Langston* (1988) and Marlon Riggs's documentary *Tongues Untied* (1988). He is the author of two chapbooks, *Earth Life* and *Conditions* (both 1985), and a collection of poerty, *Ceremonies: Prose and Poetry* (1992); and the editor of *Brother to Brother: New Writings by Black Gay Men* (1991). Hemphill narrated *Out of the Shadows*, a documentary about black gay men living with HIV and AIDS. "The *Other* Invisible Man" is from Hemphill's unpublished autobiography.

I met George by chance in the shy spring of 1975 during my senior year of high school. Had I not been preparing an article for the school news magazine, George and I would never have connected.

Our intimacy began innocently enough. My journalism instructor assigned me to interview the reverend of a local Episcopal church. Under his pastorship, volunteers from the congregation were providing daily meals for the poor and homeless. I phoned the church later that afternoon to schedule an appointment. George answered my call.

His thick baritone voice overwhelmed me. I stammered through my introduction, my purpose for ringing the line. As I explained myself, his breathing sounded as inviting as his supple, leathery voice. I had not felt desire like this even when I was messing around, a few years earlier, with a grocery clerk who was also named George, an older, white homosexual who lived and worked in my neighborhood in Washington, D.C. As this new, brown-like-me George breathed in and out of the telephone, there was nothing for me to clutch, nothing to grasp, no way to resist him. I didn't really want to resist.

When at last I finished my rambling, George politely said, "The reverend isn't in at the moment." I paused. I was becoming increasingly aroused by his soothing baritone. His mellifluous voice lingered long after he ceased speaking. The phone sweated in my hand as I regained the focus of the conversation, which was loping away from me every time he spoke.

I asked could I leave a message and George replied, "Yes, you can." The notes resonated, in my loins and in my imagination. I was called to answer those startling, enticing blue notes. I was called to receive them, to claim them, to own them proudly. I would later discover that this music between men can be sacred, worth fighting and dying for, but at that moment my mind and reasoning weren't in control—my hormones were. I was enchanted and curious. I allowed the liberal hand of pleasure to rule.

After giving George all the necessary information to pass on to the reverend, we lapsed into a momentary silence. Sensing the imminent good-bye, George lowered his saxophone voice a half octave and brashly asked, "Why don't you come on up here and meet *me*?"

I feigned protest, but he pursued me anyway, neutralizing the little resistance I halfheartedly pretended. I wanted very much to meet the man possessing such a voice—a voice offering possibilities I had not yet dreamed of or considered. But I wasn't completely sure. I wasn't convinced of his motives—or my own.

"My name is George—George Hart," he continued, just as I said, "I don't even know your name."

"Well, now you know it. I'm George," he offered again. "Where are you calling from? Home?"

"No, I'm at my part-time job, downtown."

"Where at?" he insisted.

"I work on Seventeenth Street,"

"Near Seventeenth and K?" he asked.

"Yes," I replied.

"You're not too far from the church. You can take the S2 or the S4 uptown and get off at Newton. The bus stop is on Sixteenth Street, a block east of where you are. What time do you get off?" he asked.

"I get off at five-thirty."

"Where do you live?"

"I live in Southeast, off Martin Luther King Avenue."

"Anacostia?"

"No, I live a couple of blocks from Ballou. That's where I attend high school."

I wanted to stop the information from flowing, but I couldn't. Everything he asked me, I answered. Every breath he released, each syllable, every enunciation, beckoned me.

I would be leaving the office in another hour. I considered the possibility of meeting him and getting home by eight. I figured I could call and tell one of my sisters my magazine assignment would delay me. I could then scoot up Sixteenth Street, meet George, race back down Sixteenth, cross the Eleventh Street Bridge, the Anacostia River, and walk in the front door around eight, and not create unnecessary suspicion. That wouldn't be too hard to pull off; I reasoned all the factors suggested that I could.

"So, Mr. Essex, what's your decision?"

He was purring again, coaxing and calling me out. I can hear his breathing even now, as I remember him effortlessly. I considered the risk variables and concluded that the odds were in my favor that I would be relatively safe with him. The possibility of danger could be minimized by agreeing to meet him at the church instead of his apartment.

I was about to meet a black man with a sexy voice, in a church, in a city famous for its churches *and* the black men who reside in the city. Was I excited? Yes! Yes! Yes! Was I overwhelmed?

No. *I* was deciding to take this chance on meeting him, and the thought of being able to do so thrilled me. As much as I was intrigued by George and drawn to him, *I* made the decision to see him. The devil didn't make me do shit, it can't be blamed on my mother's single-parent love, and no gun was placed to my watermelon head to force me into George's bed.

My dick went bone as I sat behind my desk in an office with six black women, who were like aunts or mothers or older sisters to me, advising me and loving me, teaching me some of the ways to be friends with women. They had no idea that at that moment I was getting my life on the office phone. And if they had known it is likely they would have snatched the phone out of the wall and whipped my tail blue with the cord. They cared for me that way, and they wanted to see me succeed in the world. To have discovered me on the phone listening to a man luring me into his arms was not their idea of "success," nor were they any more ready than my own mother to accept an announcement that "I am a homosexual." Had I announced my sexuality then—or, more important, had I possessed the confidence to announce this truth to any of these women—all hell would have broken loose. So, on that fateful afternoon, I began playing more earnestly with masks, adopting new practices of deception that I would eventually, thankfully, discard.

When I later left for college, the women I worked with gave me an ample supply of multicolored condoms as a going-away gift. It tickled them more than it tickled me. I recall their acting so silly and giddy over this particular gift. It implied certain presumptions about my sexuality, and it also conveyed their concern that I be responsible. They fully expected me to use those condoms heterosexually. I recall putting one of those latex socks on and masturbating into it, but I also remember thinking it a rather dull and boring experience.

Now I think how prophetic and wise it was of them to give me protection against risk and infection. I dismissed their gift as simply inappropriate for the person I was becoming—a black male erotically attracted to other males. To my mind, condoms were for preventing pregnancy. They were for males to use with females, and for that reason, the gift was eventually thrown away, not out of ingratitude, but because the condoms weren't useful at the time.

I was then a part-time file clerk at a civil service outpost and a part-time senior high school student with only morning classes to attend. The afternoons belonged to me—or, more specifically, they belonged to Uncle Sam, which allowed me to *earn* money honestly and not flood my neighborhood with drugs and terrorize it with gunfire. In a few months, I would graduate from high school and attend the University of Maryland for a year. But at that moment, I was seventeen—*seventeen*—a clumsy waif of a boy, in possession of raging hormones and an embarrassing erection, listening to the husky breathing of a man named George, a man I imagined I could love, just from the sound of his voice. If my supervisor had needed my attention while I was getting turned on over the telephone, if she had summoned me at that moment from the spell of my sexual enchantment, I would have been unable to rise to her call without exhibiting a complete lack of composure and self-control.

"I will come to visit you—I mean, I will come visit the church," I corrected myself. "Maybe the reverend will have arrived by the time I get there."

"Very good," George enthused. "I look forward to meeting you, Mr. Essex. I anticipate us having a pleasurable meeting."

"Good-bye," I croaked, my mouth and throat cotton dry. I rang off the line and sat hidden behind my desk, I needed to calm down and call home. Yes, I was going to the church. Yes, I wanted to meet George, to see what size and shape of a man he was. I expected him to be tall and broad, upright, older.

And he was. He was all that. He was more than I could have imagined.

I arrived at the church shortly after leaving the office at the end of the day. The bus ride took about twenty minutes. He was right: The church was sitting on the same side of the street as the bus stop when I disembarked at Newton. I entered the church from Sixteenth Street, stepping into a quiet, but noticeably busy, sanctuary. I asked for Mr. Han. I was politely shown down a dimly lit hallway to a small office, where a nutmeg-brown, broad-shouldered man sat crowded behind a fragile desk. He simply overwhelmed it: His hands, his face, his body swelled up over that desk and soon shadowed it, when he rose to shake my hand as the person who'd delivered me to his office departed, leaving the door open.

George stared at me for the longest time. Thick brows waved above his brown eyes. I stared back as intensely, as candidly, taking in his salt-and-pepper mustache and his full crown of salt-and-pepper hair. He was wearing dark trousers, a white shirt open at the collar, and a light gray sports jacket. He was significantly taller than me, and I imagined he weighed at least two hundred pounds. I believe George was cruising into his late forties when we met, although he never told me his exact age.

I could see that his body retained some of its tautness and definition from his youth. I could also see his stomach easing over his waistband to peek down at the tops of his shoes. His jacket constrained obvious arm muscles and an expansive chest. His hands and fingers were thick and strong, capable of beating and punching, but I would never know his hands for those reasons. I would know them only for tenderness, caresses, touching. I would know them as teachers of pleasure, I would watch his hands, so capable of violence, turn the pages of books he would sometimes read to me.

In front of his desk was a chair, which he offered. "Please, have a seat," he suggested, his sound filling the room, changing that small space into a concert hall featuring his voice, which triggered arousal in me at every sibilant octave and every husky pitch.

"Thank you," I replied as I sat appreciatively. Sexual desire crackled through the room, popping and snapping like queens, but I was not frightened. There was no danger. I sensed there would be no harm.

I studied George. Standing before me was a powerful black

man. A man clearly interested in me. His round, moonlike face glistened under a sheer veil of nervous sweat. His solid, thick-boned body seemed so overwhelming, so completely mysterious. I was in awe. I could have been standing in Memphis, and before my eyes flowed the sensuous, secretive Nile, undulating and hypnotic.

George slowly proceeded to tell me about the services the church offered to the surrounding community. This ten-minute explanation allowed him to use his voice to great effect. Masked beneath his intricate intimate detail was a subtext of desire, encoded in his mellow tones and body language.

"Now, let me take you down to the community dining room," he said. "Any person who comes to our door seeking food is fed. We turn no one away. We find a plate, or a bowl, or a cup of something to serve. We feed nearly two hundred people a week. Many single-parent families and elderly people come to us, as well as the homeless. The food is donated and prepared by volunteers from the congregation. For six years—that's how long we've been doing this—and still it's not enough"

"How long have you been working here?" I asked as we rose to leave. Just then an awesome growl let loose loudly from my stomach, rudely interrupting our conversation.

"Are you hungry?" George quickly asked, then smiled with just a bit of slyness. "I can have a plate prepared for you when we get to the dining room."

"No, thank you," I said. "I'll be going home to dinner when I leave. Please, finish telling me about how you came to this church."

"I joined this church eight years ago," he proudly continued. "I immediately volunteered to work in one of the community programs. Prior to this I was a boxer, prancing and pounding my way around the ring. I'd been stepping to fellas since I was sixteen up and down the East Coast. I did come Southern gigs, too. I made a bit of a name for myself. The promoters told me I had promise. I was quick with my hands and my feet, swift with my fists, and graceful. But an automobile accident forced me to give it up. My leg was permanently damaged in that accident. My left leg is mostly made of pins and luck," he said, as he dislodged himself from behind his desk.

I walked out of the office ahead of him, then turned back to watch him catch up to me after he locked the door. He did favor his left leg, with a slight limp that you barely noticed. He smelled of English Leather or Brut—it was difficult to determine the aftershave. He was pleasant in his manner as he showed me around the church, introducing me to some of the volunteers and diners. When we completed our tour, we returned to his office.

"How would you like to see the reverend's office?" he asked.

"Do you think he's in?" I questioned as we left George's office again.

"We can find out right now," he replied.

I followed him a short distance down the hall to an arched doorway with a heavy wooden door filling out the frame. It was a simple door: functional, no unnecessary adornments. It suggested privacy and strength. George took a ring of keys from his jacket pocket, located one from what appeared to be a dozen, and unlocked the door. It creaked open, yawning quietude as we stepped inside.

This room was filled with tall standing cases lined with books. There were a few comfortable-looking chairs, and floor lamps for reading. George ambled the short distance across the room and unlocked and opened a second door. We stepped inside a smaller room, the reverend's private office, and shut the door behind us.

The walls here sagged with religious paintings depicting the Last Supper, Jesus on the cross, the Resurrection. Crucifixes and palm fronds were in evidence. White candles stood on wrought iron holders, like unlit streetlights. Several Bibles of different sizes and colors lay open on top of the desk, like Pandora's boxes. This was the quietest, the most soundproof room in the church. No noise, other than our breathing and our heartbeats, could be heard. The cacophonous eating utensils of the hungry could not be discerned. Only our hunger was now apparent, already the most naked thing between us, louder than gnashing teeth and clashing silver.

"Take down your pants," George suddenly instructed me.

I was startled.

"What?"

"Take down your pants," he repeated. He watched me patiently. I could feel my erection growing again.

"I'm not taking my pants down in here!" I said incredulously.

"I want to suck your dick," he said. "Have you ever had your dick sucked?" He went behind the reverend's huge desk, sat in the creaky chair, there called me to join him.

"I can't do this here," I protested. "What if someone comes? What if the reverend returns?"

"The reverend won't be returning tonight," he interrupted. "Come here," he called to me. "Come here, let me look at you. Come on."

I finally walked over to him, carefully measuring my eager steps. I stood on one side of the reverend's crowded desk and stared across at George, suggestively rubbing his hand in his lap. I could see his crotch bulging and straining like my own.

"Come on," he urged. "This is why you came up here. I could tell you would check me out when I talked to you this afternoon. You know what's going on. You have nothing to fear from me. Come on. Come on over here."

And he was right. I was feeling fearless. I *definitely* knew what was going on. I walked around the desk and stood in front of him, arms akimbo, legs apart.

He rubbed his hands inside my thighs and over my crotch. He rubbed his hands up and down my chest, pinching at my tender nipples, pulling at my tight flesh. I was soon trembling, soon out of control. He unbuckled my pants and pulled them down, along with my undershorts. My dick sprang out in front of us, striking about in the air until he lowered his mouth over it like a net over a panther cub. A sigh escaped my chest and resonated throughout the room like an organ note.

I couldn't believe that only a few hours earlier we had met on the telephone, and now, in the belly of this church, we were fervidly making out, driven on to orgasm and high-spirited ecstasy, driven by the force of different thirsts and different hungers. Behind a locked door in this sanctuary, I was drunk with passion as his hands had their way with me, then I had my way with him.

After we spent ourselves like lottery money, we tidied up in the reverend's private bathroom. George then walked me to a nearby bus stop, but not before writing down his phone number.

"I don't live far from here, but at the moment I share an apartment with my sister. I do have guests over occasionally. Perhaps you'll pay me a visit—soon," he urged, as he handed me the hastily folded slip of paper.

We stepped from the church into a mild, lavender-hued April evening. As we approached the bus stop, he turned to me and asked, "Can I call *you*?"

"I can't give you my phone number at home," I quickly replied. "My mother might suspect something. She doesn't know—"

"She doesn't know *what?*" he interjected.

"She doesn't know I . . . I . . . I like men."

"You mean she doesn't know you're *homosexual*," he corrected me with slight amusement. "My sister doesn't know I chase around after brothers, either," he revealed, "although I sometimes believe she suspects that I do. I haven't found it necessary to tell her. I don't know if she'd understand."

"I may tell my parents," I blurted out. "In time, I might tell them. I've given it some thought, but I have to be sure."

"Think about it carefully before you do," he warned me. "Sometimes families can react very strangely when a son tells them he's homosexual. Not everyone can handle that. They may act like you're supposed to cut that part of yourself off and hide it away. You'll see what I mean. The life will show you many things."

We stepped to the bus stop in silence after these remarks, oblivious to pedestrian and automobile traffic. George's warning would be echoed in subsequent conversations about "the life." I was too inexperienced to understand then that the warnings he uttered were meant for us both, not simply stated to eradicate my naïveté.

"Well, Mr. Essex, I won't pressure you for your phone number. You just be sure to call me. Come back and visit me when you're sure you want to see me."

"I will," I assured him as I boarded the bus headed south into the unfolding twilight.

It didn't matter that I had lied in order to make this evening a reality. The only issue that mattered was that the meeting had been consummated.

When I paid my first visit to George's home, it was clear that the household was struggling to stay afloat—mostly on the income of his sister, I would learn. His residence in the apartment they shared was really an act of sibling kindness. George wasn't ever going to move out on his own, unless he could earn the money to do so on a regular basis. For reasons still unknown to me, George's primary employment seemed to consist of working administration for the church. God was his employer and, materially speaking, meager was his reward.

My involvement with George lasted nearly two years. During that time I learned more than sexual practices from him. By late spring, our time together became planned and frequent. By late spring, I was borrowing my mother's royal blue Dodge sedan to drive uptown from far Southeast to spend a few hours with George. I borrowed the car under pretenses such as needing to go to the library to study.

I *was* studying, but I couldn't explain my subject as clearly then as I now can. From this reflective place in my present life, this place of measured solitudes, I am able to look back and count my many blessings, not to determine how many I have, or how many there have been, but to acknowledge my thankfulness to George, in this instance, for being as interested in my mind and its workings as he was in my then-sweet, coltish body. He demanded pleasure from my intellect with the same intensity I used to demand pleasure from his body. I was hungry to know his mystery, his power. He was also hungry, hungry to know what existed between my ears other than my face and its expressions.

George discussed Shakespeare's plays and Plato's philosophy,

Langston Hughes's poetry and Dr. King's dream. We argued local and national political issues. He read some of my early poems and encouraged me to write more. He never offered me money for my body. He didn't offer me drugs and alcohol. He gave me pleasure at times when I was too selfish to return the same. He gave me pleasure in ways that at times had nothing to do with my body. Eventually, I learned that he ranked training the mind to think and reason over training the body in sexual practices. This didn't disappoint me; it expanded the quality of our interactions.

George loved to read and debate. He loved to discuss the meaning of life in terms particular to his experience but common to every soul faced with the struggle to live and maintain dignity. He was the best-read adult black male I knew at the time, other than my schoolteachers. His mind was a beautiful, stimulating place to visit. His mind had not died the common zombie death that plagues ghettos. His mental faculties were lean and well muscled, as alert and as inquisitive as my own. He nurtured his intelligence in utter contrast to the evidence of poverty that surrounded him.

I told no one of George until after we ended our relationship. In some ways I knew, and he knew, too, that the thirty-odd years between us posed a tremendous barrier, an obstacle our passion could not diminish.

I was fortunate to have met George and to have learned some *real* truth about caring for a man horizontally *and* vertically. Driven by my hormones and my imagination, my horniness was easily exploitable, but George wasn't interested in playing games. I could have been corrupted, but instead, George treated me like a student, an apprentice, a man ultimately responsible for his actions. When he entered my then homo-secret world like a gust of forceful wind, George diverted me from making foolish choices just so my life could be defined as typically black and typically male. He blew all that shit away. He pointed me toward the only acceptance that matters: acceptance of myself. He intervened, not to interrupt my destiny but to take his place in it. His kisses upset the predetermined path that seemed to await me had I adopted the rigid identities a black male is supposed to embrace. I didn't want to strike cool poses on the corner and father numerous children to prove my manhood. I didn't want my anger to disfigure me with various kinds of self-abuse and self-hating behavior. I could not use exaggerated bravado and butch drag to smother my homo yearnings.

George didn't make me feel like a sissy or a punk because I enjoyed reading. He didn't think I was "acting white" because I enunciated clearly and conjugated my verbs. These were defining signs of manhood and intelligence, and George respected both qualities, and to the extent that he could, he nurtured these qualities in me while expanding my sexual knowledge. George understood my curiosities and my fears. He pointed out a different way to me, hinting at others who had gone before us, suggesting a tradition, a history, ways of being.

I was twenty-five years old when I read of George's death, over breakfast one morning. My first live-in relationship was breaking down after three years. My partner and I would make attempts to mend the damage, the wear and tear, but that only temporarily forestalled the inevitable. I can say we were fortunate men; we lived together openly and flagrantly, our families and friends fully aware that we were a gay couple.

I was stunned by the unexpected death notice in the paper, flooded with sudden memories as George gazed at me from the obituary page. He was pictured in a dark suit which made him appear successful, a winner; he looked like a champion, the victor of all his fights. It was clearly an early photo of him; his face was not as weathered as I remembered. I hadn't thought about George in quite a while, consumed as I was with my boyfriend, a military man with a lifetime commitment to the navy but not to me.

George's obituary made me pause and consider heart attacks. Even now, I ask, *What does that mean?* I want to know what exactly attacked his heart and caused him to die. The obituary didn't mention the loneliness for a man's love as a possible accomplice in George's death. The commentary about his life didn't mention the blue note longing for a companion. It didn't say the factors of his death were complicated not only because he was black and male, but complicated because he was also homosexual, which I would later understand to mean he had managed multiple identities oftentimes contentious and contradictory. Each identity was capable of causing him profound pain and profound invisibility. Each mask he wore could put him at risk, even as it served to protect him. He carefully used masks to avoid danger, accusation, discovery. But each false identity was a chosen denial, and the same masks could bring sorrow to his heart without warning. His boxing was the ultimate cover he used, to discount any speculation about his manhood and his sexuality.

George Hart—another black male, another native son, the *other* one, *the* funny one, the *truly* invisible one—dead in America before sixty-five. Whatever really killed him, I knew, was much more complicated, much more insidious, much more deadly, than a mere heart attack.

"Washington Writer"

CHRISTOPHER BUCKLEY (1952–   )

> New York City–born Christopher Buckley worked a $20-a-week
> job aboard a Norwegian freighter before enrolling in Yale
> University. After his graduation, he worked in various positions
> at *Esquire* magazine, eventually becoming managing editor. He
> took to the sea again in 1979 on a 78-day journey aboard a
> tramp steamer, working as a deckhand. His seafaring would
> later serve as the basis of his memoir, *Steaming to Bamboola:
> The World of a Tramp Freighter* (1982), which met with critical
> success. He returned to his work at the magazine but in 1980
> became a speechwriter for President George Bush, a position he
> held for eighteen months. His 1986 *White House Mess*, a "fake
> memoir," drew on this experience. Among his other publica-
> tions are the novels *Thank You for Smoking* (1994), *God Is My
> Broker: A Monk-Tycoon Reveals the 7½ Laws of Spiritual and
> Financial Growth* (1998), *Little Green Men* (1999), *No Way to
> Treat a First Lady* (2002), *Boomsday* (2007), and *Supreme
> Courtship* (2008). Buckley is a frequent contributor to the *New
> Yorker* and other magazines. Buckley is the son of William F.
> Buckley, founder of the *National Review,* and syndicated col-
> umnist. The following essay first appeared in the *Washington
> Post* in 1996.

Writing brought me to Washington. I was sitting at my desk at
Esquire magazine in New York, eating my New York bagel,
musing New York thoughts—rent control, the newest twenty
hot restaurants that had opened that day, and whether I could
get a reservation—when the phone rang. It was a desperate vice
presidential press secretary calling from—cool!—Air Force Two.
He needed a speechwriter, needed one fast, needed one cheap.

What the hey, I said to myself philosophically. Could be an
interesting gig. I've always thought of writing as a journeyman's
trade; perhaps the way a studio musician might think of his own

craft. Here was a chance to work on a new album with George ·
Bush. (*Voodoo Economics Lounge?*) Do it for a year, go back to
the Apple with neat Secret Service stories.

That was fifteen years ago. Here I still am, with every intention of staying, despite having spent the last forty-eight hours in
inane Sisyphean battle with minor functionaries of the D.C. government over—oh never mind. I like it here.

I wrote my first novel. It had the words "White House" in the
title, and that somehow fixed me, if not pigeonholed me, as a
"Washington novelist." At first I was quite delighted with this
appellation. Me, a "Washington novelist." I don't think we're in
New York anymore, Toto.

I wrote a second novel that didn't have "White House" or
"Washington" or "Potomac" or "Power and Principle" or any
other denotative code words in the title. There was a disappointed sound from the gallery when it came out (despite good
reviews). *It's very nice and all, but frankly we were rather expect-
ing another Washington book. . . .*

I wrote a third novel. It didn't have D.C. buzzwords in the
title, but it was certainly a "Washington novel." (Main character: a K Street tobacco spokesman. Washington enough for you?)
The gallery expressed satisfaction: *Now* that's *more like it.* Once
again I was, in the reviews, a "Washington novelist," or just
"Washington writer." "Washington satirist" followed. I guess
whatever my feelings about the Department of Public Works,
this effectively rules out fleeing to the burbs. "Bethesda novelist," "Chevy Chase satirist" just doesn't have the same oomph.
There's this, too: if you live somewhere where renewing your car
registration is automatic and painless, you won't be inspired to
write satire. Efficient government—local and federal—would
only wreck my career.

Washington was my writer's capital, as Melville put it in a
more aqueous context, my Harvard, my Yale. I was quite innocent when I arrived here with my houseplants, Hermes type-
writer, and *Bartlett's Familiar Quotations.* I'd seen a bit of the
world; rather a lot of it, actually. But oh what a brave new world

was Washington, that had such people in't! A few weeks after I arrived that suffocating July, 1981, I soon found myself in the White House mess, that is, the Navy-run dining room in the basement, listening to two (grown) speechwriters arguing furiously over who had had more "face time"—face time! oh brave neologisms!—in the "Oval" with "POTUS." (The first term is synecdoche, of course; the second acronym for President of the United States.) All this I watched in fascination and in wonder. Here was a ritual that had been acted and reenacted since the first royal court was established thousands of years ago in the palmly deserts of the Fertile Crescent, when the first Rosencrantz and Guildenstern squabbled over who had spent more time sucking up to Assurbanipal.

I don't think my two messmates were familiar with Alexander Pope's "Epitaph for one who would not be buried in Westminster Abbey":

> Heroes and kings! your distance keep,
> In peace let me poor poet sleep,
> Who never flattered folks like you:
> Let Horace blush, and Vergil too.

The little episode was my first inkling that I had found my proper place in the universe. There's a Spanish word my father taught me early on: *querencia.* Literally "favored spot." It's used in bullfighting. When the bull enters the ring, the matador watches very intently as the bull seeks out the spot where it feels safe. Once he finds it, he will continue, as the anger and pain increase, to return to it. The matador must therefore take care not to put himself between the bull and his *querencia,* for once he has set his charge for this—to put it in a Washington way— safe house, he will keep going, no matter what stands in his path. He will not be tempted by a proffered cape. Woe to the matador who has misjudged the invisible spot in the sand. At any rate, I had found my *querencia.* Or, as these things happen, it had found me.

I was surprised to find myself so contentedly situated. I was a New Yorker, and New Yorkers—for the most part—are programmed to disdain Washington as a third-rate burg with not enough first-rate restaurants. Of course, Reagan changed that, for a time. The Eastern Shuttle was crammed with **boldfaced** names from "Suzy Says." There was a touch of mink about the place for a while until the new tenants, a Greenwich Episcopalian and his what-you-see-is-what-you-get wife moved in and the ethos changed from Rodeo Drive to—go figure—Country Western. But all that was merely ebb and tide. It was permanent Washington, with its solemn absurdities, its motorcades of vanity, its noisy earnestness, its pomp and mitigating circumstance, its serene solipsism—to say nothing of its perfectly good, even terrific restaurants—that held me here.

Otherwise, I suppose, I would have given the houseplants to the lady next door, dropped off *Bartlett's* at the Vassar book sale, and caught the last shuttle back to New York.

I'm still perplexed about this elusive thing, the "Washington writer." Is Charles McCarry a "Washington novelist" because he has written about spooks? Larry McMurtry spent a quarter century here—though he did keep a place in West Archer, Texas—but managed never to become a "Washington writer." *Lonesome Dove* isn't about Strobe Talbott at the disarmament table. Is Anonymous a "Washington writer?" Apparently not, as one hears he's just bought a new house in Pelham, New York. It would be a stretcher to call my British chum Christopher Hitchens a "Washington writer," though he has certainly created the most interesting, or as we used to say in foreign policy speeches, "vibrant" Washington literary salons going, with a Vermouth splash of Hollywood glam, owing to his *Vanity Fair* gig. Very casual. Martin Amis, Salman Rushdie, Julian Barnes, Kevin Costner's coming. Barbra Streisand may drop by. Come early and have a drink, shall we say *vers sept heures?* Doesn't *sound* like a "Washington writer," does he? What about Edmund and Sylvia Morris, the Nick and Nora of biography (Reagan—Clare Boothe

Luce). Are they "Washington writers?" Nah. Too exotic. But they're here, thank heavens.

Was Gore Vidal typed as a "Washington writer" after *The City and the Pillar?* He seems more of a Washington writer now, in his umpteenth decade as a resident of Ravello, Italy, than he did after that first shockeroo of a novel appeared. He writes oftener and oftener these days about Washington. *Nostalgie de la boue?* An aspect of his narcissism? It was here, after all, that he grew up and first fell in love, with, now he tells us, a Saint Alban's schoolmate. Perhaps in the end, you don't have to live here at all to be a "Washington writer." Perhaps—how does it go?—Washington is a moveable beast.

from *Supporting the Sky*

PATRICIA BROWNING GRIFFITH (1935–   )

> Born in Fort Worth, Texas, playwright and novelist Patricia
> Browning Griffith earned a bachelor's degree at Baylor University
> and studied at the University of Texas and at Texas Christian
> University. She currently lives in Washington, D.C. Among her
> publications are *The World Around Midnight* (1991), *Tennessee
> Blue* (1981), and *The Future Is Not What It Used to Be* (1970).
> Griffith is an associate professor of English at George Washington
> University. A frequent contributor of stories, articles, and reviews
> to *Harper's*, the *Paris Review,* and the *Washingtonian,* Griffith is
> a past president of the PEN/Faulkner Foundation and a founder
> of the *Washington Review of the Arts.* Following is an excerpt
> from her 1996 novel *Supporting the Sky.*

In the neighborhoods of the District of Columbia in the month
of August, the air is filled with the cloying sweetness of confederate jasmine, a vine that grows wildly in the humidity of this
partially refurbished swamp. Downtown, in the federal area of
the city, well-tended, color-coordinated flower beds are mar-
shaled like platoons at attention around the government buildings. There the air is filled with the smell of vendor hot dogs and
the sounds of tourists, who seldom penetrate the narrow streets
and broad alleys of the surrounding neighborhoods. But that
particular hot morning in late summer I saw a bus of tourists
when I went out to retrieve the newspapers off the steps of my
old row house and see if there was any sign at all of my sixteen-
year-old daughter, Shelly, lately of the partially bleached hair,
paste-on fingernails, and nose ring, who'd failed to come home
the night before from a trip to an amusement park in rural
Virginia. I had spent the night waiting for a phone call or the
slam of a car door followed by a key in the lock, all the while
going through every possible catastrophe a parent might imag-

ine. The mental images in Technicolor with sound had grown
more vivid over the years. They seemed always hovering just
outside my consciousness, like a committed stalker on the
periphery of my vision. But rather than some sign of Shelly, that
morning there was only the surprise of the tour bus, hulkingly
oversized for our street and moving slowly like an invading
tank. Inside, the tourists were hidden behind dark-tinted windows, gazing no doubt at the native sighted there in front of her
slightly tattered but gracious old Victorian townhouse, a vision
of tousled disorder in a pink-flowered robe.

It had been so hot that summer of 1991 that my patio tomato
plants produced only a few blossoms, which grew into tomatoes
while the vines themselves shriveled around them as though
dying in childbirth. Thirty days over ninety degrees, and as we
headed toward September it was not looking much better. Before
we could buy liquor on Sunday and had fancy nouvelle cuisine
restaurants with cowboy decor, D.C. was considered a hardship
post for foreign diplomats. Even now our area in political-speak
is often referred to derogatorily as "inside the Beltway" and the
local citizens' concerns are dismissed as skewed and unimport-
ant, unlike the concerns of, say, Truth or Consequences, New
Mexico. And while there may be actual proximity to the U.S.
government, the fact is we live here like fleas on the federal dog,
sometimes producing a momentary discomfort but more often
ignored. When newspaper columnists denounce the city as middle-class and dull, they are, of course, talking about the minority
white population, approximately a quarter of the male lawyers,
who march along K Street in button-down shirts and suits beside
women, who are often lawyers too, in panty hose and running
shoes. If those columnists would look at the majority of the population, which is assorted hues of black and brown, they'd find
more flamboyance and diversity, but the cameras are programmed mostly for pale images. Especially that one image, that
large white Georgian mansion on Pennsylvania Avenue surrounded by a tall iron fence with stone buttresses around it and
a hidden rose garden. If you've lived here long enough, you've

heard older people tell about the days when they'd cut across the
White House lawn on their way to town. Or when Eleanor
Roosevelt tossed cheap throw pillows that said "Aloha" around
the Green Room. What does it mean that today the place is a
fortress? Has the world changed, or just us? Questions no doubt
pondered in that house, as in so many houses over dinner, before
newscasts, before and after meetings, and even on many beaches
in the warmer months.

Night or day you can drive by the White House, two miles
from my house, and see the newsman or newswoman caught in
an intense circle of television light as if experiencing a heavenly
visitation while addressing the small red light of a camera as he
or she tries to report on the puzzling world around us, which so
often seems on the brink of disaster.

Meanwhile, in deep background are the rest of us—queuing at
bus stops and riding down steep escalators into the caverns of our
neat Metrorail system, moving to and from our various tasks of
cleaning buildings, patrolling the streets, teaching the children,
lobbying, litigating, attempting to keep the peace. All of us labor-
ing alongside the trouble ghosts of Washington past that, according to one of my neighbors, Mrs. Anita Nance, haunt the city. The
ghost of Lincoln, we all know, resides in the White House, but
there are others, according to Mrs. Nance, such as the noble ghost
of Frederick Douglass, who haunts A Street Northeast, near the
Capitol, and the ghost of Duke Ellington, who haunts our very
own neighborhood. According to Mrs. Nance, Avon salesperson,
oral historian, and charter member of our Neighborhood Watch
group, often in the night when the wind is from the south one can
hear, wafted from the bridge named for him, the mellow strains of
an Ellington song such as "Satin Doll."

But despite our proximity to Duke Ellington's ghost, the local
citizens are never seen to be in an enviable position. Indeed, a
recent poet-in-residence at the Library of Congress who com-
muted three days a week from New York City, where for some
reason he seemed to feel safer, signed his books in Washington
with his name and the location, "Ground Zero."

For one thing, the War of Independence didn't do a thing for us along the Potomac. We would be perfectly justified in pouring tea into the Tidal Basin, but with the pollution of our waterways and the addition of foreign algae that expand and choke the natural wetlands, multiplying like magic, it is uncertain whether or not anyone would notice. "The Last Colony," the signs say as you enter our territory along Kenilworth Avenue. Which means that we inhabitants of this beautiful and sophisticated world capital where thousands come to demonstrate for their rights have no voting representation in Congress and so in these last years of the twentieth century are still subject to taxation without representation.

Later on that day of my long, hot vigil, trying to ward off panic while considering at what point I would phone the police, I lay on a chaise longue in my back patio, going perfunctorily through *The New York Times* and *The Washington Post*. Beside me, what Shelly called my boom box was tuned to a public radio fund-raiser playing old June Christy records between pitches. The program host had just played "Midnight Sun" and then offered, for a pledge of fifty dollars, a black coffee mug he claimed would protect a home from burglars. If somebody breaks into your house, he said, when they see that mug they'll leave. I realized immediately that this was a form of airwave extortion, generated by desperation in recession times, but I did adore that announcer, who each weekend regaled us with stories as well as music, and I had to appreciate the whimsy of the idea. Oh, if only the world were so simple, I thought, and wondered how many coffee mugs I'd have to buy before I saw my own dear daughter walk safely through that steel-reinforced door with so many locks it looked like a devotee of S&M.

Arlo, our formerly homeless, generic gray cat with a notched ear—Shelly had taken him in some years back—appeared at the top of my ten-foot patio fence. He leaned forward, surveying the landscape before leaping down and sidling up to me for petting. Then he settled in the shade of my chair, and scratched a flea before curling into a midday nap. Arlo was a free spirit, who days pretended allegiance to us, and nights, driven by passion, roamed in search of love and excitement. Much like my daughter.

Shelly had phoned the previous evening to say, in the sweet voice she uses when she's about to do something she knows I wish she wouldn't, that she was going to the amusement park and she'd be home around midnight.

"Who are you going with?" That seemed a reasonable question. She said she was going with some people she'd met. "Where?" I asked, since supposedly she'd spent the night with her girlfriend Miranda.

"In Georgetown," she said, mentioning an area of posh federal-style homes and tourist restaurants where teenagers cruised the streets and jammed the bars on weekends.

"Names?" I suggested.

"They're friends of Noel's," she replied, and announced she had to run, they were waiting on her.

Now that is a typical conversation with Shelly. And I had never heard of a "Noel." And when Shelly says she'll be home around midnight, what she supports is the notion of coming home may occur to her about then. We have battled about this over the years, but as all nonfascist parents know, you have to choose your battles. Her reluctance to tear herself away from a party in Potomac or some go-go dub in Southwest is a part of her life as a free spirit. And by free spirit I mean I've tried to trust her and let her become the unique person she could be, not realizing what I may be getting myself or her into. Let's face it, you'd have problems if you were bringing up baby nuns nowadays—let alone an exuberant sometimes blonde who matured early.

Where I grew up, in East Texas, in the era of "Make love, not war" (a principle I've tried to adhere to, along with "Save water, shower with a friend"), I may not have received a superior education in those public schools, but, I always thought, I'd at least grown up knowing all types of people. Yet what I have learned over the last seventeen years is that all types of people—meaning the public at large—have become considerably more varied than what I was faced with as a rather rambunctious teenager in East

Texas, who started smoking at thirteen and fell madly in love all too easily. Those days wouldn't hold a candle to the intricacies, the variables, the possibilities of disaster available in this last decade of the twentieth century. It is crazy out there, it often seems, with a gun in every hand, and all the people I know are struggling, indeed battling, for decency, civilization, and survival for themselves and their children.

So here it was, the last week in August, hot and humid with the late-summer katydids, crickets, and cicadas shrill amid the impatiens and crepe myrtles tucked about the city's townhouses. It was supposed to hit the nineties again that day, and I was still trying to tan my legs enough so that I could, maybe one day of the year, as a symbol of freedom and my southwestern origins, go to work at my Santa Fe–style office of Harrison & Associates, Public Relations Consultants, without having to wear panty hose.

Lying there on my hot chaise, I could see the rear of my neighbors' second and third floors above their decks or patios, all of us lined up in our efficient row houses, going about our complicated lives in intimate proximity. That's what I loved about living in the city—the economy of that proximity. Where I grew up, the middle class thought they had to live with a couple of acres surrounding them, a moat of green Bermuda grass broken only by neatly coiffed flower beds and shrubs. Living here was like being at the beach, all the people conducting their sometimes messy lives on small rectangles of colorful towels or quilts, pretending to ignore the half-naked bodies around them. There was something sweet and respectfully humane to me about that. This is a racially and economically diverse neighborhood where we know one another's cars and cats. When it snows we push one another's cars out of snowbanks and shovel the older people's walks. When we see suspicious movement around one another's doors we phone 911, though sometimes the line is busy.

Next door, my neighbors Dan and Don, back from their early-morning AIDS walkathon, were ferrying drinks onto their deck. Shielded only by the privacy fence and the lacy leaves of a diseased elm tree, they were serving coffee and tequila sunrises to an assembling brunch group. I knew that when I turned off my radio they would turn on their tapes of pre-AIDS nostalgic rock from the sixties and seventies. Meanwhile, my neighbors on the other side, an older retired couple, were gone to church, and their Doberman was left to prowl and protect the premises. Directly behind me stood the stately home of Reverend Ezra Thompson, minister of the New Southern Rock Church of God, a man of towering principles and generous humor who exercised secretly by running circles in back of his townhouse.

Around noon the radio host started "Something Cool," my very favorite, with June Christy's soothing voice relieving somewhat the heat of the day. Suddenly I heard a sound inside the house, and my heart leaped—it might be Shelly! I strained toward the door, hoping. With my inner-city crime-stopper's caution, I had to consider the possibility of some unwelcome intruder. But the door to the patio was pushed open, and accompanied by something like an electrical charge before a storm, there appeared Shelly, sixteen, turbulent, and bordering on beautiful, pulling a young man after her. She's safe, I realized, clutching my bluebonnet T-shirt over my heart. Shelly, fine-boned and tall, built more like her father than me, with his broad sensuous mouth. Her wide brownish-green eyes seemed to gaze at the world with a calm detachment that gave her a challenging appeal. She had the tawny, compelling attraction of a lion cub that on second glance would cause you to hesitate, sensing the presence of something dangerous, maybe even fierce. But before I could feel full relief, before my stomach could calm the volcanic buildup of the past fifteen hours, the early stages of a whole new anxiety arose as I took in the figure of the young man behind her.

Now I do not consider myself a street-wise person, and if I prayed I would pray with all my heart to escape the racial prejudice rife in this country. But the minute my eyes settled on his red sweatsuit and gold chains, his immaculate white sneakers and the handsome bronze face commonly referred to as black, I knew I was looking at trouble. First of all, who in the world would wear a sweatsuit in this heat? I made a quick mental search for familiar signs of substance abuse, the contemporary litany of parenthood. As I stared into his pale brown eyes, I felt my disadvantage lying there below them, my bare white legs gleaming and smelling of the piña colada of Shelly's tanning lotion, my bare feet sticking up like a corpse's. I knew even before I saw the round love bite on Shelly's neck that he might as well have worn a signboard saying "Brace yourself—more complications to come!" After all the depths of emotions I had experienced in the past hours, here was another looming threat, a minefield I had yet to traverse.

In a few brief seconds I read the easy carelessness of his body as they moved toward me holding hands. Across the street, a neighbor's dog, who hears sirens before humans do, began an extended howl. A second later he was joined by a siren down toward Sixteenth Street, where a squad car would have to weave its way through the streams of cars parked and double-parked at churches all along that broad boulevard. From the Tibetan meditation temple to the Buddhist temple on down to the Baptist church where Jimmy Carter once taught Sunday school, people assembling with dreams of salvation, what we all hope and search for in our various ways. And here I was, confronted with the red sweatsuit, symbol of an L.A. drug gang that had spread nationwide, I'd read in the paper, and within it the careless motion of a young man's body, a no-restraints looseness, a formidable sexuality in his easy-flowing movements that women are never too old to read. And with Shelly, caught in the hormonal tumult of sixteen, the possibilities took my breath away. Not the fear of sex for my precocious teenager, that crisis having been addressed more than a year before. It was a kid thing then, and this man before me was much more than a kid; rather, sex underlined, moving in big boots across a vast, hot, and complicated canvas. Then again, it rushed at me that I was being prejudiced, assigning him an attitude before I knew him at all. In the midst of my confusion, Shelly said, "Moms, this is Dee." "Moms," an annoying term she pretends to use with affection to get on my good side.

"Hey." Dee smiled with a glow that could light Pittsburgh, and moved forward to shake my hand.

I paused, lost in the uncertain etiquette of disapproval. After all, it wasn't too many years ago that you didn't just sail into a girl's house holding her hand when she'd been out all night unaccounted for and smile as if you were offering a free trip to China. However, remembering from my churchgoing East Texas background that Jesus recommended consorting with the Pharisees, and deciding it wiser to stifle my anger and bide my time, I raised my hand in a compromise: I proffered a hand shake but no smile, rather a wary study of his marvelously intriguing face. Dee met the admonishment of my unsmiling eyes and clasped my hand indifferently for only a second, indicating to me that my approval was of no great importance.

"I wish you'd phoned at some point," I told Shelly. "I've been crazy with worry."

She answered with a kind of wave of her head, her way of launching into a story. "I'm sorry, Moms," she began, looking not at me directly but down toward Arlo, who had roused himself and was rubbing against her legs. She bent to pet him, revealing the top of her buff stretch bra under her blue T-shirt. She straightened up and moved her hand to the back of her neck and lifted her long two-tone hair—the first four inches soft brown at the roots with natural golden highlights some women pay big bucks for, and the remaining flow of hair which settled below her shoulders bleached blond and less lively. She fanned her neck a moment as she talked and then let her hair fall, tossing her head gently and readjusting the five inches of silver bracelets she always wore up her left arm.

"We went to Kings Dominion and we had the best time!" Shelly glanced at Dee, made a brief reading of his reaction. "But on the way home the car broke down, so we had to get a tow truck, and we didn't have enough money and . . ."

I listened, desperately trying to find—in what I knew would be a long and fuzzy story—some specific time, place, or name.

". . . and by then it was after three and I didn't want to wake you up." Her eyes widened with innocence to demonstrate her consideration, met my own. *Call me no matter what time*, was the rule. And when she saw the familiar traces of anger and skepticism in my face, she turned away. The sirens grew louder behind her words and she looked at Dee, searching for his approval of this meager, vague report.

"When we got to Dee's cousin's house the phone was broken . . ."

Ah, the number of broken phones in this area of the nation, and Shelly seemed bound to discover them all. It was just as she turned to look at Dee that I saw the round reddish love bite on her neck, tanned to perfection from her summer lifeguard job, where she reigned on a wooden throne. And then she smiled her lovely perfect-teeth smile, repaying me some of those hundreds of orthodontist dollars in the kind of slow beautiful smile I hoped to enjoy for the rest of my life.

Then, having fulfilled her duty and being satisfied with her performance, Shelly caught Dee's hand and started toward the door. As if I needed more reassurance of her presence, I called out, "Well, ain't it hot?" knowing the "ain't" would rile her, her mother's crude Texas ways. Sometimes I used it for effect. I had been known to stop a dinner party by saying "reckon." But it sailed past her.

"Listen, we're starving, is there something to eat?" She spun on her bright blue stretch sandals that matched her shorts and shirt still hanging on to Dee's hand. He smiled at me with a touch of humor, as if he were being jerked around helplessly by this dear child. Just then "Something Cool" ended and I realized I hadn't even heard it. I again watched the liquid, easy sexuality of this young man's movement. The door thudded behind him and I sat up at attention like a general both energized and horrified at having sighted the enemy over the hill. For half a minute I wished I were elsewhere, at a beach, any beach, even a Delaware beach rife with jellyfish in the afternoon, even a sweltering Texas beach where you find not diamonds but tar on the soles of your feet.

I turned off the radio and the cordless phone I'd kept beside me those past hours rang. I rifled through the newspapers to find it beneath *Book World*.

"Rosemary, how ya doing?" It was Doreen, major organizer of our neighborhood orange-hat patrol, calling to report that the Alcohol Control Board hearing planned for the next week had been postponed. Our neighborhood was trying to rid itself of the Bluebird Bar & Grill, a haven for drug dealers, by opposing the renewal of its liquor license. Doreen lived behind me and down two houses. Had she been looking out her bedroom window through her daisy-print balloon curtains, we might have waved at each other. She asked if she could count on me for orange-hatting the next weekend, and I told her I'd patrol if I didn't have to maintain surveillance of my teenager.

"Oh, I know what you mean," Doreen, mother of three exemplary daughters, said with real feeling.

"Maybe you could get Dan and Don," I added.

I always suggested Dan and Don, though I suspected that some of the male orange-hats didn't welcome the prospect of patrolling neighborhood streets with an interracial gay couple.

"Well, see you later," Doreen said. "Have a good week."

Doreen is a nurse. When Shelly and I first moved in, she appeared at our door introducing herself and offering to help if I ever needed emergency medical assistance. I passed that on to my mother, who immediately felt better about our being in what she considered a godless, strife-torn city. Of course when Mama came to visit I drove her down Sixteenth, pointing out the churches and synagogues and temples, showing how it was the opposite of a godless city. And Mama felt some relief, despite the number of what she considered off-brand religions. Mama had never before seen a Buddhist temple. Indeed, you can live in East Texas your entire life and not see a Buddhist temple.

I stacked the newspapers. Beyond the dying elm Dan and Don started "Stairway to Heaven," and I moved toward the sliding glass door, readying myself for guard duty, wondering if I'd have to wait a whole year for the haunting sound of June Christy singing "Something Cool." At the door I paused, hoping for a miracle, that I might walk inside and find not this stranger in my kitchen, but Shelly's father, who would kindly take my hand and help me prepare for the next campaign.

"The Tunnel"

ALAN CHEUSE (1 9 4 0 –   )

New Jersey–born Alan Cheuse taught at Bennington College and at the University of the South in Sewanee, Tennessee, before his current position in the creative writing department of George Mason University in Fairfax, Virginia. He is the author of ten books of fiction and nonfiction, among them the novels *The Grandmother's Club* (1986), *The Light Possessed* (1990), and *To Catch the Lightning* (2008), and the short story collections *Candace* (1980) and *The Tennessee Waltz and Other Stories* (1992). As a book commentator, Cheuse is a regular contributor to National Public Radio's *All Things Considered*. The selection below is from Cheuse's story collection *Lost and Old Rivers* (1998).

One week after their candidate lost the election Jas and her roommate Sharon were getting ready for a party, Jas stepping into her flashiest skirt, the silver-sequined wraparound, and wondering about a blouse. She was a tall girl, so skirts like this looked good on her. She had narrow hips, long legs—good, firm breasts, that was true, and a long neck. My swan, her dad used to tease her lovingly. My swan. Who wanted to be a swan? Swans were oddly beautiful, but were they happy? That was the question that bothered Jas whenever she recalled her father's pet name for her.

When she thought of her mother, it was another sort of memory, much more deeply tinged with emotion. Her mother had told her nearly every day of her life that her eyes were beautiful, and Jas felt her chest constrict—and seem to turn to ice at the same time—at the picture in her mind of her mother, just before she went into that last surgery, unable to speak but blinking hard at her, blinking, blinking, which meant, your eyes, your eyes. All she needed was to have a boy look her in the eyes and he'd be a goner. That was her mother's constant refrain. But so far no one tall enough to look properly into her eyes—and there had only been a few of those anyway—was anyone she wanted to look back at. There had been one or two guys at school whom she had gone out with more than once, but nothing happened with them. All they wanted was sex, and she just couldn't, not yet, not so soon, she told herself, after her mother's death. There had been no one in the year after graduation when she had worked in downtown Detroit. No one these last six months when she had worked on the Committee to Re-Elect the President, first in Michigan and then—because of a little fling Sharon had had with a committee man passing through the state, a two-night stand, actually—here in Washington.

"Fletcher said it's going to be a great party, even if we did lose," her roommate said, stepping up next to her in front of the mirror.

Jas gave her a queer look.

"You didn't ask him to bring a friend for me, did you?"

"No." Sharon looked at her in the mirror looking at her.

"Look me in the eye and say that," Jas said, turning to Sharon and touching a hand to her friend's shoulder.

"I'll call a taxi for us," Sharon said, moving toward the telephone.

"I knew it!"

Jas stalked past her, went to the window, pretended to study the dark street below.

In the taxi, Jas enjoyed seeing the wide marble buildings lining the wide avenue, and as they approached Georgetown, the narrow but stately colonial brick houses with an occasional wood-frame mansion between. Up toward Dumbarton Oaks the vehicle carried them, the driver listening intently to the scratchy radio calls in a language neither girl could put a name to.

"Good address," Sharon said when they pulled up in front of a three-story house with a wonderful white porch on R Street.

"Whose house again?" Jas had forgotten.

"Daughter of Senator Whoosis," Sharon said slyly as they stepped from the cab into a gutter full of crackling leaves.

"Republican or Democrat?" Jas said.

"What do you think?" Sharon said. "Democrats have all the good parties."

"To make a bad pun," Jas put in.

"Ouch," Sharon said. "But it's true. Fletcher knows her husband, a photographer. They met on some trek or other in the Himalayas."

"Tibet or not Tibet, that is the question."

Sharon gave her a playful shove as they climbed the steps to the front porch.

"You have a great sense of humor. And such great eyes."

"Thanks," Jas said, noticing heads bobbing past the large picture window. Through the glass panes in the door they could see a thick curtain of coats hung on hooks along the wall.

Sharon rang the bell. Jas felt a little jolt, the old pain in her chest. Ever since the end of sophomore year at college it had visited her regularly. Will I ever be happy the way other people seem to be happy? And then, as usual—fortunately—her mind danced away from the thought.

There was a lot to distract her once they went inside. Their hostess, a petite woman wearing a long black dress and a Tibetan necklace of some sort—Sharon asked, so they learned that it *was* from Tibet—introduced them to the nearest group of people: a broad-chested national correspondent for a chain of midwestern newspapers, his mousey wife, a weak-chinned professor of philosophy from Georgetown—maybe he'd been a priest once, Jas figured from the way he spoke and looked at her—and a sour-faced fellow who wrote a political column for one of the local newspapers, the one with the lowest circulation. None of the men came up to Jas's collarbone.

"I understand you're going to be out of a job," the philosophy professor said.

"That's right," Jas said. "We lost."

"Poignant," said the professor.

"Are you looking around?" said the wife of the national correspondent. "There's always something else to do in this town."

Before Jas could think of a response the circle of people shifted,

and the national correspondent's wife led him across the room but
not before Jas caught a whiff of his foul-smelling breath. A thick-
necked, shifty-eyed bull of a man the color of maple syrup drifted
past; people said hello, hello, and then he was gone to another
room. Then Sharon appeared, accompanied by the tallest guy Jas
had seen in town in the past six months of her stay.

"Jas, this is Charles. Charles, Jas."

"My name is actually Josephine," Jas said, "but nobody calls
me that."

His eyes were level with hers and she stared a moment,
watched him blink.

"Can I get you a drink?"

"Oh!" Jas laughed and swept her right arm out to the side,
knocking someone's shoulder with her outstretched hand.

"Excuse me," she said as the man turned to stare at her with
cold blue eyes, glaring at first and then smiling, his cheeks crin-
kling up in a charming way.

"Of course," he said and turned back to his conversation with
the national correspondent and his wife.

"Easy on my boss," the tall guy said.

"That's your boss?"

"That's my Senator," he said. There was something about this
young man's eyes Jas noticed now—they were red-rimmed, as
though he lacked moisture for his contacts or had been up all
night talking, and whatever else. "Something to drink?"

And she said, yes, fine, and he brought her a glass of wine and
asked her questions about the office and commiserated with her
about its imminent closing. He managed to ask if he could call her.

"May I?" he said, like some lanky little boy in grade school
asking for permission for a bathroom pass.

He called a few days later, catching Jas and Sharon in the
middle of clearing out their closets.

"Oh, my God," she heard herself say, trying to dig herself a
little cave amidst the pile of sweaters and old running clothes. "I
can't, I just can't."

"You mean you won't?" His voice sounded mournful at the other end of the line.

"I'm just so busy," she said. "We're closing our office, and I've got tons of work before I even start looking for another job."

"So you're going to stay in the city?"

"I don't know," Jas said, her voice turning a little childish. "I don't know."

"It's something to do," Sharon said after Jas had hung up.

"I am not going out with someone just because we are the same height."

"I know people who've gotten together for worse reasons," her roommate said.

"Who?"

"Our parents."

"If he calls again, I'll see," Jas said, plucking at the collar of an old sweater from college with her sorority letters embroidered on the sleeve.

But she must have really put him off, she decided. Weeks went by, and they were nearly out of a job when Rosaliza, the secretary-receptionist in their soon-to-be-former office, suggested that Jas do a little research on government agencies where they all might look for something. That's what you were reduced to in this town if you worked for the party out of power and you had little experience and fewer contacts. So she found herself in the Library of Congress spending hours going over lists of possibilities. The high-ceilinged room where she sat suggested such promise, the gilt of its decorations, the names of the greats, that she worked on and on in the midst of many others, from the elderly with noses pressed to their books to girls new to college whose purposes would in a few years turn out, she guessed, to be similar to her own. Find a job, hope for love—oh, Jas, she chided herself, get on with the work and leave the daydreaming to those with the time to do it. She fingered the collar of her blouse while she read and made her notes, closing her eyes now and then and wondering, as a chill spread across her neck and down her spine, just what she was going to do with herself.

When she left the reading room and made her way to the elevators, the air around her chilled her and she pulled her coat close to her chest. A stout black guard watched as she stopped at the elevator door. She smiled at him. He looked the other way.

The car arrived and she stepped inside, pushing what she took to be the button for the ground floor. Alone in the descending car, she breathed hard and sighed, for what reason she could not figure, just the general sadness of it all, she supposed—from the loneliness of independence, of course, her father might say.

Down she went, down past the first floor and the ground floor. Oops! Wrong button after all! It would have been comical, she decided in that instant, typical of her life—if when the door opened she hadn't felt a sudden surge of fear. But there was only a cream-colored wall and a sign with an arrow pointing to the right. She shrugged and stepped out of the car and with some caution followed the arrow along a narrow corridor with peeling paint and peeling pipes overhead. Somehow the arrow gave her comfort.

An angular woman with skin the color of brown velvet appeared around the corner, an identity card dangling from her neck on a long metal chain.

"Is this the way out?" Jas said.

"Follow the signs." The woman looked her over and walked around her.

Jas marched forward, finding herself in a room with vending machines and the odor of coffee hanging in the air. A few young library workers—she noticed their identity cards—lounged about on plastic chairs, food scattered on tables before them, papers on the floor. A thick-necked boy with braids and a bright red comb jutting out from behind his ear stared up at her as she passed. He signaled to his companion, an older fellow wearing one of those hooded sweatshirts Jas had noticed were all the rage. She hurried from the room, finding herself in another curving passageway that led in two quick turns to a broad tunnel whirring with the hum of turbines and the echo of distant voices.

The tunnel was broad and wide—rectangular rather than tubular as she might have imagined it—and sloping slightly upward several hundred yards as though it were a roadway beneath a river and led to another shore. From that distance a gaggle of formidable women, their faces ranging in color from onyx to near-purple, charged toward her down the incline, laughing, waving hands at each other. The tallest was only three quarters of Jas's height, and they glanced up at her—the shortest of them openly stared—as they passed her by.

Jas quickened her stride, passing doors on either side marked PERSONNEL ONLY and EMERGENCY ONLY. Within a few minutes she had walked halfway to the other end. The exit to the street had to be somewhere off in the distance where a group of men in suits now turned the corner and came walking swiftly toward her down the incline. As they approached—five of them, all of them fairly tall and most of them with a full head of hair— Jas instinctively glanced down at her breasts, and then, fixing a serious expression on her face, straightened up and kept walking forward.

"Hey," the tallest of them said from a distance of about thirty feet or so. The man nearest him used his elbow on the tall one while the others stared at her. "Hello," she said as they passed.

"Just a minute," the tall one said to the others, another of whom, the man in the center, she recognized by his cold blue stare: the Senator.

"Hey," the tall guy—it was Charles—slowed down and tilted his head to one side.

"Hey," Jas said, stopping to speak.

"You never called me back." Charles said.

"I didn't?"

"Nope."

"You never called me again," Jas said.

"I will now," he said, giving her a little wave and then making clear with his hands that he had to hurry after the others. "Ceremony over at the Adams building. Got to go."

"B-bye," Jas said, watching for a moment as he rushed along the wide corridor to catch up with his group. Then she was moving again, her mind full of new questions, stopping only when startled by a dark-headed young black man who stepped sideways out of one of the side doors.

"Excuse me," she said, afraid she'd made some sound of distress. The young man kept on walking ahead of her as though she were not there. On the street, at night, say, this might have seemed sinister. In the brightly lighted tunnel, Jas thought nothing of it. The black man stopped at the elevator. When she came near she noticed that despite his wiry build the top of his head was barely level with her shoulder. The elevator door slid open, he stepped inside, and she followed. She said a hello and only then did he look at her, his eyes full of veins and flecks. He wore a brown cardigan nearly the color of his flesh and a pair of neatly creased brown trousers. His two smooth cheeks gave off an appealing odor of a familiar aftershave, the name of which she could not recall. Almost as if he could read her mind, the man raised a hand and touched a finger to his cheek—all this in what seemed like absolute slow-motion—revealing a gold band on an appropriate finger.

"Floor?" the man said, his voice high-pitched and almost boyish.

Before Jas could answer they both turned at the sound of running feet and saw Charles charging up to the car.

"Whoa!" he said and leaped inside. "Nearly missed you!" He pressed a button. The other man pressed another button. The car gave a shudder as the doors closed and it began to rise.

"What are you doing?" Jas said, eyebrows raised, her hands balled nervously into fists at her sides.

"Coming after you," he said.

The other man threw her a furtive look, then glanced at Charles.

"You okay?" the man said to Jas.

"She's okay," Charles said.

The black man shrugged as the elevator car jerked to a halt and the doors slid open. He took one more look at her and stepped out of the car.

"Thank you," she said.

"I have a proposition for you," Charles said as he moved along with Jas out of the car.

"What?"

"Don't get worried. This is business. Come with me and listen to what I have to say."

So they left the Library and walked back along the street toward the Senate Office Building. It was one of those days near winter when the sun beat brightly down and there was little wind. Jas felt warm enough to open her coat and she swung her arms freely as she walked and listened to Charles's proposal.

"The Senator wants me to work for him?" she said when he had finished. "He doesn't even know who I am."

"In fact, he does," Charles said, moving his arms in wide arcs as he explained.

"Sharon sent over our resumes?"

"Uh-huh."

"And he wants to hire her, too?"

"If she's willing."

"So this is how it's done?" Jas shook her head. Standing at the curb before the Supreme Court Building waiting for the cars to pass, the Capitol dome glowing in the sun at a distance across the street, she felt as though she were waiting in a dream—the marble buildings all around her, the bare tree branches overhead, the sun splashed across the white-pale sky.

She returned to the apartment so full of news she could scarcely speak. Sharon had the same look in her eye, the same trembling in her lips and hands.

"You got two job offers!" Jas couldn't believe the coincidence. It was like living in a story, it was like a soap opera. Except that this was her life—their real lives.

"I write a great letter, let's face it," her roommate said. "Fletcher helped, of course. He's got the knack. So what about Charles? Do you think he has it too?"

Jas could feel the heat of a blush rising to her cheeks, but she talked right through the sensation.

"If he's not just bullshitting, it's a good job. You ought to think about coming with me. I—"

"Fletcher thinks the Education Association is a good entry for me," Sharon said.

Jas cared about Sharon, so she backed away from the subject.

"So you think I should take this job?" Jas asked.

"I think you should jump at it."

She jumped. She went to the office and filled out the forms. She met the staff. She endured the obligatory interview with the Senator himself, who fixed her with those stone-blue eyes for about twelve seconds before nodding and offering a soft hand and saying, "Welcome aboard."

"When do you begin?" her father asked her when she went home for Christmas. His eyes seemed different from the way she remembered them—soft, glassy, threads of red running out from the dark pupils.

"Soon as I get back," she told him.

"I was worried when the campaign committee shut down," he said. "I didn't know what you were going to do."

"It's a big town, Papa," she said, "with a lot of opportunities."

"I worry about some of those opportunities," he said. "I sit at home and worry quite a bit about some of those opportunities."

It went like that for a couple of days more, whether they were sitting in the old renovated train station turned restaurant watching the snow fall onto the rarely used tracks, or in the living room watching *McNeil-Lehrer* before she cooked his favorite meal, or in the car to the airport.

"Say hello to the President for me," he said.

She laughed. "At least I'll say hello to the Senator."

"Just be careful," he said. She could still hear his sorrowful voice as the airplane tilted its nose into the snow and edged upward toward the clouds.

Back in her empty apartment Jas found sleeping difficult with Sharon still away at her parents' house. The apartment became a theater of suspicious noises, threatening sounds. The next day when Sharon returned they killed two bottles of wine as they sat up late, talking, drinking; the warm glow seemed to soften Jas's holiday blues.

New Year's Eve: the two of them back at the house of the daughter of Senator Whoosis. Jas had never met her hostess the first time; now she spent the first few minutes discussing the city's winter weather with her. Her husband, the photographer, wasn't at home, she learned. He was somewhere in Tibet, chasing some elusive mountain goat with his camera. The Senator stood on the other side of the room, his wife in tow, a doll-like woman with bright made-up eyes, a slash of crimson across the place where her mouth would be. Even at this distance Jas had to look away from his stare. She was relieved to see the burly foul-breathed national correspondent and his wife, and the sour-faced philosophy professor, and the political columnist.

"Hi," she said, and they made polite noises and asked her questions. They all seemed to know about her new job. She spoke, her mind replaying the events of the past year—that's what this time of the night did for her, especially after she'd had a few glasses of wine—the dissolving of her old job, the meeting with Charles in the tunnel—but where was he tonight? Not that she cared. She looked around. Somehow midnight had crept up on them and music filled the room. Sharon was dancing with a pink-faced stranger in a beautiful blue jacket. Jas's mood picked up. She shuffled her feet in place to the music.

Next morning, her stomach gurgling, her eyes filmed over with cataract-like veils, she yanked herself out of bed and went stumbling toward the bathroom only to find Sharon's dance partner sitting on the toilet. She backed out of the bathroom and stood at the window of the living room. Two men in hooded sweatshirts came loping along the street, tapping on car hoods as though they were steel drums. Jas crawled back into bed and stayed awhile.

That New Year's Day, a day full of physical discomfort and the resumption of the winter blues, led off a raw January, a month when Jas spent little time outdoors. She was having doubts about her political beliefs, and it wasn't a great time for someone who had worked to reelect the ousted President to stroll about the streets. Either she holed up in her new cubicle at the Senate Office Building or—the week of the inaugural, when she was hit with a terrible cold—she burrowed into her bed at home with reports to read, and now and then a novel to clear her mind. She read about the environmental impact of coal processing plants in her Senator's home state, and she read about an honest young lawyer chased through the streets of Memphis on the run from killer partners. Neither was entirely real; neither was at all satisfying.

Sometimes, though, she and Sharon—just as alone now, it seemed, as she was—had a good laugh together, and now and then they went out to the Hawk and Dove. Late nights, all smoke and beery air, it seemed jovial enough at first. Eyes meeting glances of men at the bar, men Jas recognized from the corridors of the office building, other men strangers with a familiar look, thin steel-rimmed glasses, ties askew, dark hair slicked back with either water or pomade. They glanced at her, she glanced back, then looked away. The end of a basketball game on the television screen mounted above the bar. Black men, much taller than she, galloping along the court in one direction and then tuning on a dime and galloping back again.

Hurrying home through the dark and chill, Sharon jabbering away about something, how one of the guys at the bar had said something to her, Jas wondering about the street ahead, the dark, the cold days to come. Soon it would get lighter earlier, stay light longer. Something to look forward to. Shoes squeaking on the pavement. The sound of their voices, their breathing. At the corner a taxi dropped some people at the hotel. Jas and Sharon crossed the street. Suddenly out of an alley shot a man on a bike. He wheeled around in front of them, a wide-faced man, his eyes lost in the darkness of his hooded sweatshirt.

"Girls," he said.

"Let's go," Sharon said, and Jas nearly tripped as they made a wide berth around him, fast-walking in the street for the next half block.

"Ladies," the rider said, coming up behind them.

"Go away," Jas said as she broke into a trot.

"Wait for me," Sharon said, hurrying along behind.

Rushing to their building, rushing up the steps. Jas at the top of the stoop dared to look back and saw an empty street.

"The phantom rider," Jas said.

"Don't even joke," Sharon said. "I hate this."

"My father has a word for it," Jas said as she let them inside. "Modern girls in the modern world. He calls the dangers we worry about 'opportunities.'"

"Very funny," Sharon said.

"He lost his sense of humor when my mother died," Jas said.

A week later Sharon came into her room late at night and sat down on the edge of the bed.

"Fletcher ask you to marry him?"

"Not exactly," she said. "But I'm moving in with him."

Jas switched on the bedlamp and grabbed her friend's hands.

"I'm so happy for you!"

"I feel like a shit," Sharon said.

"I won't say a word about the guy who stayed over."

Sharon shook her head.

"Not about that, dummy," she said. "About you. About abandoning you."

"You're not," Jas said, feeling herself sink into the bed.

"I just can't live here anymore," Sharon said. "It makes me too nervous. I know I'm being a coward."

"You're not," Jas said again, something shifting in her chest as Sharon went on with her explanation.

A week later and she found herself alone in the apartment, with no immediate financial need for a new roommate since Sharon, in her guilt, had written her a check—God knows where she got the money, maybe borrowed it from home—for half of the next three months' rent. But Jas had other worries. The night noises of the building kept her constantly in a state of nerves. Walking home alone, she focused on her demeanor, walked in a way that she took to be determined, street-wise, like someone with a mission, not one of those day-or-night dreamers who get knocked off by roving muggers. Sharon called her often those first few weeks, and they talked a lot, almost as much as when they lived together. Jas watched television for company, silly shallow TV movies that made her sniffle, sometimes even weep at the most ludicrous and artificial circumstances. With respect to her own circumstances, she kept herself tough, only now and then indulging herself with chocolate and an occasional call to her father.

"You're alone?" he asked the first time they talked after Sharon's departure.

"Don't sound so worried. I'm a big girl and it's a safe building."

"That's not what I was thinking."

"What then, Pa?"

"I know all about being alone. Take care of yourself, please, would you?"

She wasn't sure how she was supposed to do that. But just after the first day of spring when Charles came up to her desk out of the blue and leaned over and asked if she wanted to go out for a beer she said okay.

He was company, and not bad company at that. Over their beers at the Hawk and Dove he had stories to tell about the office, the Senator, about a number of odd and amusing occurrences among the denizens of the same halls they walked each day. A trivial thought, she knew, but she didn't even have to lean over when they talked. At eye-level with Charles she felt more relaxed than with most people toward whom she had to stoop. Wandering back along Pennsylvania Avenue, she felt safer than she had in months. Even when they walked past the entrance to the Capitol Hill Suites where she saw a hooded bike rider flash past in the dim glow of the street lamp she felt secure, pointing him out to Charles, though the rider disappeared around the corner before she could explain. Charles kept close to her, and she bumped hips with him once or twice as they walked.

And talked about the new President.

"A bum," Charles said. "Runs well, but if these first few months are indicative, he sure as hell doesn't know how to govern."

"But he's smart, don't you think?" Jas said, tasting beer on her words.

"Yeah, sure," Charles said. "But that's not always a good thing to be in this town. Most of the elected officials are just average brains. They don't like it when anybody stands out too much above them. It's like . . . being our height, you know what I mean?"

"I guess I do," Jas said.

They had reached Jas's block and she slowed down, holding onto Charles's arm, and settled into a stroll, as though it were full-blown spring out here and light, maybe eleven in the morning or three in the afternoon.

"Nice night," Charles said.

"Thank you," Jas said, stopping them as they reached her building.

"Home?" he said. "Nice building." He kept his eyes on her.

"Come up?" she said. "How about some coffee?"

Upstairs she pointed him toward the sofa while she went to the stove. Standing there she felt the oddest sensation, not a palpable feeling but more a sense of absence, as though she had left her body and floated above the burners, light and airy and buoyant, yet anchored somehow to the floor so that she could not float away. She touched the coffeepot. She touched the switch for the gas. She touched a finger to her collarbone, traced it, pushed, probed. Next thing she knew he was standing next to her.

"Maybe I'll have a beer instead," he said.

"In the fridge," she said, holding to the stove.

A few minutes later she tried to stand, only to fall back onto the sofa where he had led her with an easy looseness of bones and muscles. She stood again—the room must have moved—and then fell back—onto the bed. Her sweater and bra had disappeared. Charles licked at her nipples like a pup you might see in a pet store window. This tickled, and excited her as well. She made sounds—he worried that he might be hurting her but she reassured him—and then she was thinking, Oh, my God, I'm here with this guy and it's only because we're the same height.

"No, please, no," she said, taking him by the wrist and settling his hands back in his lap. Sitting there, naked to the waist, she felt a little chill—goosebumps!—but no embarrassment or shame.

"Jas," he said.

"I can't," she said.

"What's wrong?" He tried to look her in the eye but his glance kept slipping.

"Nothing's wrong. It's just not right."

He wasn't happy about this, but he stood up—a gentleman, which almost won Jas over, but she managed to stand, or sit, her ground. He adjusted his clothing while she scrambled into her sweater. After a few more words he allowed her to usher him out of the apartment. After she shut the door she pressed her ear to the wood and listened to his footsteps fade away down the stairs. She paced around the living room awhile, wondering if she had done the wrong thing. At the window she watched the spinning leaves, a car passing by, another car. A hooded man on a bicycle. Two late-night strollers. No one, for minutes. The bicyclist circled back. A car rolled past from the opposite direction.

Finally, she dragged herself to bed, lying there in the dark while the night sounds magnified. When she jumped at what sounded like the crack of a stick in the street—who knew what that cracking noise meant?—the clock at her bedside showed only the next half hour. At the noise of her intercom, she jumped to her feet and went to the door. The buzzing came again, steady and insistent. Going to the window, she saw no movement on the street except the blowing leaves. The buzzer again. Back at the door, she took a deep breath and pushed the button.

She listened carefully as the street door opened and then thudded closed. Footsteps on the stairs. It seemed like several minutes before the climber reached her landing.

"Jas?" from the other side of the door.

"Who is it?"

Squinting through the peephole, she could scarcely make him out.

"Charles?"

Slowly she opened the door to face him, leaving it on the chain.

"Oh, my God," she said, seeing his bleeding forehead and his bloodied hand cupped over his nose.

He'd been sitting on the stoop, he said. Hadn't gone home when she'd kicked him out.

"But why?"

"How am I supposed to know?" He shook his head before the mirror, studying his sorry face.

Jas handed him a hot damp towel.

A hooded man on a bicycle had swung past the stoop, made a quick trim, and let the bike fall onto the sidewalk as he charged, slamming Charles in the face and grabbing his wallet.

"We need to call the police," Jas said, watching him dab the deep red smears across his cheeks.

"No, no," Charles shook his head. His voice wasn't his own, it was so nasal because of his smashed, bleeding nose. "More trouble than it's worth. I'll cancel my credit cards. I didn't have that much cash." He stopped and studied his contorted face in the mirror. "No driver's license."

"You don't drive?"

"Never learned," he said, resuming his work with the towel. "Easy here. I take cabs. I take the Metro. Soon as I clean up I'll call myself a cab. Should have done that in the first place, I guess."

"No," Jas said. "It's so late." With a sigh she pulled her robe close and left the bathroom for the hall, opening the closet and dragging out some bedding that she carried into the front room and tossed onto the sofa.

"Thanks," he said, having followed her from the bathroom. "I really appreciate this." He was staring at the bedding as if sheer will alone might help to arrange it as Jas left the room. While she lay there in the dark in her own bed she heard him adjust and readjust himself on the sofa. The apartment walls creaked, but the sound didn't seem so menacing now that she was not alone.

He coughed.

She breathed deeply, trying to ignore his presence. A car passed by on the street below. The wind rattled the trees. Her breathing softened.

But at the feel of weight on the bed she sat up alert, awake.

Charles leaned over her, his breath sour and metallic from the beer and the blood.

"I have a confession to make," he said.

In the light from the other room his head seemed to quiver slightly as he spoke, as though he suffered from the onset of some neurological condition.

"Are you all right?" Jas asked.

"I have to tell you this," Charles said, leaning toward her.

"What?"

"I lied," he said.

"What?"

"I wasn't mugged."

"What are you saying?"

"I wasn't mugged. I punched myself in the nose with my own fist. That's how bad I was feeling."

"Get out, please," Jas said. "I need to sleep."

"I'm sorry," he said. "There was a black guy on a bike and he looked pretty menacing. He kept circling the block. I was afraid to walk home. It'll be worse now."

"Get out!" she said in a voice so strident that a few hours later when she awoke and dressed for work her throat still felt raw. Charles, of course, was gone, having left sometime between that terrible moment and the onset of the muted late winter dawn.

With a cup of strong coffee in hand she stalked around the apartment, sniffing, sniffing, as if she might find out the part of herself that seemed to have melted away in the throes of the night. With the cup half empty she sat down and toyed with the telephone, dialing part of her father's number and then breaking off the call. She tried Sharon.

Please leave a message when you hear the beep for either . . .

She broke that connection, too. Who wanted to hear Sharon's

name entwined electronically or otherwise with that bald-headed eagle Fletcher? It made Jas wonder. It made her shiver. It made her jealous. But she wasn't giving in to anything. Jumping to her feet, she swept up her coat from the closet, propelled herself out the door, and climbed down the stairs. Halfway down she stopped, cursed herself, and climbed back up to fetch her forgotten briefcase. Then she headed down again, her heart racing.

Her walk to the office, which she had lately come to enjoy despite the lingering cold weather, was this morning a torture. Low clouds pressed down, seeming to touch the tops of the marble buildings, wind slashing across Pennsylvania Avenue, attacking her face and ears. A voice in her ear: her father's. Saying what? She couldn't quite make it out over the noise of the wind and the passing cars. At the corner, by a line of newspaper vending machines, Jas stopped, waiting for the traffic light to change.

PRESIDENT SMILES ON—

—she caught a glimpse of a headline. On? On what? She would have searched for a coin for the vending machine but the light changed in her favor and she crossed the street. A few guards stood about laughing and joking, white breath to the wind, at the rear of the Library of Congress. Jas pushed ahead, eyes on the sidewalk the rest of the block.

At the office Charles was not around.

When Jas inquired about him in what she hoped was her most offhand manner, Carla the receptionist said he might be at the Budget Office.

There was snow coming, she told Jas. A late storm. And did she see the paper about another mugging on the hill—a black man on a bicycle had clobbered some young secretary on her way home and taken her money and keys.

"The money part I don't care about," Carla said. "But the keys? What do you do without your keys?"

Jas stood quietly, listening.

"Oh, and *he* wants to see you," Carla added, holding up a

memo. "Just buzzed me. Got some bug up his gazoobee this morning." She narrowed her eyes in a way Jas had never noticed before and said, "Watch yourself."

"Watch myself? Is there something wrong?"

Carla shook her head mysteriously, suggesting with a nod that Jas had better get moving.

"Just watch yourself," she said.

A telephone rang. Two telephones rang behind her.

"I'm going," Jas said, heading for the door leading to her boss's domain. A door slammed ahead of her and she met the brawny national correspondent, whose eyes registered a faint sign of recognition.

"He's all yours," he said, passing her on the run, the faint odor of his breath lingering in the air. Jas turned to watch him go and caught him looking back at her.

"Do you do research?" he said.

Before Jas could reply he said, "I need someone. If you're interested, give me a call."

Jas shook off the suggestion and went directly to the Senator's door.

"Come in," he called when he saw her standing there. "And close it."

She stepped inside and drew the door closed behind her, feeling the pull of his eyes. A lingering trace of the correspondent's breath yielded to the powerful odor of the Senator's cologne.

"I like to check with new staff—with everybody who works here—every once in a while." The Senator bore in on her with those eyes, and Jas made it a point of pride that she didn't turn away.

"I've been watching you," he said, "ever since that day in the tunnel."

"We met before that once, sir," Jas said. "At a party—"

"I go to too many parties," the Senator said as he stood and walked around to the front of his desk. Jas was half a head taller than the man and when he approached her she could look down through the rectangular pattern of his thinning hair and see the shining—lacquered almost—surface of his scalp. In that instant the Senator seemed to lean toward her almost as if in some practiced move from an athletic competition suddenly thrust his arms around her, at the same time raising his mouth toward hers. Before she could register what was happening his tongue slipped in between her teeth.

"Uh," Jas made a sound as she pulled her mouth from his. But she couldn't get further back—he had her trapped, bumping his belly against her pelvis.

"Please," she said, finally tearing herself free.

"Wait," the Senator said as she went for the door. He grabbed her by the shoulders, pulling her back toward him, nuzzling his mouth against the back of her neck. Jas wrenched herself loose, yanking the door as he whispered an apology behind her, and flung herself into the hall.

She spent the rest of the day at the Library of Congress— beneath it, to be exact—wandering the tunnels from building to building, stopping in a snack room for a soda and a bag of chips, then setting out again, getting as far as the next set of elevators before turning and walking back through the long wide passageway, listening to the echoes of voices and the nattering of machines. Up and along the wide corridors she dawdled, strolled, slowed to notice marked and unmarked doors along the walls, then hurried along again, changing direction, following arrows, marking her pathway by the signs on the walls. The traffic around her ebbed and flowed.

When from a long distance she saw a tall man in a great hurry coming toward her, she turned and picked up her pace. A pair of hooded workers pushed a long cart ahead of her and she ducked around them to step into a narrow passageway to the left where sawhorses and old steel bookshelves stood haphazardly along the wall. Someone called to her and she hurried along. Spying one of those doors in the wall, she stopped to pull it open. It opened—luck or stupidity or ineptitude or policy had left it unlocked—and she stepped inside, closing the door behind her. Pipes and machinery murmured overhead, all around her. Standing in the dark, hugging her arms to her chest, she heard voices raised in laughter in the narrow hall outside. She began to shudder in a sort of cold and voiceless misery, her tall body bending forward and jerking back as though she were controlled by some puppetmaster much taller than she who yanked her on a string.

In her ear a noise, a whisper, a voice: her father's. Home, it was saying, how he needed her, the safety would be a luxury but one she deserved. It became garbled then, muffled and distorted by her own sobs and coughs. One last word she could make out: swan. And she was overtaken by a series of wracking cries so deep they seemed to come up from her ankles and knees rather than her belly and chest.

The light flooded over her.

A dark man in a green sweatshirt and voluminous black trousers stood in the doorway not three feet away.

"What you doing here?"

Her heart jammed in her chest; her breathing eased only when she saw the chain around his neck with the dangling ID card that caught the reflection of the bright bulbs overhead.

"I don't know," she said. "I don't know."

Acknowledgments

Special thanks to the following individuals and institutions for their assistance in making *Literary Washington, D.C.* possible:

Jabari Asim of the *Washington Post*, Bill Broyles, the staff of the Countee Cullen-Harold Jackman Memorial Collection at the Robert W. Woodruff Library at Atlanta University, Benjamin Boyce Crader, the staff of the Special Collections Department of the Gelman Library at George Washington University, Emily Grandstaff, Jennifer Howard of the *Washington Post*, Jim Marks of the Lambda Literary Foundation, Robin Van Fleet and the staff of the Moorland-Spingarn Research Center of Howard University, Greg Varner of the *Washington Blade*, Emily White, Brett Wiley, Gabriel T. Wilmoth, and many others, as well as the authors themselves.

ALSO AVAILABLE

Literary Savannah
edited by Patrick Allen

Literary Charleston and the Lowcountry
edited by Curtis Worthington

Literary Nashville
edited by Patrick Allen